Gender and Creative Labour

The Sociological Review Monographs

Since 1958, *The Sociological Review* has established a tradition of publishing one or two Monographs a year on issues of general sociological interest. The Monograph is an edited book length collection of refereed research papers which is published and distributed in association with Wiley Blackwell. We are keen to receive innovative collections of work in sociology and related disciplines with a particular emphasis on exploring empirical materials and theoretical frameworks which are currently under-developed.

If you wish to discuss ideas for a Monograph then please contact the Monographs Editor, Steve Brown, Professor of Social and Organisational Psychology, School of Management, University of Leicester, Leicester, LE1 7RH, UK. s.d.brown@le.ac.uk.

Our latest Monographs include:

Violence and Society: Toward a New Sociology by Jane Kilby and Larry Ray
Disasters and Politics: Materials, Experiments, Preparedness (edited by Manuel Tironi, Israel Rodriguez-Giralt and Michael Guggenheim)
Urban Rhythms: Mobilities, Space and Interation in the Contemporary City (edited by Robin James Smith and Kevin Hetherington)
Waste Matters (edited by David Evans, Hugh Campbell and Anne Murcott)
Live Methods (edited by Les Back and Nirmal Puwar)
Measure and Value (edited by Lisa Adkins and Celia Lury)
Norbert Elias and Figurational Research: Processual Thinking in Sociology (edited by Norman Gabriel and Stephen Mennell)
Sociological Routes and Political Roots (edited by Michaela Benson and Rolland Munro)
Nature, Society and Environmental Crisis (edited by Bob Carter and Nickie Charles)
Space Travel & Culture: From Apollo to Space Tourism (edited by David Bell and Martin Parker)
Un/Knowing Bodies (edited by Joanna Latimer and Michael Schillmeier)
Remembering Elites (edited by Mike Savage and Karel Williams)
Market Devices (edited by Michel Callon, Yuval Millo and Fabian Muniesa)
Embodying Sociology: Retrospect, Progress and Prospects (edited by Chris Shilling)
Sports Mega-Events: Social Scientific Analyses of a Global Phenomenon (edited by John Horne and Wolfram Manzenreiter)
Against Automobility (edited by Steffen Böhm, Campbell Jones, Chris Land and Matthew Paterson)

Other Monographs have been published on consumption; museums; culture and computing; death; gender and bureaucracy; sport plus many other areas. For further information about the Monograph Series, please visit: www.sociologicalreviewmonographs.com

Gender and Creative Labour

Edited by Bridget Conor, Rosalind Gill and Stephanie Taylor

Wiley Blackwell/The Sociological Review

This edition first published 2015
© 2015 The Editorial Board of the Sociological Review
Chapters © 2015 by the chapter author

ISBN 9781119062394 and The Sociological Review, 63:S1.

All articles published within this monograph are included within
the ISI Journal Citation Reports® Social Science Citation Index.
Please quote the article DOI when citing monograph content.

Registered Office
John Wiley & Sons Ltd, The Atrium, Southern Gate, Chichester, West Sussex, PO19 8SQ, UK

Editorial Offices
350 Main Street, Malden, MA 02148-5020, USA
9600 Garsington Road, Oxford, OX4 2DQ, UK
The Atrium, Southern Gate, Chichester, West Sussex, PO19 8SQ, UK

For details of our global editorial offices, for customer services, and for information about how
to apply for permission to reuse the copyright material in this book please see our website at
www.wiley.com/wiley-blackwell.

The right of Bridget Conor, Rosalind Gill and Stephanie Taylor to be identified as the editors of
this work has been asserted in accordance with the UK Copyright, Designs and Patents Act 1988.

Wiley also publishes its books in a variety of electronic formats. Some content that appears in print
may not be available in electronic books. Designations used by companies to distinguish their
products are often claimed as trademarks. All brand names and product names used in this book
are trade names, service marks, trademarks, or registered trademarks of their respective owners. The
publisher is not associated with any product or vendor mentioned in this book.

Limit of Liability/Disclaimer of Warranty: While the publisher and authors have used their best
efforts in preparing this book, they make no representations or warranties with respect to the
accuracy or completeness of the contents of this book and specifically disclaim any implied
warranties of merchantability or fitness for a particular purpose. It is sold on the understanding
that the publisher is not engaged in rendering professional services and neither the publisher nor the
authors shall be liable for damages arising herefrom. If professional advice or other expert
assistance is required, the services of a competent professional should be sought.

First published in 2015 by John Wiley & Sons

Library of Congress Cataloging-in-Publication Data

Gender and creative labour/edited by Bridget Conor, Rosalind Gill and Stephanie Taylor.
–1 Edition.
pages cm. – (Sociological review monographs)
Includes bibliographical references and index.
ISBN 978-1-119-06239-4 (alk. paper)
1. Cultural industries. 2. Sex discrimination in employment.
I. Conor, Bridget, 1980- editor.
HD9999.C9472G46 2015
331.4′133–dc23

2015002040

A catalogue record for this title is available from the British Library

Set in TimesNRMT 10/12pt by Toppan Best-set Premedia Limited

Printed and bound in the United Kingdom

1   2015

Contents

Series editor's acknowledgements   vii

Acknowledgements   viii

Part 1: Introduction

Gender and creative labour   1
Bridget Conor, Rosalind Gill and Stephanie Taylor

Part 2: Sexism, segregation and gender roles

Sex, gender and work segregation in the cultural industries   23
David Hesmondhalgh and Sarah Baker

Unmanageable inequalities: sexism in the film industry   37
Deborah Jones and Judith K. Pringle

Part 3: Flexibility and informality

Getting in, getting on, getting out? Women as career scramblers
in the UK film and television industries   50
Leung Wing-Fai, Rosalind Gill and Keith Randle

Labile labour – gender, flexibility and creative work   66
George Morgan and Pariece Nelligan

Birds of a feather: informal recruitment practices and gendered
outcomes for screenwriting work in the UK film industry   84
Natalie Wreyford

Part 4: Image-making and representation

Blowing your own trumpet: exploring the gendered dynamics
of self-promotion in the classical music profession   97
Christina Scharff

'Egotist', 'masochist', 'supplicant': Charlie and Donald
Kaufman and the gendered screenwriter as creative worker 113
Bridget Conor

Genre anxiety: women travel writers' experience of work 128
Ana Alacovska

The heroic body: toughness, femininity and the stunt double 144
Miranda J. Banks and Lauren Steimer

Part 5: Boundary-crossing

When Adam blogs: cultural work and the gender division
of labour in Utopia 158
Ursula Huws

A new mystique? Working for yourself in the neoliberal economy 174
Stephanie Taylor

Hungry for the job: gender, unpaid internships, and the creative
industries 188
Leslie Regan Shade and Jenna Jacobson

Notes on contributors 206

Index 211

Series editor's acknowledgements

The Sociological Review Monograph series publishes special supplements of the journal in collections of original refereed papers that are included within the ISI Journal Citation Reports and the Social Science Citation Index.

In existence for over fifty years, the series has developed a reputation for publishing innovative projects that reflect the work of senior but also emerging academic figures from around the globe.

These collections could not continue without the considerable goodwill, advice and guidance of members of the Board of *The Sociological Review*, and of those anonymous referees who assess and report on the papers submitted for consideration for these collections. I would like to thank all of those involved in this process, especially Professor Kate Oakley for her very considerable input into the collection as a whole, all of the referees, and also the editors of *Gender and Creative Labour* for having produced such an interesting volume.

Chris Shilling, SSPSSR, University of Kent, UK

Acknowledgements

We would like to thank all the authors who have contributed to this book for their wonderful work and their good humour in the face of deadlines. It helped to make working on this an intellectually exciting and enjoyable endeavour. We would also like to express our appreciation to the many other academics, including colleagues, whose work has contributed to our own thinking and to the larger projects of research on gender, creative labour and inequalities.

Thank you to Chris Shilling at *Sociological Review Monograph* and to our external reviewers.

Thank you also to Simidele Dosekun for her invaluable work in editing and bringing the volume to fruition, and to Joanne Figiel for her editorial assistance. We are grateful to City University London and the CCIG research centre at the Open University for funding to assist with the manuscript preparation.

Finally we would each like to thank our friends and families – you know who you are.

Part 1: Introduction

Gender and creative labour

Bridget Conor, Rosalind Gill and Stephanie Taylor

Abstract: Inequalities within the cultural and creative industries (CCI) have been insufficiently explored. International research across a range of industries reveals gendered patterns of disadvantage and exclusion which are, unsurprisingly, further complicated by divisions of class, and also disability and race and ethnicity. These persistent inequalities are amplified by the precariousness, informality and requirements for flexibility which are widely noted features of contemporary creative employment. In addition, women in particular are disadvantaged by the boundary-crossing (for instance, between home and work, paid work and unpaid work) and new pressures around identity-making and self-presentation, as well as continuing difficulties related to sexism and the need to manage parenting responsibilities alongside earning. This article introduces a new collection which explores these issues, marking the significance of gender for an understanding of creative labour in the neoliberal economy.

Keywords: gender inequality, precariousness, sexism, self-representation, neoliberalism

Introduction

The cultural and creative industries (CCI) present a paradox. On the one hand they are famously 'open', 'diverse' and 'Bohemian', 'hostile to rigid caste systems' (Florida, 2002) and associated with work in cultures that are 'cool, creative and egalitarian' (Gill, 2002). Yet on the other, fields like film, television, the music industry and the arts more broadly, are marked by stark, persistent and in many cases worsening inequalities relating to gender, race and ethnicity, class, age and disability. The aim of this collection is to examine this paradox, focusing particularly on gender, to interrogate both the myths of equality and diversity that circulate within the CCI, and the distinctive patterns and dynamics of inequality and exclusion. Whilst gender inequality characterizes almost all sections of the labour market, it takes different forms – and may have different drivers – in different fields or settings. There are, as Acker (2006) has argued, different 'inequality regimes'. Inequalities in creative work have been relatively underexplored until recently, and we seek to illuminate the distinctive features of working in fields such as arts and media that might help to understand the persistence of inequality in the CCI.

The Sociological Review, 63:S1, pp. 1–22 (2015), DOI: 10.1111/1467-954X.12237
© 2015 The Authors. Editorial organisation © 2015 The Editorial Board of the Sociological Review. Published by John Wiley & Sons Ltd, 9600 Garsington Road, Oxford OX4 2DQ, UK and 350 Main Street, Malden, MA 02148, USA

The general failure to address inequalities in these fields is particularly striking and dissonant given the prominence attached both to 'creativity' in general, and the CCIs in particular, in national policies across the world. Creativity has become so elevated as a characteristic of individuals and nations in recent years that it has taken on a status almost beyond critique. Banks (2007) talks of 'the creative fetish'; Osborne (2003) argues that creativity has become a 'moral imperative'; whilst Ross (2009) contends that creativity is the 'wonderstuff' of our time, the 'oil of the 21st century'. The CCI are hailed in policy documents for their capacity to stimulate national economies, to regenerate depressed urban areas, to aid in attempts to build social inclusion and cohesion, to challenge unemployment, and even to improve nations' health (eg Cunningham, 2009; Keane, 2009; Power, 2009). There is nothing they cannot do, it seems. At one point it seemed that such celebratory discourse might have peaked around the turn of the century, for example with Australia's championing of a 'Creative Nation' policy, and the UK's attempt under New Labour to make Britain 'the world's creative capital' (Department for Culture, Media and Sport, 2008). However, in retrospect, this may turn out to have been just the beginning of a global trend that now includes BRIC nations (Brazil, Russia, India and China) and developing economies – namely 'post-socialist' countries' aggressive inward investment policies promoting their 'vast supply of creative labour', and China's attempt to shift its self-branding from 'Made in China' to 'Created in China'. Moreover, the enthusiasm for CCI in developed economies shows no sign of waning, and, indeed, as we write in June 2014, the UK Prime Minister David Cameron has just announced his intention to host another 'Cool Britannia' party at his Downing Street residence, with pop stars, actors and fashion designers at the top of the list of guests.

In this context of relentless celebrations of 'creativity', and promotion of the CCI within policy discourses, the lack of attention to *work* in these fields is particularly disturbing – and stands in stark contrast to areas such as bio-science or engineering which are rightly deemed to require investment and a properly trained and rewarded workforce. Not so the CCI it would appear. Into the vacuum formed by a lack of serious discussion of the CCI, a powerful stereotype has taken root and flourished. This sees the typical 'creative' as driven by passion to Do What You Love (DWYL), prepared to work for long hours for little or even no pay, and requiring minimal support. It is significant to note the potency and pervasiveness of this personalized figuration of the 'creative' and how profoundly it has displaced important questions about working conditions and practices within the CCI, let alone issues of equality, diversity and social justice.

This collection, then, aims to start a conversation about these issues that will speak to the concerns of academics, policy makers, activists and people working within the CCI. Whilst attempting to address concerns across domains as diverse as architecture, museums and theatre, it is focused most centrally upon film and media industries – including on screenwriters, production staff and stunt men and women. In part this reflects the existing small but important literature on which the collection builds, and to which it also contributes articles on classical

The Sociological Review, 63:S1, pp. 1–22 (2015), DOI: 10.1111/1467-954X.12237

musicians, travel writers and creative entrepreneurs. Above all, the collection is animated by an interrogative that questions the similarities and differences across the varied fields designated as 'creative'. What do 'creatives' in advertising, in heritage and in television have in common – if anything? To what extent is it meaningful to mark out a territory called 'creative labour'?

The aim of this introductory article is to define key terms, to outline and take stock of gender inequalities within the field of creative labour, to review existing research and to highlight the thematic areas to which this collection makes a contribution. The remainder of the introduction is divided into four sections. First, we report on some of the 'headline figures' relating to gender and other inequalities within the CCI. Next we move on to examine some of the existing research about work in the CCI, exploring definitions of creative labour, and issues about the informality, precariousness and 'bulimic' working patterns (Pratt, 2002) which characterize much creative endeavour. The third section discusses the key areas to which this collection contributes an understanding. It focuses on questions about freelancing, informality and 'network sociality' (Wittel, 2001); on new contributions to the understanding of sexism; on identity-making and self-representations of workers within the CCI; and on questions about boundary crossing – including the boundaries of home and work, above the line and below the line labouring, paid and not paid work, amongst others. We draw together the threads of the distinctive contributions of the collection, highlighting our intersectional approach, our interest in questions about the dynamics of inequality as a psychosocial phenomenon (Gill, 2007, 2014a; Taylor, 2015), and our aim to contribute to understanding labouring subjectivities in neoliberalism. Finally we offer a brief summary of each article in this collection.

The creative and its associations

Various terms have been deployed to describe the work that is undertaken in the production of art and forms of culture, two primary categories being cultural work (Banks, 2007) and creative labour (Hesmondhalgh and Baker, 2011). Various neologisms have proliferated which situate work between or across previously discrete categories of production and consumption, including produsage, prosumption, playbour and co-creation. These are now often conflated in the term 'cultural and creative industries' which we use here, and in the term 'creative labour'. Drawing on Hirsch (1972), Banks and Hesmondhalgh define 'creative labour' as that work which 'is geared to the production of original or distinctive commodities that are primarily aesthetic and/or symbolic-expressive, rather than utilitarian and functional' (2009: 416). A 2001 publication from the UK government's Department for Culture, Media and Sport (2001) offered a specific list of the 'creative industries':

> Advertising, architecture, the art and antiques market, crafts, design, designer fashion, film and video, interactive leisure software, music, the performing arts, publishing, software and computer services, television and radio.

The Sociological Review, 63:S1, pp. 1–22 (2015), DOI: 10.1111/1467-954X.12237
© 2015 The Authors. Editorial organisation © 2015 The Editorial Board of the Sociological Review

This already broad reference is extended in a recent academic source which claims:

> 'Creativity', once associated with the 'natural' or 'acquired' fits of the artist, has expanded to include virtually all the performative labours producing the information economy, from computer coding to legal research. (Fuller *et al.*, 2013: 144)

One critical question here might be: how do we define what or who is creative and therefore, what or who is included and excluded from creative labour? Mato (2009) presented this critique in an argument that 'all industries are cultural' and questioned prevailing creative labour scholarship which privileges film and television production over toy or garment production for example. More radically and following particularly from innovations in media technologies which are central to many CCI, there have been challenges to the classic distinction between production and consumption, signalled by terms like 'produsage', 'prosumption', 'playbour' and 'co-creation'. Mato (2009) similarly argued that it is at the myriad point(s) of consumption that products (and arguably any products) can be analysed as cultural as well as material entities. Miller (2009) rebutted with his own question: 'Are all industries primarily cultural?' He noted that Mato's assertion sits very closely alongside neoliberal and celebratory creative industries policy discourses which decontextualize terms such as 'creativity' in order to mobilize them 'through the neo-classical shibboleth of unlocking creativity through individual human capital' (Miller, 2009: 94). So just as studies of creative labour could be argued to be unintentionally aligned with those who fetishize creativity and privilege 'creative' occupations, the opposite tendency is just as visible: the assertion – through picking particular occupations and arguing they are creative or cultural – that *anything* can be creative, that anything which turns a profit can be creative and cultural. Creativity again seems beyond critique. What is particularly galvanizing for the authors in this collection is that whilst creativity and creative labour are often framed as open to all, by dint of their universalism ('everyone is creative'!) in fact, inequalities are rife in these industries and at times of economic crisis and instability, are worsening.

Further to these points, it is useful to attempt to recontextualize some of the multiple terms in play by looking more closely at their reference and associations. One common point here and elsewhere, for instance in Florida's now-classic reference to the creative class, is that creative people, creative work and creativity itself are all positively valued. This valuing derives partly from the association with specially talented, even genius figures, particularly from the 'high culture' fields of the arts, as in Fuller *et al.*'s definition (above). A number of writers have reviewed the transitions by which the creative and the cultural came to be viewed not as aesthetic but as economic 'goods' (eg Hesmondhalgh, 2007; O'Connor, 2007); nonetheless, the earlier associations remain and continue to shape many of the expectations and conflicts around creative work. Psychology has played an important part in expanding the reference of creativity. Brouillette (2013: 43) describes the contributions of US-based psychologists in the 1950s and 60s to a model of a new economic actor as a 'flexibly creative individual',

The Sociological Review, 63:S1, pp. 1–22 (2015), DOI: 10.1111/1467-954X.12237

based on a non-conforming artist figure. These psychologists included Abraham Maslow, who famously proposed self-actualization as the apex of a hierarchy of human needs, and Teresa Amabile who investigated the contexts and factors that facilitate and promote creative activities. Their work became important in organizational psychology and management theory, including through the 'guru' Tom Peters. As Brouillette's (2013) account indicates, both the creativity and non-conformity of the artist were celebrated as qualities that supposedly enable the ideal worker to contribute to business innovation while tolerating the flux and uncertainties of the economic conditions of the late 20th century. The focus on an individual artist matched well with the rising popularity of liberal economic theories centred on an individual economic actor. Yet Amabile's (1983) social psychological model of the creative individual also emphasizes the importance of context, including relationships with others. Subsequently, sociocultural psychologists have extended this to encompass the importance of creative collaboration (eg John-Steiner, 2000) and the creative productivity of groups, including in business and other organizational contexts (eg Sawyer, 2007). Their work therefore undermines a focus on the individual. In addition, Amabile's (1983) model of 'creativity in context' challenges the elite figure of the gifted artist by suggesting, first, that creativity is a capacity which is applicable to a huge range of human activities (she cites chess playing as one example) and second, that it is a universal potential. Although some people may have special, even extraordinary talents, a premise of her model is, seemingly, that anyone can be creative, given the right circumstances.

This complex background has contributed to still-current notions. Creative work retains some of its elite associations as positive and special; it is understood to offer the possibility of personal fulfilment or self-actualization, albeit in return for considerable hard work and an absence of financial security. The imagined individuality of the artist or auteur figure (McRobbie, 1998) remains central to the personalized associations of creative work (Taylor and Littleton, 2012); however, in departures from the elite image, the reference of the creative has expanded to a wide range of fields, as already noted, and the capacity for creative work is assumed to be widespread, extending to (raced, classed, gendered) categories of people who were traditionally excluded from 'high culture'. This, of course, is one basis for myths of equality and diversity in the CCI. Moreover, in a further twist, education systems have tended to promote academic subjects over supposedly creative ones so that a creative career is often regarded as the less prestigious alternative to the conventional professions (medicine, law and so on) and therefore one more accessible to students who are less successful at school, including of course those who are from less privileged backgrounds (Taylor and Littleton, 2012). Contributions to this collection explore some of the continuing implications of these conflicting associations. For example, David Hesmondhalgh and Sarah Baker consider the persistence of the stereotype of 'masculinist creativity' (Nixon, 2003) in relation to sex segregation in the music, magazine publishing and television industries. George Morgan and Pariece Nelligan discuss how for aspirant creatives the flexibility to tolerate employment uncertainty is difficult to reconcile with a personal commitment to a vocation and hard-won skills.

Inequalities in the cultural and creative industries: mind the gap

The late 20th and early 21st centuries have seen dramatic changes in work and employment in affluent Western economies. With the shift from Fordism to post-Fordism, workers have been required to adapt to less secure employment and relinquish any expectation of a career for life (Sennett, 1998). A seemingly more positive change has been a major increase in women's participation in labour markets but, as Adkins notes, this has not brought about the social and political changes which feminists had once anticipated; the hope that 'paid employment may offer women emancipation or liberation from problematic arrangements of gender' has not been realized (2012: 623; see also McRobbie, 2011). One complication was the end of the 'family wage' associated with Fordism and another the associated expectation that women with childcare responsibilities will now also be earners. The rise of the CCI has therefore taken place in a context of general employment change and in this sector too, hopes have not been realized, even outside the period of the recession.

Despite the myths of the CCI as diverse, open and egalitarian, inequalities remain a depressingly persistent feature of most fields. Whatever indices one considers –relative numbers in employment, pay, contractual status or seniority – women as a group are consistently faring worse than men. This is true in advertising, the arts, architecture, computer games development, design, film, radio and television; it is also true in 'new' fields such as web design, app development or multimedia. Of course, caution is needed in making such an assertion, in part because the picture varies transnationally, with some countries (not surprisingly) doing better than others – and the articles presented here provide some insight into that. But care is also needed for a second reason, because of the shortage of relevant data which, we argue, both reflects and *contributes to* enduring inequalities. If what governments choose to measure and audit is a reflection of their concerns and priorities for action, then inequalities in the CCI seem to be low on the list. Contributors to the collection have collected and explored the currently available evidence but gaps remain. The lack of national (let alone cross-national) statistics and information about, for example, the numbers or pay of women compared to men in the CCI is symptomatic of a lack of interest and care in a postfeminist moment in which, as Jane Holgate and Sonia Mackay (2009) argue, even the relatively hollow statements of good intentions – such as 'working towards equality' – seem to have all but disappeared. But it also reflects a genuine difficulty in collecting data about businesses and organizations that are predominantly small-scale, temporary and which rapidly recompose for different projects.

The sources which contributors have been able to access – the data variously collected by universities, foundations, or trade unions, by the United Nations or national bodies (such as skills sector councils or SSCs in the UK) and NGOs –

The Sociological Review, 63:S1, pp. 1–22 (2015), DOI: 10.1111/1467-954X.12237

offer a bleak picture of gender inequalities in the CCI. In the UK, the Fawcett Society's annual *Sex and Power* (Centre for Women and Democracy, 2013) audit report indicates that there is not a single female Chair or Chief Executive of a Television company; men outnumber women by more than 10 to 1 in decision-making roles in media companies; and women constitute only 5 per cent of editors of national newspapers. The only senior roles where women outnumber men are in women's and lifestyle magazines. Similarly, the British Film Industry's *Statistical Yearbook* (2013) records that only 7.8 per cent of films were directed by a woman and 13.4 per cent written by a woman – figures that resonate with Lauzen's annual *Celluloid Ceiling* report auditing the top 250 films made in Hollywood. Lauzen's US research is valuable in offering not only a snapshot of the stark inequalities in key creative roles but, crucially, in highlighting how little these fluctuate year on year. As she summarizes it, 'Women comprised 18 per cent of all directors, executive producers, producers, writers, cinematographers, and editors working on the top 250 domestic grossing films of 2012. This percentage represents no change from 2011 and an increase of 1 percentage point from 1998' (Lauzen, 2012: 1). These figures are not dissimilar from those in industries as diverse as architecture and classical music. Sang *et al.* (2007) noted the percentage of women architects in the UK was 14 per cent in the mid-2000s and this figure has not risen above 20 per cent since, and Roan and Stead (2013) write that 23.3 per cent of architects were women as reported in the 2006 Australian census. Christina Scharff discusses the parallels in classical music (this collection).

Both horizontal and vertical segregation by gender are striking. For example, women dominate in wardrobe, hairdressing and make-up roles in film and television but are dramatically under-represented in sound and lighting departments as well as key creative roles such as screenwriter, cinematographer and director (Skillset, 2012). Another emerging axis of stratification that has gendered implications is that between 'above the line' and 'below the line' workers in a range of industries (eg film, advertising, television) (Scott, 2005: 121; Miller *et al.*, 2005). More complex intersectional inequalities are also emerging as significant. For example, it is becoming increasingly clear that gender is mediated by age and parental status, with women concentrated in the youngest cohorts of the CCI workforce, and less likely than their male counterparts to have children. An optimistic explanation might be that gender inequality has become a problem of the past, and the current unevenness is simply a matter of women not yet having had time to work their way into older cohorts or more senior roles. However, not only is this not supported by the evidence, but it also relies upon a problematic 'progress narrative' (Edley and Wetherell, 2001) which suggests that progress towards equality is somehow inevitable and requires no active intervention. In fact, this is far from the situation indicated by the available evidence: some inequalities are getting more rather than less pronounced year on year (for example in computer games), and, moreover, the global financial crisis and associated recession and austerity in some countries has disproportionately impacted on women (Fawcett, 2009). In the UK, for example, the resulting contraction of the TV industry saw women lose their jobs at a rate of six times that of men, falling to only 27 per cent of the workforce in 2010 (O'Connor, 2010). Although during the slow economic recovery women's overall employment increased, the way in which recessionary pressures were mediated by gender cast a long shadow on women in – or trying to get into – some fields, resonating with an existing sense of women as somehow more 'disposable' to the (creative) workforce than men.

Gender inequalities are not the only inequalities in the CCI; these fields also demonstrate stark patterns of exclusion, segregation and inequality in relation to class, disability and race and ethnicity (Holgate and McKay, 2009; Randle *et al.*, 2007; Thanki and Jeffreys, 2007). Black, Asian and minority ethnic (BAME) individuals are dramatically under-represented, leading to accusations of 'institutional racism' (Thanki and Jeffreys, 2007). Far from having a better representation of minority ethnic groups than other sectors, as early research and policy visions suggested (Peck, 2011; Oakley, 2013), the CCI are in fact performing worse. In London, perhaps the creative city *par excellence*, BAME individuals represent more than a quarter of the workforce, but fewer than one in ten of the creative workforce. This proportion has declined systematically over the last few years, and is now, at 5.4 per cent, the lowest since records began. In 2014, a BAFTA speech by black actor and comedian Lenny Henry vividly summed up this sobering picture:

> Between 2006 and 2012, the number of BAMEs working in the UK TV industry has declined by 30.9% ... The total number of black and Asian people in the industry has fallen by 2000 while the industry as a whole has grown by over 4000. Or to put it another way – for every black and Asian person who lost their job, more than two white people were employed. (quoted in Khaleeli, 2014)

An appreciation of the extent to which inequalities are entangled and cross-cut by different axes of identity contributes to the adoption of an intersectional ethic in many articles in this collection. By this we mean an understanding that multiple axes of oppression constitute distinct experiences and subjectivities. As Brah and Phoenix put it, the concept of intersectionality signifies 'the complex, irreducible, varied and variable effects which ensue when multiple axes of differentiation – economic, political, cultural, psychic, subjective and experiential – intersect in historically specific contexts. The concept emphasizes that different dimensions of social life cannot be separated out into discrete and pure strands' (2004: 76).

In the next section we turn to research on the CCI more broadly, highlighting how some of its distinctive features may contribute to inequalities in the CCI.

Creative labour: informality, precariousness and the bulimic career

Over the last decade, a substantial body of research on fashion, digital games design, film and TV production, theatre and music performance, museums, advertising and web design has produced a relatively consistent picture of 'creative' labour – whilst also noting significant differences within and between different fields and occupations (Banks, 2007; Blair, 2001; Caldwell, 2008; Deuze, 2007; Hesmondhalgh and Baker, 2011; McRobbie, 2002; Ursell, 2000). One of the shared experiences of growing numbers of people working in the cultural and creative field is of precariousness and job insecurity. Increasingly, cultural and media workers are freelancers or work on extremely short-term contracts that are counted in days or weeks rather than months or years. Zero hours contracts are not unusual. For large numbers of people in the CCI pervasive insecurity and precariousness are therefore the norm, with individuals very often unsure how they will survive beyond the end of the next project, and living in a mode that requires constant attentiveness and vigilance to the possibility of future work. This has been well documented in recent years (Gill, 2009, 2010; McRobbie, 2002, 2004, 2007; Neff *et al.*, 2005; Taylor and Littleton, 2012) with cultural workers becoming the poster children of 'precarity' (Neilson and Rossiter, 2005; Ross, 2009), iconic exemplars of a group that lives individualized, 'risk biographies' (Beck, 2000), in which all the uncertainties and costs are borne by them rather than by employers or the state (Sennett, 1998, 2006).

The absence of social security benefits to tide people over periods of unemployment, and the lack of sick pay or pension are major sources of anxiety. In most European countries, not being in employment also profoundly impacts on entitlements to maternity benefits, a factor that contributes to the under-representation of women, and particularly mothers, in fields like media, where freelancing or extremely short contracts predominate. As one freelance scriptwriter, quoted by Skillset (2010) put it 'I dream about having sick pay, never mind maternity pay'.

One of the consequences of this pervasive work insecurity amongst cultural workers is the prevalence of second-jobbing or indeed multi-jobbing – frequently in teaching or in the hospitality industries. This is necessitated by insecurity and by low pay, as well as by the deeply entrenched culture of 'working for free' (eg Figiel, 2012; Hope and Figiel, 2012; Kennedy, 2010), not only in unpaid internships at the start of a career (eg Perlin, 2012) – which represent the most well-documented example – but *right across working lives*. The 'privilege' of working in a particular orchestra, theatre or media production is frequently presented as reward in its own right, and silencing mechanisms include the commonly held view that it would somehow be in 'bad taste' to ask about money/pay, implicitly calling into question one's commitment to the project – whether it be performance, recording, film or a new online publishing venture (Ross, 2000).

Generally speaking, freelancers in the media and creative fields live by the aphorism that 'you can't say no to a job'. This in turn leads to extremely long hours and to what Pratt (2002) has termed 'bulimic' patterns of working – feast or famine, stop-go, long periods with little or no work followed by intense periods of having to work all the time, in some cases barely stopping to sleep. These characteristic working patterns have also been accompanied by a general marked intensification of work across the cultural and creative field so that patterns that were once associated with 'crunch times' – such as getting a game into production or finishing editing a film – are increasingly normalized (de Peuter and Dyer-Witheford, 2005). All the time is 'crunch time' now. As Gregg (2011) puts it, workers are expected to be 'always on' and 'always connected'.

One of the most enduring and powerful images of creative organizations is that they are 'hip' and informal. From the legendary environments of Google and Apple, through well-known games companies and web design agencies, all the way down to tiny start-ups, creative workplaces are held to be 'funky', 'Bohemian' and playful (Lloyd, 2006; Ross, 2003). McRobbie (2002) talks about an ethos from 'club to company', and Florida (2002) famously argued that 'creatives' dislike 'rigid caste systems' and prefer flat and informal organizations, without obvious hierarchies. This principle of informality is not just a feature of working *environments*, but also – crucially – of *hiring practices* which largely exist outside formal channels and are enacted through contacts and word of mouth.

In these settings reputation becomes a key commodity, and networking and maintaining contacts a key activity for nurturing it. This is achieved face-to-face at regular drinks and other social occasions, but also in the affective labour of updating profiles, tweeting, blogging and engaging in diverse self-promotion activities (Cote and Pybus, 2011). One characteristic of cultural work labour markets is their 'network sociality' (Wittel, 2001) – thin, shallow relations. In such 'reputation economies' wherever you go, whoever you meet, represents a work opportunity. 'Life is a pitch', as one of Gill's (2010) interviewees put it pithily.

In this introduction we have discussed the contested definitions of creativity, creative labour and the CCI, outlined a broad picture of inequalities in these fields – particularly those relating to gender and offered an overview of some of the existing literature about the distinctive nature of work in the CCI. In the next section we turn directly to four broad themes to which this collection makes a particular contribution. Our contributors represent a broad range of interests, industries and national contexts (though with particularly strong representation of film and media, as noted above). The articles refer to work in Western Europe, the UK, USA, Canada, New Zealand and Australia, offering both theoretical and empirical analyses. They are organized under four thematic headings: informality and flexibility; new approaches to understanding sexism; identity making and representation; and boundary-crossing. In addition to these key themes, the collection is distinctive in its psychosocial focus, and in its attention to the intersectional nature of inequalities.

Gender and creative labour: taking the debates forward

As already discussed, a key theme of research on the CCI concerns the extent to which work environments, work organizations and working practices are governed by notions of informality and flexibility. The collection builds on the insights of this research to consider how these much vaunted and in many cases highly valued (see Taylor this collection) features of work may also be implicated in the persistence of inequalities in the CCI.

The problems of informal recruitment are becoming increasingly well documented, with evidence that women fare better in settings in which there is both greater formality to the hiring process and greater transparency. In the CCI, outside large organizations, this is relatively atypical, with 'word-of-mouth', reputation-based decisions by far the most common way of securing or distributing work. These practices lead to what Thanki and Jeffreys (2007) call a 'contacts culture' that disadvantages women, people from BAME groups and working-class backgrounds.

In this collection, informal hiring practices are discussed in some detail. Natalie Wreyford considers the process through which screenwriters get taken on and commissioned, arguing that informal networking is a key mechanism for reproducing gender and other inequalities. Her work is valuable in featuring those who do the 'hiring' or selecting as well as those who are seeking work. Her article illuminates how homophily works in practice. She demonstrates the way that notions of 'the market' and of 'risk' and 'trust' together come to constitute a situation that reproduces the status quo (see also Conor, this collection).

Leung Wing-Fai, Rosalind Gill and Keith Randle highlight similar issues in relation to film production. Noting the dominance of freelancing in this field they unpack the significance of networking, to understand what one interviewee described as 'men … feeling more comfortable with their own … The peer on peer thing, and the stories they relate to'. Deborah Jones and Judith Pringle's article (discussed further in the next section) highlights the way in which inequalities become 'unmanageable', existing as they do in an informal and unregulated zone, despite all the relevant instruments and statutes designed to protect equality of opportunity.

A number of articles discuss how the 'flexibility' of flexible work is designed around the needs of the job rather than those of the worker and, like risk, is transferred onto individuals. As Perrons (2000) has noted acerbically, there exists a 'very flexible' account of freelance working in fields like these (her own focus is on new media). George Morgan and Pariece Nelligan look at how responses to this demand may be both gendered and classed. Flexibility may, they suggest, be particularly challenging for young working-class men steeped within the cultural codes of blue-collar manual work, and struggling to become what they term 'labile labour'. Morgan and Nelligan's work highlights nicely the psychosocial dimensions of working in the CCI – the notion that in order to thrive it is not only particular skills but also particular kinds of subjectivity that are needed: flexible, networked, adaptable and entrepreneurial. The collection as a whole offers different vantage points into the psychic life of neoliberalism (see also Gill, 2014a; Scharff, forthcoming).

A second set of themes, closely related to the above, concerns how we understand gender inequality, and its connection to sexism, an issue which is the focus of a newly revitalized interest, seen in popular culture in the Everyday Sexism Project and in energetic campaigns around sexual violence and media representation. The prominence of sexism as a focus is striking, especially compared with writing about gender and work from a decade ago, and may be part of what Gill (2011) has described as the need to 'get angry again'. Sexism, gender roles and segregation are connected concerns in this collection and Hesmondhalgh and Baker, and Jones and Pringle contribute articles that address these issues.

Many writers have noted the extra difficulty that women confront around combining precarious employment with parenting responsibilities, yet this may not be the only issue, and there are dangers in perpetually reinforcing the women-childcare link (Gill, 2014a). As theorists we have to be aware of both the 'realities' of gendered lives, and, simultaneously, of how our own stories may cement or challenge these. Moreover, the expectation that women will maintain responsibility for caring roles conflicts with the immersion required for creative making and conventional female orientation to the needs of others. Taylor (2011: 367–368) has argued recently: 'Creative working, as unbounded immersion and personalized, emotional labour, demands the masculine selfishness of the conventional creative artist and this conflicts with long-established gendered positionings of women as other-oriented, attending to the needs of others and heeding their preferences'.

The CCI, it has been observed, are better at recruiting women than at keeping them (O'Connor, 2010) and the contributions across this collection offer some insight into why this might be the case. Hesmondhalgh and Baker take as their topic the persistent segregation found within media work, a segregation that often seems underpinned by stereotypes, including positive ones such as the notions that women are caring or are good listeners. They assert the need not simply to challenge the stereotypes, but to move beyond the very dichotomies themselves. In this way their work contributes to a growing body of analyses that explore the flexibility and dynamism of sexism (Gill, 2011, 2014a, 2014b; Kelan, 2009; Scharff, 2012) revealing it to be far more malleable, agile and subtle than traditional definitions allow. Gill's work on 'new sexism' also informs Wing-Fai's article which is notable in considering motherhood not only as presenting practical challenges for women but also in constituting a central theme of sexist discourse – in such a way as to present discrimination as 'reasonable' and 'rational' – albeit regrettable.

Jones and Pringle also make a novel and important contribution to understanding sexism in their study of below the line workers in the New Zealand film industry. Their analysis highlights both continuities and breaks: on the one hand there are traditional sexist stereotypes of 'gung ho jocks' and 'girly girls', and so on, yet on the other there is an acceptance of sexism as just how it is – in a context in which inequalities are largely 'unmanageable'. These pieces (as well as those by Conor, Scharff and Wreyford) point to the distinctiveness of the operation of sexism in the current post-feminist moment – a moment in which feminism has been both taken into account but also repudiated (McRobbie, 2009) and in which an 'overing' (Ahmed, 2012) or 'gender fatigue' (Kelan, 2009) makes inequalities increasingly unspeakable.

A third, key set of themes for this collection relate to identity making and self-representation. Late 20th-century market-focused accounts of work emphasized the importance of cultivating 'Brand You', in Tom Peters' term (cited in Brouillette, 2013: 41) and a recent account of 'new work' proposes that gender has now become 'an act, one which moreover is fused into production, indeed should be understood to be part of what is produced' (Adkins and Jokinen, 2008: 143). Both points would suggest that enacting gendered occupational identity is a requirement for all contemporary workers. However, we argue that these themes have an additional and special relevance for contemporary creative workers.

This is partly because of the general importance of representations and presentation in the media, advertising and many other industries in this sector. But an additional reason is the absence of collective workers' organizations in the CCI. This absence both follows from and reinforces the precariousness and informality of employment in the sector, in that people in short-term and informal employment are less likely to form collective organizations, and without such organizations they will have less protection from informal and irregular employment practices. Traditionally, both the professional organizations associated with higher status fields of employment and the unions associated with workers' 'trades' have played an important role in defining and conferring occupational identities. Professional organizations did this, first, by ratifying formal training and entry requirements, conferring professional recognition on entrants to a profession, and second, by policing standards, for example, through the threat of expulsion for non-compliance with regulations or behaviour deemed to discredit the profession as a whole. Within the CCI, architecture is probably the most prominent field to have retained this model of a profession. Trade unions, although weakened during approximately the same period that the CCI have come to prominence, have had a similar role in defining particular employment roles and setting conditions for membership. For example, in the UK context, entry to journalism or acting depended on obtaining membership of the relevant union (the National Union of Journalists, NUJ; Equity). In the absence of such organizations, the collective definition of what it means to be a (particular kind of) creative professional or practitioner will be replaced by *individual* claims. In other words, in the absence of some ratified qualification or certification, there will be a greater requirement for an individual project to construct and enact a particular creative occupational identity, for instance, by conforming to the stereotypes and myths attached to it, including by looking the part.

One distinctive feature of contemporary creative work may therefore be the *extent* to which it depends on self-presentation (in person, through websites, on *Twitter* and so on) as part of an individual claim to a professional status (see also Conor, 2014: 7–8) and occupational identity. This opens as an area for investigation how creative workers must negotiate received and accepted (gendered, raced, classed) images, practices and personae. Conventionally, the artist/creative maker is male and in addition, areas of creative practice often divide into a professional or elite form, dominated by men, and the domestic version(s) carried out by women (such as chef versus home cook; fashion designer versus home dressmaker). Taylor and Littleton (2012) have previously suggested that these domestic associations can carry over to stigmatize women's creative work. In this collection, the articles by Bridget Conor, Christina Scharff, Ana Alacovska, and Miranda Banks and Lauren Steimer discuss the problems faced by women presenting themselves as, respectively, screenwriters, classical musicians, travel writers and stunt workers, including problems related to the requirements for 'self-mythologising' (Conor, 2014: 7) and 'representational strategies' (2014: 8) which prevail in a particular field. These contributions all signal that it is crucial to consider the vigilant self-monitoring needed to maintain or expand individual professional biographies, and the impact of conventional representations on such biographies. One issue becomes the extent to which images, representative figures and other depictions of a creative worker become a barrier to the recognition of particular categories of people, including women, as creative practitioners or professionals, perpetuating their exclusion and under-representation. Another is the conflicts around psychosocial identification which occur when occupational self-presentation must be reconciled with other values and identities. As examples, Scharff discusses how the requirement to 'sell' themselves professionally is problematic for women musicians, and Morgan and Nelligan consider the conflicts between 'brittle' working-class masculinities and the fluid self-presentation required to get on in the new economy of the CCI.

The new circumstances of the contemporary cultural and creative industries thus return us to the problems which have been named in relation to more conventional occupations and areas of work: prejudice, glass ceilings and 'sticky floors' so that, for example, women are required to be exceptionally good in order to receive the notice and reward which would be granted to a man for more ordinary achievements. For women in precarious creative employment, there is often no redress through formal appeals and an additional problem, discussed by Wreyford in her article, becomes the need to avoid looking like a trouble maker so as to avoid 'scaring off' those who might offer work in the future.

Our final theme is boundary-crossing and here, contributors have highlighted the myriad ways in which gendered work in creative industries travels across and within established (but perhaps, shifting, morphing, even disintegrating) boundaries: home and work; paid work and unpaid work; production and reproduction. The 'boundary crossing' potentialities of creative labour may be a potential attraction for women, both as a turning away from the perceived banality or suppression of individuality associated with conventional workplaces, and also as an unconfident response to anticipated difficulties. Creative work may therefore be attractive to women as 'not work' (Taylor and Littleton, 2012) – a concept which links up to Banks' (2007) notion of the morality of cultural work. There is also a resonance here with the 'refusal of work' movement in parts of Europe in the 1960s and 70s, a movement that heavily influenced Operaismo authors (such as Hardt and Negri, 2000 and Virno, 2003, those authors criticized by McRobbie for neglecting gender as a definitional category). We note that Weeks (2011) has recently called for a utopian form of 'anti work politics' as a feminist response to excessive neoliberal productivism. Stephanie Taylor, Ursula Huws and Leslie Regan Shade and Jenna Jacobson all contribute articles that consider the blurring of traditional boundaries in creative work, forms of blurring which then illuminate the gendered dynamics of those boundaries.

Structure of the collection

The first section in the collection focuses on sexism, segregation and gender roles. **David Hesmondhalgh and Sarah Baker** look beyond industry-wide statistics on the under-representation of women in the cultural industries in order to investigate how women and men are disproportionately concentrated, or confined within particular roles, such as 'the creative side' or marketing. The article suggests that this gendered segregation is sustained by stereotypes. For example, claims that women are more caring and better organized or superior listeners and communicators can justify their presence in administrative and PR departments. Similar stereotypes can function oppositionally when set against various modes of masculinity, including the 'masculinist creativity' noted by Nixon (2003), so that the very 'qualities' that women supposedly bring to the non-creative roles, such as their capacity to mother or nurture, become evidence that they are not suited to more prestigious creative work.

Deborah Jones and Judith Pringle draw on their research in the New Zealand film industry to demonstrate how gender inequalities are produced and reproduced in this field of work, especially 'below-the-line' professions. Drawing attention to a 'deficit model' in statistical reports on discrimination and gender inequality in creative industries which can imply that 'women are the problem', they argue for the usefulness of a case study approach to an industry in which there are few of the traditional indices by which sexism might be identified. Their research reveals a number of patterns: workers accept inequalities as par for the course, as simply a matter of 'getting on' in the 'blokey' worlds of film production, and as not easily enabling life choices such as parenthood. Below-the-line professions fuel very traditional forms of sexism and classism and stereotypically gendered job roles (for instance, 'technical' roles are masculine, make-up is feminine). Jones and Pringle argue that a film industry suffused with the connected language(s) of national pride and creative freedom is, ironically, still apt to perpetuate gendered forms of discrimination.

The next section of this collection is focused on themes of informality and flexibility in creative work and the gendered consequences of these working conditions and practices. In their article, **Leung Wing-Fai, Rosalind Gill and Keith Randle** discuss the gendered nature of freelancing in the film and television industries, using the term 'scramblers' to evoke the challenges faced by freelancers as they attempt to 'get on' and stay in these sectors over time. Rather than only focusing on gender, the authors highlight that an analysis must also be attentive to other personal characteristics of industry 'scramblers': age, class, family status. They examine the ways in which freelancing exacerbates exclusions in this industry across these different axes. Bringing together data from over 100 interviews, the authors are able to identify consistent patterns that affect current working practices around freelance screen production work and render it unsustainable for many, especially women.

George Morgan and Pariece Nelligan discuss the gendered nature of vocational identities and the constraints experienced by aspirant creative workers negotiating the forms of self-presentation which are required in the new economy of 'postmodern capitalism'. The article argues that success in contemporary creative careers, for instance in the design world, requires fluidity, ease of self-presentation and a readiness to dissimulate. For young working-class men, these behaviours conflict with the cultural codes of manual labour, craft and apprenticeship, in which authenticity is based in skills acquired over time, and masculinity is taciturn, protecting its integrity through a refusal to perform to the crowd. A case-study approach is used to present the conflicts between the working-class masculinities of Fordist production and its associated communities of practice, on the one hand, and the requirements for new workers to become 'labile labour', ready to transfer and re-brand their skills, adopt an individualistic and competitive ethos, and grasp serendipitous opportunities as they arise.

Natalie Wreyford argues that the film industry offers an exemplary case for understanding the dynamics of inequality and exclusion that are seen right across the cultural and creative industries. Whilst most research focuses on the production side of filmmaking, with its project based networks, Wreyford (like Conor in this collection) is interested in screenwriters – a group, she argues, who (theoretically) can work from home and arrange their working lives and schedules autonomously and therefore should be equally open to women and men. Why, then, are contemporary screen productions in the UK so dominated by male writers? To explore these questions Wreyford draws on more than 40 interviews with contemporary screenwriters and those who commission or hire them. This article shows compellingly how ideas of 'meritocracy', of 'what the market wants', of 'trust' and of 'risk avoidance' systematically work to disadvantage women. Indeed, even when the film industry considers itself to be searching for 'new talent', 'something different' or 'the next big thing', its informal practices of choosing screenwriters most frequently mean that the 'new' looks remarkably like the 'old'.

In the third section of the collection, the focus is identity making and representation. **Christina Scharff's** article investigates the lives of classical musicians – an underexplored occupational group in the context of the CCI. She argues that they face many of the same challenges as other cultural workers; the field is casualized, precarious, characterized by low pay and scarcity of work, and requires multiple jobbing. It is also deeply shot through by sexism, heterosexism and by intersecting class and racial inequalities, including newer forms of inequality that relate to the informal and entrepreneurial nature of the classical music sector. Discussing the requirement for them to become entrepreneurial subjects, Scharff considers the implications for musicians of having to see themselves and their work as 'businesses' in need of constant promotion. She explores the gendered difficulties inherent in the need for musicians to see their performances and their selves as products to be sold. Whilst most musicians – irrespective of gender – disliked 'selling themselves', women negotiated particularly fraught relationships with branding and self-promotion.

Bridget Conor discusses the film *Adaptation*, written by Charlie Kaufman, as an example of identity making and self-representation in the 'invisible' creative profession of screenwriting. Conor draws out the implications of the film's teasing depictions of a screenwriter called Charlie Kaufman, who has a more successful twin brother, also a screenwriter. She notes that these characters occupy a narrow range of subject positions that, although superficially negative ('egotist', 'masochist', 'supplicant'), nonetheless reassert the masculinity of the professional screenwriter. Reviewing statistics on Anglophone film industries, she draws parallels between the disproportionately low numbers of women who contribute to production, including through screenwriting, and the limited on-screen representations of women, in terms of both the numbers and range of female roles. The article argues that Kaufman's depictions of screenwriting exemplify and reinforce the taken-for-granted 'unspeakable' nature of the gendered exclusions and inequalities of the film industry more generally.

In **Ana Alacovska's** article, gender inequalities in media industries are examined through the unusual lens of the concept of genre. This refers to the categories, such as romance or news and current affairs, through which products and their majority audiences are matched in industries like publishing and television. Alacovska notes that although creative and media research has tended to link genre to reception through audience studies, it is primarily a category of 'labour and production'. She argues that there are 'gendered and gendering' ideologies attached to media genres that result in occupational segregation within institutions so that, for example, women producers are under-represented in 'male' genres in television and film. More subtly, genres have biographical implications, resulting from gendered stereotypes of producers' professional identities and gendered norms and cultural prescriptions for life courses and behaviours. Alacovska discusses the example of women travel writers, presenting findings from an interview study to show how genre-related conflicts around production practices, professional standing and careers are experienced at the most personal and emotional level, for example, as anxiety and feelings of inadequacy.

Finally in this section, **Miranda Banks and Lauren Steimer** foreground the work of the female stunt double in Hollywood film, a figure who challenges traditional notions of on-screen femininity through the display of physical power and strength. This case study highlights the ways in which stuntwomen's identities and bodies are simultaneously displayed and erased, not only on-screen, but in media coverage of the work of female stars who rely on the work of their stunt doubles but seldom acknowledge it. Histories of stunting highlight the particular gendered dynamics of the profession, including that the key position of the stunt coordinator (which often ensures career longevity) was traditionally white and male, and women were excluded from the profession until well into the 1970s. Women stunt doubles working today encounter ageism and a requirement to constantly diversify their portfolio of strengths and abilities.

The Sociological Review, 63:S1, pp. 1–22 (2015), DOI: 10.1111/1467-954X.12237

The fourth and final section of this collection is centred on notions of boundary-crossing, between home and work, paid and non-paid work, production and reproduction. **Ursula Huws** first discusses how activities corresponding to cultural and creative labour have been envisioned in Utopian models of society, past and recent. Her comparison of Rousseau and Morris, among others, draws attention to recurring conflicts and still-relevant problems. A central issue is that prioritizing cultural and creative work inevitably raises the question of who will carry out less worthy or enjoyable activities. Utopian models generally choose one of two solutions. The first is to propose some mechanism for sharing out the good and bad or creative and non-creative tasks, which raises problems of allocation and enforcement. The second solution is a division of labour based on different categories of persons, with the less privileged doing the less desirable work. Either solution involves inequalities, between the enforcers and the enforced, or the creatives and non-creatives, or both, and most of the Utopian models replicate the gendered and classed inequalities of the modeller's own society, usually unwittingly. As Huws notes, there is a failure here and elsewhere to recognize how 'unpaid reproductive work' underpins both productive work in a capitalist economy and 'satisfying creative work' in 'an idealised pre-industrial economy'.

In her article, **Stephanie Taylor** takes as a starting point for discussion a newspaper article profiling people working for themselves and at home. The 'working from home' trend has increased in coverage and popularity and encompasses the self-employed, freelancers, small business owners and 'mumpreneurs'. Taylor discusses the 'discursive drift' that has seen discourses of entrepreneurialism and new forms of creative working 'converge' on the workplace-in-the-home. She suggests that working for yourself, far from offering freedoms, potentially further excludes those who may already be on the margins of neoliberal workplaces and spaces because of 'caring responsibilities, maturity or work history'. Taylor argues that this drift is associated with a feminized creative figure and that the coverage of the 'working from home' trend is particularly insidious for women and for those who do not conform to a masculine creative and entrepreneurial ideal, encouraging a retreat to the home like that deplored by Betty Friedan in her original framing of the feminine mystique.

Lastly, **Leslie Regan Shade and Jenna Jacobson** discuss unpaid internships which have become ubiquitous in the CCI, regarded as key entry level positions. Previous criticisms have focused on class issues but Regan Shade and Jacobson argue that 'internship injustice' (Perlin, 2012) is also connected to gender. This can be seen both in the kinds of industries that have unpaid internships (eg publishing not techno-science), and in the kind of work expected of female (not male) interns. The article examines young women's experiences of unpaid internships in Canada's creative sector. Regan Shade and Jacobson's interviewees spoke of the difficulties of finding work and the concomitant pressure to take on multiple unpaid internships, whilst also recognizing that being able to do so was a sign of their relative privilege (eg being able to rely financially on parents for food and rent, etc.). Those with less support worked part-time alongside the unpaid internships, with little time off. The article offers a nuanced account of how young female interns navigate these difficulties and challenges and their high personal costs, in a world in which even getting an unpaid internship in the CCI has become extremely competitive.

References

Acker, J., (2006), 'Inequality regimes: gender, race and class in organisations', *Gender and Society*, 20 (4): 441–464.

Adkins, L., (2012), 'Out of work or out of time? Rethinking labor after the financial crisis', *South Atlantic Quarterly*, 111 (4): 621–641.

Adkins, L. and Jokinen, E., (2008), 'Introduction: Gender, living and labour in the fourth shift', *NORA – Nordic Journal of Feminist and Gender Research*, 16 (3): 138–149.

Ahmed, S., (2012), *On Bring Included: Racism and Diversity in Institutional Life*, Durham: Duke University Press.

Amabile, T.M. (1983), 'The social psychology of creativity: a componential conceptualization', *Journal of Personality and Social Psychology*, 45 (2): 357–376.

Banks, M., (2007), *The Politics of Cultural Work*, Basingstoke: Palgrave Macmillan.

Banks, M. and Hesmondhalgh, D., (2009), 'Looking for work in creative industries policy', *International Journal of Cultural Policy*, 15 (4): 415–430.

Beck, U., (2000), *The Brave New World of Work*, Cambridge: Polity Press.

Blair, H., (2001), '"You're only as good as your last job": the labour process and labour market in the British film industry', *Work, Employment and Society*, 15 (1): 149–169.

Brah, A. and Phoenix, A., (2004), 'Ain't I a Woman? Revisiting intersectionality', *Journal of International Women's Studies*, 5 (3): 75–86.

British Film Industry, (2013), *BFI Statistical Yearbook*, available at: http://www.bfi.org.uk/sites/bfi.org.uk/files/downloads/bfi-statistical-yearbook-2013.pdf

Brouillette, S., (2013), 'Cultural work and antisocial psychology', in M. Banks, R. Gill and S. Taylor (eds), *Theorizing Cultural Work: Labor, Continuity and Change in the Cultural and Creative Industries*, 30–43, Abingdon: Routledge.

Caldwell, J.T., (2008), *Production Culture: Industrial Reflexivity and Critical Practice in Film and Television*, Durham, NC: Duke University Press.

Centre for Women and Democracy, (2013), *Sex and Power 2013: Who Runs Britain?* available at: http://www.fawcettsociety.org.uk/wp-content/uploads/2013/02/Sex-and-Power-2013-FINAL-REPORT.pdf

Conor, B., (2014), *Screenwriting: Creative Labour and Professional Practice*, London: Routledge.

Cote, M., and Pybus, J., (2011), 'Learning to immaterial labour 2.0: Facebook and social networks', in M.A. Peters and E. Bulut (eds), *Cognitive Capitalism, Education and Digital Labour*, 169–193, New York: Peter Lang.

Cunningham, S., (2009), 'Trojan horse or Rorschach blot? Creative industries discourse around the world', *International Journal of Cultural Policy*, 15 (4): 375–386.

Department for Culture, Media and Sport, (2001), *Creative Industries Mapping Document*, London: HMSO.

Department for Culture, Media and Sport, (2008), *Creative Britain: New Talents for the New Economy*, London: DCMS.

De Peuter, G. and Dyer-Witheford, N., (2005), 'A playful multitude: mobilising and counter-mobilising immaterial game labor', *Fibreculture* 5, available at: http://journal.fibreculture.org/issue5.html

Deuze, M., (2007), *Media Work*, Cambridge: Polity Press.

Edley, N. and Wetherell, M., (2001), 'Jekyll and Hyde: men's constructions of feminism and feminists', *Feminism and Psychology* 11 (4): 439–457.

Fawcett Society, (2009), 'Are women bearing the burden of the recession?', Fawcett Society.

Figiel, J., (2012), 'Work experience without qualities? A documentary and critical account of an Internship', *ephemera* 13 (1): 33–52.

Florida, R.L., (2002), *The Rise of the Creative Class: And How it's Transforming Work, Leisure, Community and Everyday Life*, New York: Basic Books.

Fuller, G., Hamilton, C. and Seale, K., (2013), 'Working with amateur labour: between culture and economy', *Cultural Studies Review*, 19 (1): 143–154.

Gill, R., (2002), 'Cool, creative and egalitarian? Exploring gender in project-based new media work in Europe', *Information, Communication and Society* 5 (1): 70–89.

Gill, R., (2007), 'Technobohemians or the new cybertariat? New media work in Amsterdam a decade after the web', Amsterdam: Institute of Network Cultures, available at: http://www.networkcultures.org/_uploads/17.pdf

Gill, R., (2009), 'Creative biographies in new media: social innovation in Web work', in A.C. Pratt and P. Jeffcutt (eds), *Creativity, Innovation and the Cultural Economy*, 161–178, London: Routledge.

Gill, R., (2010), 'Life is a pitch: managing the self in new media work', in M. Deuze (ed.), *Managing Media Work*, 249–262, London: Sage.

Gill, R., (2011), 'Sexism reloaded, or, it's time to get angry again!', *Feminist Media Studies*, 11 (1), 61–71.

Gill, R., (2014a), 'Unspeakable inequalities: postfeminism, entrepreneurial subjectivity, and the repudiation of sexism among cultural workers', *Social Politics*, doi: 10.1093/sp/jxu016, first published online: 24 July.

Gill, R., (2014b), 'An ideological dilemma: the resurgence of sexism and the disappearance of "sexism"', in C. Antaki and S. Condor (eds), *Rhetoric, Ideology and Social Psychology: Essays in Honour of Michael Billig*, 109–121, London: Routledge.

Gregg, M., (2011), *Work's Intimacy*, Cambridge: Polity Press.

Hardt, M. and Negri, A., (2000), *Empire*, Cambridge, MA: Harvard University Press.

Hesmondhalgh, D., (2007), *The Cultural Industries*, London: Sage.

Hesmondhalgh, D. and Baker, S., (2011), *Creative labour: Media work in Three Cultural Industries*, Abingdon: Routledge.

Hirsch, P., (1972), 'Processing fads and fashions: an organization set analysis of culture industry systems', *American Journal of Sociology*, 77: 639–659.

Holgate, J. and McKay, S., (2009), 'Equal opportunities policies: how effective are they in increasing diversity in the audio-visual industries' freelance labour market?' *Media, Culture and Society* 31 (1): 151–163.

Hope, S. and Figiel, J., (2012), 'Intern culture', available at: http://www.artquest.org.uk/uploads/recovered_files/Intern%20Culture%20report.pdf

John-Steiner, V., (2000), *Creative Collaboration*, New York: Oxford University Press.

Keane, M., (2009), 'Creative industries in China: four perspectives on social transformation', *International Journal of Cultural Policy*, 15 (4): 431–443.

Kelan, E., (2009), 'Gender fatigue: the ideological dilemma of gender neutrality and discrimination in organisations', *Canadian Journal of Administrative Sciences* 26 (3): 197–210.

Kennedy, H., (2010), 'Net work: The professionalisation of web design', *Media, Culture and Society*, 32 (2): 187–203.

Khaleeli, H., (2014), 'Lenny Henry: diversity in the TV industry "is worth fighting for"', *The Guardian*, 20 June, available at: http://www.theguardian.com/culture/2014/jun/20/lenny-henry-interview-diversity-tv-industry

Lauzen, M., (2012), 'The celluloid ceiling: behind-the-scenes film employment of women in the top 250 films of 2012', available at: http://womenintvfilm.sdsu.edu/research.html

Lloyd, R., (2006), *Neo-bohemia: Art and Commerce in the Post-industrial City*, London: Routledge.

Mato, D., (2009), 'All industries are cultural: a critique of the idea of "cultural industries" and new possibilities for research', *Cultural Studies*, 23 (1): 70–87.

McRobbie, A., (1998), *British Fashion Design: Rag Trade or Image Industry?*, London: Routledge.

McRobbie, A., (2002), 'From Holloway to Hollywood: happiness at work in the new cultural economy', in P. du Gay and M. Pryke (ed.), *Cultural Economy*, 97–114, London: Sage.

The Sociological Review, 63:S1, pp. 1–22 (2015), DOI: 10.1111/1467-954X.12237

McRobbie, A., (2004), 'Creative London-creative Berlin: notes on making a living in the new cultural economy', *Atelier Europa*, available at: http://www.ateliereuropa.com/doc/creativelondberlin.pdf

McRobbie, A., (2007), 'The Los Angelisation of London: three short-waves of young people's micro-economies of culture and creativity in the UK', *European Institute for Progressive Cultural Politics*, available at: http://eipcp.net/transversal/0207/mcrobbie/en

McRobbie, A., (2009), *The Aftermath of Feminism*, London: Sage.

McRobbie, M., (2011), 'Reflections on feminism, immaterial labour and the post-Fordist regime', *New Formations*, Winter, 70: 60–76.

Miller, T., (2009), 'From creative to cultural industries: not all industries are cultural, and no industries are creative', *Cultural Studies*, 23 (1): 88–99.

Miller, T., Govil, N., McMurria, J., Maxwell, R. and Wang, T., (2005), *Global Hollywood 2*, London: BFI Publishing.

Neff, G., Wissinger, E., and Zukin, S., (2005), 'Entrepreneurial labour among cultural producers: "cool" jobs in "hot" industries', *Social Semiotics*, 15 (3): 307–334.

Neilson, B., and Rossiter, N., (2005), 'From precarity to precariousness and back again: labour, life and unstable networks', *Fibreculture* 5. Available at: http://five.fibreculturejournal.org/fcj-022-from-precarity-to-precariousness-and-back-again-labour-life-and-unstable-networks/

Nixon, S., (2003), *Advertising Cultures: Gender, Commerce, Creativity*, London: Sage.

Oakley, K., (2013), 'Absentee workers: representation and participation in cultural industries', in M. Banks, R. Gill and S. Taylor (eds), *Theorizing Cultural Work: Labour, Continuity and Change in the Creative Industries*, 56–67, London: Routledge.

O'Connor, J., (2007), *The Cultural and Creative Industries: A Review of the Literature*, London: Arts Council England.

O'Connor, K., (2010), 'Speech to Women in TV debate', BAFTA, London, 17 March, Available at: http://www.bafta.org/access-all-areas/women-working-in-tv-is-it-a-young-girls-game,1048,BA.html.

Osborne, T., (2003), 'Against "creativity": a philistine rant', *Economy and Society*, 32 (4): 507–525.

Peck, J., (2011), 'Creative moments', in E. McCann and K. Ward (eds), *Mobile Urbanism: Cities and Policymaking in the Global Age*, 41–70, Minneapolis: University of Minnesota Press.

Perlin, R., (2012), *Intern Nations: How to Earn Nothing and Learn Little in the Brave New Economy*, London: Verso Books.

Perrons, D., (2000), 'Living with risk: labour market transformation, employment policies and social reproduction in the UK', *Economic and Industrial Democracy*, 21 (3): 283–310.

Power, D., (2009), 'Culture, creativity and experience in Nordic and Scandinavian cultural policy', *International Journal of Cultural Policy*, 15 (4): 445–460.

Pratt, A.C., (2002), 'Hot jobs in cool places. The material cultures of new media product spaces: the case of south of the market, San Francisco', *Information, Communication and Society*, 5 (1): 27–50.

Randle, K., Leung, W., and Kurian, J., (2007), *Creating Difference: Overcoming Barriers to Diversity in UK Film & Television Employment*, Report to European Social Fund.

Roan, A., and Stead, N., (2013), 'A "new institutional" perspective on women's position in architecture: considering the cases of Australia and Sweden', *Architectural Theory Review*, 17 (2–3): 378–398.

Ross, A., (2000), 'The mental labor problem', *Social Text*, 18 (2): 1–31.

Ross, A., (2003), *No-collar: The Humane Workplace and its Hidden Costs*, New York: Basic Books.

Ross, A., (2009), *Nice Work if You Can Get It: Life and Labour in Precarious Times*, New York: New York University Press.

Sang, K., Dainty, A. and Ison, S., (2007), 'Gender: a risk factor for occupational stress in the architectural profession', *Construction Management and Economics*, 25: 1305–1317.

Sawyer, R.K., (2007), *Group Genius*, New York: Basic Books.

Scharff, C., (2012), *Repudiating Feminism*, Farnham: Ashgate.

Scharff, C., (forthcoming), 'The psychic life of neoliberalism', *Theory, Culture and Society.*

Scott, A.J., (2005), *On Hollywood: The Place, the Industry*, Princeton, NJ: Princeton University Press.

Sennett, R., (1998), *The Corrosion of Character: The Personal Consequences of Work in the New Capitalism*, London: W.W. Norton.

Sennett, R., (2006), *The Culture of the New Capitalism*, New Haven: Yale University Press.

Skillset, (2010), *Women in the Creative Media Industries*, available at: http://www.creativeskillset .org/uploads/pdf/asset_15343.pdf?3

Skillset, (2012), *Creative Skillset Employment Census*, available at: http://www.creativeskillset.org/ research/activity/census/article_9235_1.asp

Taylor, S., (2011), 'Negotiating oppositions and uncertainties: gendered conflicts in creative identity work', *Feminism and Psychology*, 21 (3): 354–371.

Taylor, S., (2015), 'Discursive and psychosocial? Theorising a complex contemporary subject', *Qualitative Research in Psychology* 12 (1), in press.

Taylor, S. and Littleton, K., (2012), *Contemporary Identities of Creativity and Creative Work*, Abingdon: Ashgate.

Thanki, A. and Jeffreys, S., (2007), 'Who are the fairest? Ethnic segmentation in London's media production', *Work Organisation, Labour and Globalisation*, 1 (1): 108–118.

Ursell, G., (2000), 'Television production: issues of exploitation, commodification and subjectivity in UK television markets', *Media Culture and Society*, 22 (6): 805–825.

Virno, P., (2003), *A Grammar of the Multitude*, London: Semiotext(e).

Weeks, K., (2011), *The Problem with Work: Feminism, Marxism, Antiwork Politics and Postwork Imaginaries*, Durham, NC: Duke University Press.

Wittel, A., (2001), 'Toward a network sociality', *Theory, Culture and Society*, 18 (6): 51–76.

Please quote the article DOI when citing SR content, including monographs. Article DOIs and "How to Cite" information can be found alongside the online version of each article within Wiley Online Library. All articles published within the SR (including monograph content) are included within the ISI Journal Citation Reports® Social Science Citation Index.

The Sociological Review, 63:S1, pp. 1–22 (2015), DOI: 10.1111/1467-954X.12237
© 2015 The Authors. Editorial organisation © 2015 The Editorial Board of the Sociological Review

Part 2: Sexism, segregation and gender roles

Sex, gender and work segregation in the cultural industries

David Hesmondhalgh and Sarah Baker

Abstract: This chapter addresses work 'segregation' by sex in the cultural industries. We outline some of the main forms this takes, according to our observations: the high presence of women in marketing and public relations roles; the high numbers of women in production co-ordination and similar roles; the domination of men of more prestigious creative roles; and the domination by men of technical jobs. We then turn to explanation: what gender dynamics drive such patterns of work segregation according to sex? Drawing on interviews, we claim that the following stereotypes or prevailing discourses, concerning the distinctive attributes of women and men, may influence such segregation: that women are more caring, supportive and nurturing; that women are better communicators; that women are 'better organized'; and that men are more creative because they are less bound by rules.

Keywords: work segregation, cultural industries, stereotypes, sexual division of labour

Introduction

This chapter is underpinned by the following assumptions: sexism in society and culture creates conditions of profound difference and inequality between men and women; this has marked effects on all forms of work; and that such difference and inequality are likely to take particular forms in the cultural industries, because of certain distinguishing features of the cultural industries vis-à-vis other industries. We draw on some secondary, statistical sources, but ours is primarily a qualitative approach aimed at understanding the experiences of workers, and their understandings of these experiences, and so we do not focus on statistically demonstrating this inequality in its various forms. Instead, we focus on a particular aspect of how gender inequality makes it harder for women to have good experiences of cultural work than men: division of labour in the cultural industries according to sex.

According to a census produced by the UK government's skills training body, Skillset (2010), about 42 per cent of the UK 'creative media industries' workforce is female, compared with 46 per cent in UK industry as a whole. However,

The Sociological Review, 63:S1, pp. 23–36 (2015), DOI: 10.1111/1467-954X.12238

this masks a considerable disparity between industries, with very low levels of female representation in the interactive content (5 per cent) and game industries (6 per cent), high levels in industries such as book publishing (61 per cent female – the only subsector where female employment was above 50 per cent) and ra- dio (47 per cent). Two other industries that we discuss below were at or above the national average, and therefore relatively 'feminized': television (41 per cent women) and magazine publishing (48 per cent women). A third industry that we discuss below, the music industry, was not included in the Skillset census. But a figure circulated by the UK rights society, PRS for Music (2013), and attributed to research conducted by another Skills Council, Creative and Cultural Skills (2012), cites a figure of 32 per cent women and 68 per cent men in the music industry, including the recording and live sectors. These figures almost certainly represent increases on previous eras.

Behind these employment statistics regarding the concentration of women and men lurks a different but related problem: what is generally known by researchers as occupational and job *segregation* by sex – which we will call sexual work seg- regation for short. There is a tendency in perhaps all existing societies for some occupations and jobs to be strongly associated with women and some with men, though there is significant cultural variation in the categories. Examples of occu- pations associated with women in Europe and North America in recent decades include nursing, primary teaching, hairdressing and other 'beauty work', and cer- tain kinds of manufacturing work involving 'manual dexterity' (Bradley, 1989). Occupations strongly associated with men include mining, driving, professional catering, plumbing and car sales. With the entry of more women into the work- force over the last forty years in many countries, some occupations and jobs have become 'feminized' – Wharton (2012: 194) names public relations, systems anal- ysis, bartending, advertising and insurance adjusting as examples. But 'feminiza- tion' rarely refers to a predominantly male occupation becoming predominantly female. Instead it tends to denote an increase in the concentration of women within that occupation. Segregation, as Browne (2006: 5–6) emphasizes, is not the same as inequality. It can be thought of as having vertical (inequality) and horizontal (difference) components. As Browne points out, however, 'segregation tends to possess a messy combination of both horizontal and vertical dimensions' (2006: 5).

There is a considerable research literature on work segregation by sex (eg Bradley, 1989; Blackburn *et al.,* 2001; Hakim, 1979). Most books on gen- der and work devote some space to it. 'Segregation' is not necessarily used to mean full segregation – it is a relative concept, and takes different degrees in different occupations and jobs (and also in organizations – see Halford *et al.*, 1997 for relevant discussion). We use the rather awkward phrasing 'by sex' to avoid confusion with the issue of 'sex work' (such as lap dancing and sell- ing sexual services). Our concern is not sexuality, though of course this has an important role to play in sex inequality in the workplace. Rather it is the sexed division between men and women, which of course is hugely affected by gen- der. Like Browne (2006: 3), we prefer the term 'sex' to that of 'gender' in the

The Sociological Review, 63:S1, pp. 23–36 (2015), DOI: 10.1111/1467-954X.12238

context of goals of equality and justice, because we seek equality between men and women rather than equality along the dimension of identification with socially constructed notions of femininity or masculinity. As Browne points out, 'this would be neither possible nor particularly desirable in the pursuit of any practical notion of societal justice' (2006: 3). This is in no way to suggest that gender is unimportant; this is emphatically not based on a desire to return to biological or Lacanian theories of sexual difference. Gender is fundamental to our analysis below, as it is to Browne's. But equality of men and women, regardless of their biological sex, rather than the hazy and confused concept of gender equality, is the goal. (Equality of transgendered people with other people is a separate issue, but is absolutely compatible with that goal of sex equality in our view.)

The reasons why feminists (of both sexes) should be concerned with work segregation by sex are, surprisingly, rarely made explicit. We will suggest some here. First, it is strongly linked to inequality. For example, jobs and occupations carried out by women rather than men tend to be paid less. This is made strikingly clear when pay rates between countries where a certain occupation is dominated by men (such as dentists in the United States) are compared with a country where women have a more equal or even dominant share of jobs in that occupation (such as dentists in parts of Europe). Pay tends to be considerably lower for the same job in the latter case. Second, work segregation by sex limits the autonomy, freedom and recognition accorded to individual women and men. When a woman has a set of talents that would make her well suited to thrive in a particular occupation, but that occupation is considered 'male', then this makes it much more likely that she will not pursue that occupation. The same is true of men who wish to pursue occupations that are gendered female, but given the extra limitations on women entering labour markets, occupational segregation as a whole disadvantages women more than men, and this exacerbates inequality. Third, work segregation by sex limits collective flourishing, because it leads to a situation where it is harder for people to match their talents to occupations, thus inhibiting the way in which people's talents might serve the common good. Fourth, work segregation by sex both draws upon, and in turn contributes to, social 'stereotypes' which limit women and men's freedom and recognition – reinforcing the problem of gendered occupational segregation. We return to this important issue of stereotypes in what follows, as it has a considerable bearing on sex segregation in the cultural industries which is itself the key source of social representation, whether stereotyped or otherwise.

There has been a great deal written on work segregation by sex, but very little of it concerns the cultural industries. One major exception is Browne's (2006) fine study of 'vertical occupational sex segregation' at the BBC. But Browne, who is not a cultural analyst, pays no attention to how the specific nature of the BBC as a culture-producing organization might be the source of factors that influence sex segregation dynamics there – a major focus of our contribution here. In turn, very little of the considerable literature on cultural production has addressed sexual work segregation in any detail. Some of the rare exceptions are discussed below (such as Banks, 2009; Frölich, 2004; Nixon, 2003). Although there are many other important aspects of sexual inequality and gender dynamics in cultural work, our theme in this chapter, then, is work segregation by sex, which of course is one aspect of the more general problem of division of labour by sex. In the next section, we provide a brief overview of our research methods. We then outline some of the main forms which, according to our observations, work segregation by sex takes in the cultural industries: the high presence of women in marketing and public relations roles in the cultural industries; the high numbers of women in production co-ordination and similar roles; the domination of men of more prestigious creative roles; and the domination by men of technical jobs. Next, we move from problems to possible explanations of them: what gender dynamics drive such patterns of work segregation by sex? Here we consider some of our interviewees' explanations of such segregation in their cultural workplaces, reflecting on what this tells us about the effects of stereotypes, or prevailing discourses, concerning the distinctive attributes of women and men. A theme that emerges from the discussion, which we briefly consider at the end, is as follows: to what extent does the attribution of particular strengths and styles (such as an ability to deal with emotion and intimacy) actually serve to limit women's quality of working life?

Methods: interviews and participant observation

This chapter extends the analysis of the quality of working life in the cultural industries presented in our book *Creative Labour* (Hesmondhalgh and Baker, 2011) by drawing out the gendered dimensions of this work. Theoretically, the book sought to bring together the 'turn to cultural work' in recent social and cultural research (Banks, 2007; Ross, 2009) with contributions to the sociology, anthropology and philosophy of work, and thereby address the question 'to what extent do the contemporary cultural industries offer good work?' The simplicity of that adjective 'good' represented a deliberate attempt to evoke the importance of ethics and normativity. The turn to cultural work, we were suggesting, would benefit from greater clarity about evaluation of working life in the cultural industries, and therefore about what reforms might be argued for. Empirically, the book drew on interview and participant observation research conducted in three industries – music, magazine publishing and television – in order to provide a spread of case studies. We also drew extensively on other sources to contextualize those industries, and to understand their specific organizational dynamics.

Gender was a significant concern from the start. In our interviews and case studies, we attempted to balance the proportion of men and women, and to talk to workers at different levels of the industries we studied. We paid careful attention to gender in coding the results, and intended to write a separate chapter on gender. While gender issues appeared at various points throughout the book, such as our chapter on emotional and affective labour in the cultural industries, we did not find time to integrate our findings with existing theoretical and empirical research on gender and work in general (or with the very small number of studies on gender and cultural work). This chapter therefore seeks to remedy

The Sociological Review, 63:S1, pp. 23–36 (2015), DOI: 10.1111/1467-954X.12238

this fault at least partially, by drawing on our empirical material, and on previous research on gender and work, gender and cultural production, and cultural production and work.

The fieldwork for the study was conducted in 2006–7 (and was funded by the Arts and Humanities Research Council). Both of us have continued to research the cultural and media industries and, in our view, while these industries have continued to change, as they always do, they have not changed so much that our fieldwork does not cast interesting light on present realities. The fieldwork was done entirely within England. We make no claims about the international generalizability of the data. However, based on our familiarity with cultural industries in other Anglophone countries, we believe it likely that some of these patterns would be reproduced elsewhere in the (over) developed world.

Forms of segregation by sex in the cultural industries

In the cultural industries, as in many other sectors, the tasks most often carried out by women rather than men include public relations and marketing. In 1984, Steward and Garratt noted that 'In the big, happy record company family, a woman's place is in the press department' (quoted in Negus, 1992: 115). Things have changed somewhat – there are other roles that women have begun to take on. But across all three of the industries that we studied (television, magazine journalism and music) many of the marketing and PR staff we talked to were women, working in departments where women were in a majority. As Negus (1992) explains in relation to the UK recording industry, it was not always this way: in the early 1970s, nearly all 'publicists' were men. PR and marketing were among those occupations that were feminized in the 1970s, both inside the cultural industries and more generally. PR and marketing can be seen as cultural occupations that exist in many – indeed most – industries and in many firms, including in the cultural industries themselves. Aldoory (2005) claimed in 2005 that the PR profession in the USA had developed to a point where over 70 per cent of practitioners were women, though as Frölich (2004) points out, an even higher proportion of trainees in PR and journalism are women, and there is evidence that women leave these industries much more than men.[1] The feminization of journalism (Franks, 2013) has almost certainly further contributed to the feminization of PR, as many journalists migrate to work in the often more secure and better-paid world of public relations.

A second area of cultural work that is markedly female in the composition of its workforce is, broadly, those types of work concerned with the co-ordination and facilitation of production. And this relates closely to a third area of occupational segregation: that 'creative' jobs tend to be taken by men. On visiting an independent television production company, one of us noticed that the first half of the office area, nearest to the reception, was all male. Our interviewee said 'this is the creative side' and told us that the other half of the office area, which was entirely female, was for 'production' (Esther, Interview 40). This was by no means atypical in television production, and importantly, the creative side is more prestigious. One company that we researched in some detail was based around two men 'in the business of actually putting the programmes together' and 'everyone else who facilitates that process is female' (Gary, Interview 24). A female documentary producer and production manager told us: 'There are far more male directors than women and there are more women enablers, kind of bossy boots. Totally, totally crap that is, isn't it?' (Lilith, Interview 43). Such hierarchization is also apparent in the case of public relations and marketing, which, like production co-ordination, are less prestigious occupations within the cultural industries than are creative roles.

Nevertheless, some interviewees noted shifts in segregation by sex. 'Creative management' roles in television seem to be increasingly occupied by women – especially the key roles of commissioning editor or commissioner (though this is partly dependent on genre, as indeed are many of the phenomena that we observed). These are rather more managerial than they are creative – the core of the job is to organize and handle the creative outputs of others. The job is not dissimilar to that of the commissioning editor in publishing, a role that was feminized relatively early, in the 1970s and 1980s (see Henry, 2009).

The gendering of creative and 'non-creative' roles echoes findings in research on other cultural industries that we did not have the opportunity to study, such as advertising.[2] Sean Nixon (2003) cited figures showing that, by the year 2000, there was a considerable range in the presence of women in the various roles in advertising: 60 per cent of finance and administrative workers were women, 54 per cent of account handlers (up from 33 per cent at the start of the 1990s) and 44 per cent of media planners/buyers. But only 18 per cent of creatives were women, and this percentage actually declined in the 1990s. Combined with problems for women in gaining promotion, endemic in most industries (and which we will discuss below) this in turn meant that very few women achieved the position of creative director. Yet, because marketing had become increasingly feminized, as discussed above, the marketing managers to whom advertisers were presenting were often female: an imbalance of which agencies were strongly aware. According to figures cited by Nixon (2003: 96), 50 per cent of marketing managers were female by the end of the 1990s.

There is a fourth form of work segregation by sex in the cultural industries, which will perhaps come as no surprise, because of the long and problematic relationship between gender and technology (see Wajcman, 2011): as in other industries, men tend to dominate technical and 'craft' jobs, such as camera operators and editing in television, engineering and 'road managers' or roadies (technical staff handling equipment) in the music business. What is more, as Miranda Banks (2009) points out, craft and technical occupations associated with women, such as costume design, tend to be relatively unrecognized and undervalued. This can happen to the degree that such occupations are not even recognized as involving craft or technical skills at all.

In pointing to the marginalization of women from key creative roles, we should be wary of simplification about the relations between 'above the line' creative and

The Sociological Review, 63:S1, pp. 23–36 (2015), DOI: 10.1111/1467-954X.12238

'below the line' technical and craft occupations. While creative roles might sometimes be more prestigious, and more recognized publicly, actual creative workers receive very unequal rewards and have very different levels of power and autonomy from each other. Creatives are highly hierarchized, in 'winner take all' markets where the successful few are disproportionately rewarded (see Hesmondhalgh, 2012, for discussion of this phenomenon). Technical and craft jobs can in fact be of higher quality, and receive greater levels of union protection than 'creative' ones and can be relatively prestigious, especially compared with facilitation and marketing roles. These issues are important in the present context because technical and craft jobs tend to be taken by men – and there may be divisions within the creative jobs, whereby occupations with high numbers of women, such as acting, are prone to uncertain work conditions. We are likely to understand the complexities of segregation by sex better, the more we drill down to specific job levels, rather than looking at occupations or occupational groupings (such as creative or craft workers) as a whole.

Explaining work segregation by sex in the cultural industries: caring and communicating

So, we have presented a number of ways in which work segregation by sex is manifested in the cultural industries. How, though, do we *explain* such patterns? To ask such a question invokes the broader problem of explaining work segregation by sex in general. Anker has discussed how some dominant social science theories, notably neo-classical, human capital and institutional labour market models, tend (a) to treat occupational sex segregation as though it is the same thing as sex-based pay differentials, when it is not; (b) fail to provide an explanation of how occupational sex segregation comes about.[3] Anker (2001: 139) claims that feminist gender theory 'makes a valuable contribution to explaining occupational segregation by sex by showing how closely the characteristics of "female" occupations mirror the common stereotypes of women and their supposed abilities'. He provides a list of such 'stereotypes' and the occupations that tend to be affected by them. Some of them are positive, such as the idea that women have a caring nature, that they are skilled in domestic work, or that they have greater manual dexterity, trustworthiness and attractiveness. Such views feed the gendering of occupations such as nursing, teaching, social work, hairdressing, dressmaking, book-keeping, reception and shop assistant work, and so on. Some are negative, such as ideas that women are less able to supervise others, that they have less physical strength (many women have greater physical strength than many men), that they are less able in science and maths, that they are less willing to travel, or to face danger and use physical force. This affects the gendering of occupations such as management, mining and construction work, engineering and transport, and security work. Then there are other, more 'neutral' or ambivalent characterizations of women as being less inclined to complain, more willing to take on monotonous or repetitive work, and more interested in working at home. These

The Sociological Review, 63:S1, pp. 23–36 (2015), DOI: 10.1111/1467-954X.12238
© 2015 The Authors. The Sociological Review published by John Wiley & Sons Ltd on behalf of the Editorial
Board of The Sociological Review

tend to push women in the direction of jobs that are low paid, unprotected and often repetitive.

The term used by Anker, 'stereotype', merits some consideration. Questions of culture, meaning and discourse have been an important element of feminist theory in recent decades (see Fraser, 2013, for an incisive discussion of this issue). The concept of stereotyping may seem to some rather basic compared with sophisticated debates about issues such as the gendering of language itself. Certainly, it has fallen from favour in media and cultural studies over the last 30 years (though see Pickering, 2001, for a defence and clarification of the concept) and in feminist media studies. We would argue, along with feminists such as Robeyns (2007), that stereotyping is an important concept for considering the way in which prevailing and repeated categorizations might influence the treatment of individuals and groups, provided it is applied with sufficient critical rigour, and provided it is combined with other factors in any explanation.

Wharton (2012) discusses two other factors identified by researchers as causes of sex segregation: workers' own preferences, shaped by their own histories; and effects of workplace processes such as recruitment and assignment of roles. Wharton, who does not explicitly discuss stereotypes, argues that there is evidence that the effects of early 'socialization' are sometimes exaggerated, and the importance of employers' actions consequently downplayed.[4] Policy is also a vital consideration, as Browne (2006) shows. All these factors are important and need to be combined with the effects of stereotypes in understanding sex segregation in the cultural industries. But here, for reasons of space, and because of the nature of our own data, we focus on gender stereotypes, or prevailing discourses about the characteristics of women and men, as potential explanations of sex segregation.

Let us start from the case of PR and marketing. Observing the relatively high numbers of women in recording industry PR, Negus (1992: 114) suggested some of the reasons for this phenomenon: PR work 'involves the employment of skills which have traditionally been associated with women rather than men: looking after sensitive artists, maintaining personal relationships, providing support, and acting as a facilitator and catalyst'. The idea that women are more capable of caring, supportive and nurturing work than men (already mentioned above in relation to Anker's list, and widely recognized as a factor in understanding women's work) may lie behind the presence of women in PR. But related ideas were also invoked by some of our interviewees as a factor behind other forms of work gendering. Here, for example, is how one woman we interviewed sought to explain why documentary researchers were often women:

> I think a lot of women tend to put people more at ease. They're not so threatening in some situations. They can make themselves quite vulnerable, just physically vulnerable. They're smaller. I think each film dictates its own approach. It's a journey and every film makes itself in a way. So maybe a good woman filmmaker would use whatever she needed to use. I think any good filmmaker really, but some of the men I know seem to have more of an agenda on their films and more of a kind of bigger view. (Lilith, Interview 43)

The Sociological Review, 63:S1, pp. 23–36 (2015), DOI: 10.1111/1467-954X.12238

Closely linked to this idea of women as more caring, sympathetic and able to put others 'at ease' is the association of women with greater communication and presentational skills, which supposedly allow them to maintain personal relationships and prevent conflict. Here is an explanation by a male executive producer of factual television of why more and more women were working in this genre, where he claimed that talking to people 'in a relaxed way' was a requirement:

> I think the reason it has become very female is because women are also obviously better listeners. They have been brought up with a stronger emphasis on communication, listening. So maybe it's a gender stereotype forced upon people, but the fact is by the age of 20, 25, they are much more socially competent than men are. So if you are in an area which is predominantly people based and finding out about people and getting people to talk about themselves in a relaxed kind of way, then women tend to be better at that. (Kieran, Interview 20)

This kind of explanation may go some way to help understand the predominance of women in jobs and occupations that involve 'enabling' or 'co-ordinating', as discussed above. Whether women really are better communicators or listeners is a moot point. The key issue is that people working in television and other cultural industries have come to see gender in this way, and this has opened up a space for women, and perhaps closed one down for men.

We detected another 'stereotype' or prevailing discourse in operation in the cultural industries, which seems to have been discussed relatively little in social scientific studies of work in general, at least as far as we have been able to discern. This is the idea that women are better organized, and that they take greater care over procedure and so on. So roles such as production manager, production co-ordinator and production assistant were conceived by some interviewees, including relative newcomers working in creative fields, as 'female roles' (Gary, Interview 24). One of our interviewees used this idea to discuss why, as mentioned earlier in this piece, the role of programme commissioning in television was increasingly taken by women:

> So you have gender models. The two different genders overlap a lot but they also have different ways of succeeding. Women offer by and large a variation of skills. Men are more mercurial, often more difficult to handle. Women are often very steady, solid and organised. You can still have very creative women and very uncreative women, and very creative men and very uncreative men, but they are different. I mean these are gross generalisations. (Malcolm, Interview 37)

One head of production attributed the dominance of women in production co-ordination to women's 'ability to multi-task' and be 'very good organisers' (Esther, Interview 40).

Such organizational skills were explicitly contrasted by some of our interviewees to the kind of attributes that were supposedly necessary to be good in 'creative roles'. So one interviewee suggested that careful co-ordination and facilitation were not attributes of a 'good director' (which is a 'creative' rather than an 'organizational' role in factual production, where he worked). His reasoning was as follows:

> I suspect women are better organisers and want to feel that something is under control and well managed. Your good director, the one that's different, is actually the one who is going to want to put a wheel off the wagon and see what happens and take a risk. ... That is something you notice more with reckless males than you do with incredibly well organised and nice women. (Kieran, Interview 20)

It would only be fair to point out that Kieran was trying to explain the common sense of the industry, and how it contributes to work segregation by sex (though this was not the term he used). The line between observing common stereotypes and tendencies and seeming to affirm them is often very thin.

This can be seen when comparing such discourse with women's explanations of what they feel they, as women, can valuably bring to a workplace. One female managing director explained why she thought that 'women are incredibly good in television' in ways that relate to the above notions that women have skills which nurture other people's talents:

> We have loads of advantages. We are collaborative and we love working in teams. I mean, women really actually love working with other people, and they are very good at getting things out of other people and making them work to their best abilities. Women actually enjoy that I think. I'm not saying that men don't, but I think women particularly do. (Ingrid, Interview 11)

Is this reaffirming the stereotype that leads to work segregation by sex, or is it celebrating women's distinctive virtues in a way that opens up new spaces for women's employment? Or might it even be both?

In a rare and thoughtful discussion of such problems in relation to cultural work, here in the context of the gendering of journalism,[5] Frölich (2004: 71) conceded that 'worse things could happen to women' working in these fields 'than to be casually regarded as being able to communicate better simply because of their friendly, polite, consensus-oriented behavior'. However, she also suggested that such social sensitivity may derive from an effort to deal with a lower social status – these are 'tools that would enable them to survive and function in society'. This may have some validity, but not all subordinates are polite and sensitive, and not everyone in 'higher' social groups shows the opposite traits, partly because, in spite of what Frölich (2004) implies, not all social behaviour is competitively aimed at achieving personal goals. Nevertheless, Frölich may be right to point out how the possession by many women of 'communication skills especially oriented toward consensus and dialogue' (2004: 72) allows some women access to communication professions at the entry level, but does not necessarily influence how long they stay or how far they advance. 'Perhaps', she suggests, 'the very attributes that get women into the communications sector – sensitivity, caring, honesty, fairness or morality – are also associated with a lack of assertiveness, poor conflict management and weak leadership skills' (2004: 72). Yet it would surely be unfortunate if feminists responded to such a trap by arguing against the presence of these attributes among women. Frölich's (2004) term, 'the friendliness trap', seems an apt one here.

What of the clustering of men in the more prestigious creative roles, across many different cultural industries, noted earlier? What might explain this? Nixon's (2003) important study of advertising argued that the gendering of creative roles was protected and reinforced by a legacy of associations between masculinity and creativity. He drew on the work of art historian Griselda Pollock and others (see Parker and Pollock, 1981), who showed how features attributed to the creative artist – 'dependent, insecure, expressive, over-emotional and prone to infantile egotism' – placed the male artist at odds with more conventional versions of masculinity, but gained their power from 'being set simultaneously against representations of femininity that suggested that women could at best express taste' rather than 'true' creativity (Nixon, 2003: 100). This notion of masculinist creativity was apparent in the culture of creative departments, but it co-existed with a somewhat different masculine ethos of 'the creative as aesthete and man of taste'. But this mix of masculinities produced working cultures in which childishness and laddishness were valued (and Nixon was doing his research at a time when the figure of the 'new lad' was hegemonic in UK culture, partly as a result of developments in magazine publishing, and the rise of a new generation of men's magazines), and women were often seen as responsible for mothering and nurturing. This of course served to marginalize women from creative roles, and the 'mothering' roles became associated with account planning and other coordination roles. More recently, Proctor-Thomson (2013: 147) has discussed how the seemingly high value placed on gender diversity in the digital media sector in fact serves to 'exclude particular forms of difference and diversity from those considered to hold creative potential'.

Needless to say, perhaps, the kinds of segregation by sex that we have been describing here resulted in situations that were not welcomed by women. 'Sometimes', one head of television production put it, 'I feel I'm like a mother with hundreds of children, and that can be quite frustrating' (Esther, Interview 40). Yet for other female interviewees, caring and nurturing were valued as their distinctive contribution to cultural work. One successful female artist manager described how what she saw as a distinctive 'female management style' allowed her to mark out her own place:

> I would say that female management style is very much artist led … I really actually think my interpretation of management is to become a translator for that artist. So you are basically taking their vibe, their whole ethos, their philosophy, and you are trying to preserve as much as possible and translate it into a package that makes sense to the consumer. (Hannah, Interview 42)

This was in contrast to a more mechanical, less emotional male style that 'set[s] all your affairs by conveyor belt' (Hannah, Interview 42). It also contrasts with an almost legendary history of macho behaviour on the part of artist managers, supposedly in the service of their clients (see Summers, 2013). In valuing caring and nurturing styles as elements of their own and other women's work, are these women unconsciously reproducing stereotypes that then constrain women in the cultural workplace? That would surely be a harsh judgement. Education and employment policy needs to open up cultural workplaces to make all kinds of work available to women as well as men. And reasonable, constructive ('caring') approaches need to be more than just a niche that women feel they can occupy. Men should feel obliged to aspire to such behaviour too.

Some of the context for understanding gendered divisions of labour in the music industries, and what women working there have had to face, was provided by one music journalist:

> The music industry is still an incredibly sexist industry. I don't care what anybody says, I really would on the record say it's a blokes' industry and girls are press officers or stylists or groupies and it still is 'my best mate is my manager'. Somebody at quite a big independent label decided she was going to become a manager and they just went 'what do you want to become a manager for? Do you just want to shag loads of bands?' and she went 'no, I want to be a manager'. But still even within the independent community, there is that belief that a girl working in the music industry is just a glorified groupie. I think slowly that is changing. There are obviously a few high profile females, certainly in the publishing world.[6] I think the publishing world is perhaps not that bad as the record industry and there are a few powerful female managers and stuff like that. (Niall, Interview 17)

This suggests the same association of creativity with masculinity as discussed by Nixon (2003) in relation to advertising. Here, though, the dynamics are primarily sexual rather than infantile/maternal. Women's roles are portrayed as sexually subordinate. And when Niall points here to the greater presence of women in 'the publishing world' – by which he means 'music publishing' – he draws attention to the way in which work segregation by sex can be manifested at the level of entire industries, not just occupations, jobs and organizations.

The baby and the bathwater

Associations of various modes of masculinity with creativity, then, serve to marginalize women from the more prestigious creative roles and even sectors in the cultural industries. This, as we have shown, is just one way in which work segregation by sex occurs in the cultural industries. Others include the assignment to women of work involving the need for consensual and caring communication, and co-ordination. As we suggested above, however, it would be a mistake to argue too strongly against the high evaluation of such skills by women. Rather, we need to argue for a greater respect for such qualities, in both women and men. Similarly, when it comes to the gendering of creative roles, it would be a mistake to respond to the gendering of 'creative roles' by seeing all positive evaluations of 'creativity' as encumbered by sexism and patriarchy. For the view that creativity should be protected from commerce, that commerce should have boundaries, is an important way in which to protect the relative autonomy of aesthetic experience and public knowledge. They can and should be untied from dubious

The Sociological Review, 63:S1, pp. 23–36 (2015), DOI: 10.1111/1467-954X.12238
© 2015 The Authors. The Sociological Review published by John Wiley & Sons Ltd on behalf of the Editorial Board of The Sociological Review

gender politics. We need to examine *how* the commerce-creativity division of labour becomes attached to gendered divisions of labour, and recognize a much more varied set of modes of creativity, moving beyond dubious connections of creativity with infantilism and sexuality. As Edwards and Wajcman (2005) suggest with respect to stereotypes regarding leadership and management, dichotomies of hard and soft need to be broken down. Gender stereotypes matter hugely in the division of labour by sex.

Notes

1   See also Beetles and Harris's (2005) report on studies of the feminization of marketing.
2   It also echoes Banks and Milestone's (2011) careful consideration of how traditional gender roles both persisted and were being questioned in the digital 'new media' sector. Their references to theories of individualization and reflexivity help make links with 'service sector' jobs more generally, an issue we do not have space to consider here.
3   Jude Browne's (2006) more comprehensive review criticizes human capital and neo-classical models and also a range of other theories, including 'preference' models (such as those of the feminist sociologist Catherine Hakim, 1979), patriarchy models (such as those of Sylvia Walby, 1990), Carol Gilligan's (1982) 'different voices' concept, and biologically based theories of dominance (such as Steven Goldberg's, 1993).
4   These broader factors would be best approached by 'life history' studies (see Taylor and Littleton, 2012), rather than participation observation and interviews – the methods we used.
5   Recent discussions of cultural work have not paid sufficient attention to the formidable literature on working conditions within journalism. Although we made some efforts in this direction in our 2011 book, we did not go nearly far enough.
6   Music publishing does not, as the name might suggest, refer to the publishing of sheet music (a marginal aspects of the music business for decades now) but to a sector of the music business involving the administration of the 'rights' that inhere in composition and the secondary rights that derive from ownership of the rights to songs. It is generally seen as more administrative, more businesslike, less creative than the more glamorous recording industry. The latter has been much less 'feminized' than the former.

References

Aldoory, L., (2005), 'A (re)conceived paradigm for public relations: a case for substantial improvement', *Journal of Communication*, 55 (4): 668–684.
Anker, R., (2001), 'Theories of occupational segregation by sex: an overview', in M. Fetherolf Loutfi (ed.), *Women, Gender and Work*, 129–155, Geneva: International Labour Office.
Banks, M., (2007), *The Politics of Cultural Work*, Basingstoke: Palgrave.
Banks, M., (2009), 'Gender below-the-line: defining feminist production studies', in V. Mayer, M. Banks and J. Thornton Caldwell (eds), *Production Studies*, 87–98, New York: Routledge.
Banks, M. and Milestone, K., (2011), 'Individualization, gender and cultural work', *Gender, Work and Organization*, 18 (1): 73–89.
Beetles, A. and Harris, L., (2005), 'Marketing, gender and feminism: a synthesis and research agenda', *The Marketing Review*, 5: 205–231.
Blackburn, R., Brooks, B. and Jarman, J., (2001), 'The vertical dimension of occupational segregation', *Work, Employment and Society*, 15 (3): 511–538.
Bradley, H., (1989), *Men's Work, Women's Work: A Sociological History of the Sexual Division of Labour in Employment*, Cambridge: Polity Press.
Browne, J., (2006), *Sex Segregation and Inequality in the Modern Labour Market*, Bristol: Policy Press.

Creative and Cultural Skills, (2012), *The Creative and Cultural Industries: Music 2012/13*, available at: http://blueprintfiles.s3.amazonaws.com/1350901070-Creative-and-Cultural-Industries-Music-Statistics-2012-13.xlsx

Edwards, P. and Wajcman, J., (2005), *The Politics of Working Life*, Oxford: Oxford University Press.

Franks, S. S., (2013), *Women and Journalism*, London: IB Tauris.

Fraser, N., (2013), *Fortunes of Feminism: From State-Managed Capitalism to Neo-liberal Crisis*, London: Verso.

Frölich, R., (2004), 'Feminine and feminist values in communication professions', in M. de Bruin and K. Ross (eds), *Gender and Newsroom Cultures: Identities at Work*, 64–77, Cresskill, NJ: Hampton Press.

Gilligan, C., (1982), *In a Different Voice: Psychological Theory and Women's Development*, Boston, MA: Harvard University Press.

Goldberg, S., (1993), *Why Men Rule: A Theory of Male Dominance*, Chicago, IL: Open Court.

Hakim, C., (1979), '*Job segregation: trends in the 1970s*', London: Department of Employment Research Paper.

Halford, S., Savage, M. and Witz, A., (1997), *Gender, Careers and Organisations*, Basingstoke: Macmillan.

Henry, C., (2009), 'Women and the creative industries: exploring the popular appeal', *Creative Industries Journal*, 2 (2): 143–160.

Hesmondhalgh, D., (2012), *The Cultural Industries*, 3rd edn, London and Thousand Oaks, CA: Sage.

Hesmondhalgh, D. and Baker, S., (2011), *Creative Labour: Media Work in Three Cultural Industries*, Abingdon and New York: Routledge.

Negus, K., (1992), *Producing Pop*, London: Edward Arnold.

Nixon, S., (2003), *Advertising Cultures: Gender, Commerce, Creativity*, London: Sage.

Parker, R. and Pollock, G., (1981), *Old Mistresses: Women, Art and Ideology*, London: Routledge Kegan Paul.

Pickering, M., (2001), *Stereotyping: The Politics of Representation*, Basingstoke: Macmillan.

Proctor-Thomson, S., (2013), 'Feminist futures of cultural work? Creativity, gender and difference in the digital media sector', in M. Banks, R. Gill and S. Taylor (eds), *Theorizing Cultural Work: Labour, Continuity and Change in the Cultural and Creative Industries*, 137–148, London and New York: Routledge.

PRS for Music, (2013), available at http://www.prsformusic.com/aboutus/press/latestpressreleases/Pages/PRSforMusicpresentsWomeninMusic.aspx

Robeyns, I., (2007), 'When will society be gender just?' in J. Browne (ed.), *The Future of Gender*, 54–74, Cambridge: Cambridge University Press.

Ross, A., (2009), *Nice Work if You Can Get It: Life and Labor and Precarious Times*, New York: New York University Press.

Skillset, (2010), *Women in the Creative Media Industries*, available at: http://www.creativeskillset.org/uploads/pdf/asset_15343.pdf?3.

Summers, J., (2013), *Big Life*, London: Quartet.

Taylor, S. and Littleton, K., (2012), *Contemporary Identities of Creativity and Creative Work*, Aldershot: Ashgate.

Wajcman, J., (2011), 'Gender and work: a technofeminist analysis', in E. Jeanes, D. Knights and P. Yancey Martin (eds), *Handbook of Gender, Work and Organization*, 263–275, Maldon, MA and Oxford: Wiley-Blackwell.

Walby, S., (1990), *Theorizing Patriarchy*, Oxford: Basil Blackwell.

Wharton, A. S., (2012), *The Sociology of Gender, 2nd edn*, Maldon, MA and Oxford: Wiley-Blackwell.

The Sociological Review, 63:S1, pp. 23–36 (2015), DOI: 10.1111/1467-954X.12238

Unmanageable inequalities: sexism in the film industry

Deborah Jones and Judith K. Pringle

Abstract: This article addresses the question of how gender inequalities are produced in the film industry. In the absence of industry or organizational interventions, these inequalities seem unmanageable. We present an exploration of the gendered working lives of below-the-line film workers in New Zealand, in the context of the western film industry. Repeatedly, women activists have pointed out that a perception of gender equity contradicts the statistics, which demonstrate traditional as well as 'new' forms of sexism. In this post-feminist context inequality is typically invisible and unspoken, and there is a thriving narrative of meritocracy based on talent and determination, where 'you're only as good as your last job'. Below-the-line 'crew' are distinguished from creatives in a hierarchy of creativity. In the New Zealand film industry, they are not unionized, and there are no policies addressing gender. From their perspective, their powerlessness in terms of employment rights is taken as a given, a price they pay for doing their dream job. In spite of beliefs about merit, talent and the 'good idea', women's 'good ideas' and their work capabilities across a range of roles are less likely to be recognized and rewarded than those of men.

Keywords: film industry, New Zealand, below the line, sexism, gender

Introduction

This article addresses the question of how gender inequalities are produced in the film industry. The scholarship of gender and work has tended to assume the possibility of organizational or industry-based interventions to 'manage' inequalities, whether from the bottom-up or the top down. Although there has been a neoliberal shift towards 'individualism and voluntarism' (Özbilgin and Tatli, 2011: 1230), interventions against inequality are still typically discussed in terms of legal and programmatic changes: Equal Employment Opportunities programmes, 'managing' diversity policies, and anti-discrimination laws. Historically, women have made the greatest gains where interventions are the products of collective action, in settings where there are employers with whom to bargain, and organizations through which policies can be implemented (Heery, 2006). But these

The Sociological Review, 63:S1, pp. 37–49 (2015), DOI: 10.1111/1467-954X.12239

bureaucracy-based interventions do not seem to apply in the terrain of the film industry, where projects are ephemeral and the creative subject is framed as entrepreneurial and individualized, a free agent, not an employee. Here inequalities seem unmanageable.

Drawing on Gill's notion of sexism as 'an agile, dynamic changing and diverse set of malleable representations and practices of power' (Gill, 2011: 62), we focus on how it operates in a specific 'gender regime'. This concept 'stands for the ways that gender is part of organizational processes at a particular time, in a particular organization' (Acker, 2006a: 208), or, in our case, a local industry.[1] We present an exploration of film work on the periphery – the working lives of below-the-line film workers in New Zealand. This approach differs from most film industry research on gender, which focuses on the higher status above-the-line workers. We connect gendered processes in the film industry to those in other forms of work, arguing that they are typical of a wide range of male-dominated industries, demonstrating traditional as well as new forms of sexism.

Speaking of gender and inequalities in the film industry

A feature of contemporary creative labour is that inequalities are 'unspeakable' (Gill, 2011). A 'vocabulary of the workplace' is absent and so too is any talk of collective organizing or workplace rights (McRobbie, 2011). A second premise is the 'post-feminist' environment, where feminist analyses are refused or unknown, and there is 'no language' to make sense of 'clear divergences between men's and women's experiences' (Gill, 2002: 85). This gender episteme of the last two decades characterizes a new sexism 'in which equality is assumed, yet in which men are privileged – whether we take as our indices pay, access to jobs, social networks, or any number of other factors' (Gill, 2011: 62). The absence or marginalization of a discourse of inequality can be described in Acker's terms as a feature of a specific gender regime, enabling us to analyse the 'invisibility of inequalities, the legitimacy of inequalities, and the controls that prevent protest against inequalities' within it (Acker, 2006b: 444). So we pay close attention to how knowledge about inequality in the film industry is produced and received, its visibility and legitimacy, and to the possibilities of change mobilized in response to this knowledge.

Research on gender and work in the film industry sits in two separate, though converging, categories. The first is film and cultural studies, where the emphasis is on women as creatives. Linking women 'on-screen' with women 'behind-the-camera', it is argued that in films where women are 'decision-makers' – directors, writers and producers, the 'holy trinity' of movie-making – more women are shown on screen and as major protagonists (Smith, 2009: 2). The second is the critique of 'cultural' or 'creative labour', where feminists have asked 'how far new forms of work rely on old patterns of discrimination and exploitation' (Banks and Milestone, 2011: 87). New or renewed forms of inequality have been pinned directly to the forms and practices of creative industries work (Eikhof and Warhurst, 2013). Cultural labour is also associated with new gendered

The Sociological Review, 63:S1, pp. 37–49 (2015), DOI: 10.1111/1467-954X.12239
© 2015 The Authors. Editorial organisation © 2015 The Editorial Board of the Sociological Review

subjectivities, new tensions to be negotiated in constructing creative female selves. While conflicts between self-expression and other-directedness are long-running themes in the feminist analysis of women and creative work (eg Nochlin, 1988), their contemporary persistence may be exacerbated by post-feminist forms of 'self-making or actualization through work' (Taylor, 2011: 368).

The film industry occupies a particular place in the landscape of creative labour. While it is not 'new', its networked, project-based work organization has been seen as prototypical of wider trends in the future of work. There is a continuum of work from those working in core roles in production companies to those out on the periphery, barely retaining a toe-hold in the industry, while there is constant pressure from an 'oversupply of willing entrants' trying to get in (Randle, 2011: 149). Access to work must be sought repeatedly from project to project (Rowlands and Handy, 2012). It has been argued by those in the industry that in order to manage risk, networking must focus on trustworthy recruits who will fit in immediately and are seen as competent. The effect here is that members of the dominant group replicate themselves through 'homosocial reproduction' (Smith *et al.*, 2012). They see people like themselves as the most trustworthy and competent (Grugulis and Stoyanova, 2012). At the same time, there is a thriving narrative of meritocracy based on talent and determination, where 'you're only as good as your last job' (Blair, 2001). The assumption here is that demonstrating that you are 'good' is somehow a simple, transparent and objective process, without bias. The statistics tell another story.

The legitimating language of statistics

The language of statistics is a key legitimating tool to make inequalities visible and speakable. This knowledge is especially important in the film industry, where talk of inequality is frequently silenced or marginalized. Repeatedly, women activists point out that 'a perception of equity masks the fact that the position of women .... has not improved' for two decades, and that 'barriers to women progressing in these industries today … may be invisible'. (French, 2012: 4). Overall, the statistics obtained by activists show the patterns we might expect to see in any male-dominated industry or organization: there is both vertical segregation by gender – male dominance of high-status work – and horizontal segregation by gender – where a number of occupations within the industry are sorted by traditional gender roles (eg French, 2012; Lauzen, 2009, 2013). Activists have initiated research on inequalities in the film industry, believing that 'one reason gender is not receiving higher priority is that individuals are not aware that inequality exists' (French, 2012: 5). Researcher activists often report a fear or reluctance on the part of those in the industry to explore the issue. New Zealand film-maker researcher Marian Evans argues that: 'There's a "silence" issue for some people about the statistics, and about the realities behind them' (Evans, 2010; see also Bridges, 2013). In Acker's terms, the invisibility of inequalities, and the fears that control protest, effectively legitimate industry sexism (Acker, 2006b).

The other main source of statistics is official data linked to government rationalities. In the UK, for instance, government has followed a 'dual agenda', pairing creative industries policy with 'social goals of inclusion and equal opportunities' (Proctor-Thomson, 2012: 138). In terms of film, 'diversity' strategies with a 'business case' focus have been generated by the UK Film Council (2003) and then the BFI (2013). While statistics on gender have been collected to support these policies, the results for women have not been particularly encouraging (Skillset, 2012).

Questions of interpretation are central to mobilizing these statistical accounts of inequality. For instance, a Skillset study of women who have succeeded in film and television in the UK analyses them primarily in terms of their individual qualities and choices, although their statistics demonstrate systemic inequality (Skillset, 2008). In this account, the need for personal characteristics such as 'passion ... tenacity and effective management of rejection or disappointment' are seen as 'perhaps understandable' given a context 'of women being more highly qualified, working longer hours but earning less than men' (2008: 2). However, 'direct experience of overt sexism' was reported only by 'older participants', but 'the industry operates within a culture that makes it very difficult for women to sustain a long term relationship or start and bring up a family'. This means that 'women should be mindful of the sacrifices they may have to make before entering the industry' (2008: 2). Overt sexism is positioned as obsolete, but the industry culture is taken as given, with a 'masculine breadwinner subtext' (Kelan, 2008) in which women are the ones who must decide whether they will make the sacrifices. Most recommendations in this Skillset report are based around the ubiquitous 'deficit model' (Bebbington, 2002), whereby women are the problem, and they must change their own characteristics to solve it, for instance, through more training and education. Yet the same statistics show that these women already have more training and education than their male colleagues. Marginalized in the report was a 'vocal minority' who 'believed that a huge cultural shift' in society would be required to change perceptions of women before there could be real change (Skillset, 2008: 20).

The dominant industry response can be interpreted in terms of a post-feminist sexism 'designed to seem to take on board feminist arguments and to anticipate and rebut potential accusations of sexism' (Gill, 2011: 62). Lauzen argues that influential people in the industry exercise their ' "privilege of denial", a tactic used by powerful individuals when they encounter inconvenient and thus uncomfortable truths. By virtue of their position, they are able to disregard factual data' (Lauzen, 2012: 314), denying discrimination and any responsibility for that discrimination.

The New Zealand study

New Zealand can be regarded as a kind of extreme case study of unmanageable inequalities in the film industry, because there are very few of the conditions required whereby sexism can be identified or addressed. New Zealand's film

The Sociological Review, 63:S1, pp. 37–49 (2015), DOI: 10.1111/1467-954X.12239

industry is small and vulnerable (MED, 2012). Yet it became the jewel in the crown of local creative industries policy in the early 2000s, when the global success of the locally made *The Lord of the Rings* trilogy coincided with the inception of a government-brokered creative industries programme. At this moment, a national identity boosted by the success of *The Lord of the Rings* was spliced into the film industry in new ways. Its basis was the locally made and globally successful Hollywood blockbuster, enhancing 'brand New Zealand' not just for its landscapes but for the technical ingenuity of its craft labour, both crews and visual effects specialists (Jones and Smith, 2005).

As Conor (2011) has pointed out, 'non-unionised workers are an essential carrot' in the global competition for satellite productions. In New Zealand, Hollywood productions provide the possibility of relatively long-term project work, higher pay, and access to new skills. Unlike larger film industries where there is a history of unionism, albeit eroding (Blair *et al.*, 2003), there is no unionism in local film-making. In this environment, local film crews are advertised to international producers thus:

> New Zealand film crews are renowned for their 'can do' attitude and enthusiasm. Their approach to production is born from a non-unionised, freelance working environment based on the firm belief 'you are only as good as your last job'. (Film Auckland, 2012)

In 2010 film craft workers actually demonstrated against a threat of union organizing, fearing that this would frighten away Hollywood and endanger their jobs. Under pressure from Warner Brothers, urgently passed legislation declared that all such freelance workers were contractors, not employees, thus 'effectively "immunizing" the New Zealand film industry against union activity and legislated employment regulation' (McAndrew and Risak, 2012: 57).

Where talk of worker rights is marginalized, discussion of gender inequalities is almost absent, in spite of the fact that for many decades there has been a legitimated regime of equal opportunities and anti-discrimination in New Zealand (Jones and Torrie, 2009). There have been no diversity policies, no 'dual agenda', no official statistics focusing on gender in film industry work, and unlike other film funding bodies (eg SFI, 2012), the New Zealand Film Commission (NZFC) has had no diversity policies in relation to gender. But the presence of some high-profile female creatives in the last two decades has given the false impression of strong progress for women, if not complete equality. New Zealand film-maker Gaylene Preston described herself as 'shocked really when I did a fairly informal statistic of my own regarding women feature film makers in New Zealand because my perception of our feature film-making is that we are known for having a really good female input ...' (Shepard, 2000: 212). The statistics, such as they are, show familiar, traditional patterns of inequality, with horizontal and vertical gender segregation (Evans, 2008, 2012; MCH, 2009).

Within the local Women in Film and Television chapter (WIFT NZ, 2013) there have been debates over progress for women (eg O'Brien, 2009). Tomsic has argued that the role of women's organizations which 'marry filmmaking with feminism' is centrally important in both speaking of and addressing inequalities

(Tomsic, 2005). WIFT NZ 'works to support growth and sustainability in the screen industries with a particular emphasis on equal opportunity and participation for women' (WIFT NZ, 2013), by providing mentoring, internship and training as well as networking opportunities. This approach provides individual women with skills and support, but does not tend to push for industry change. WIFT groups typically depend on forms of industry funding (as does WIFT NZ) which can compromise their critical role. Nolan (2004) has argued that if such organizations want to create overall change for women film-makers, they need to move to a political advocacy role. Triggered by global activism, WIFT NZ has recently been more active in addressing inequality, and the New Zealand Film Commission has now produced a report acknowledging under-representation of female creatives in government film funding (NZFC, 2014).

This was the context for our study, based on the working lives of 'below-the line' film workers. A distinction is made between the creative 'above the line' talent and 'below-the line' workers, including 'technical and camera crews, logistical and non-star performers, and equipment, studio and postproduction' (Coe, 2000: 84). The 'line' has come to stand for a kind of creative class division, with 'creative labour' above and 'trade and technical labour' below (Trollunteer, 2013). The situation of 'craft labour' in creative industries has been overlooked by researchers (Banks, 2010: 317), although it characterizes the majority of film-related jobs (Blair *et al.*, 2003). Most gender and film research focuses on the 'celluloid ceiling', the elite creative jobs for women (Lauzen, 2009), reflecting a concern for women as cultural creatives, rather than as workers. This 'line' distinction is important because 'below the line' work is more obviously 'work'. One of the key issues in studying creative labour is that 'creative' identification may erase the concept of oneself as a worker, and as inevitably implicated in a labour process. This understanding of labour relations is critical to understanding gender inequality, and the price that women pay for their participation in creative labour (McRobbie, 2011). Further, 'creatives' prefer to push the label of 'worker' below the line of creativity, thus maintaining their elite status.

The study is part of a wider project exploring working lives in the New Zealand film industry. Here we draw on life-history interviews with 16 below-the-line film workers, and follow up interviews about 12 months later. We understand life history methodology as 'the accounts of situated individuals' (Cohen *et al.*, 2004: 413) in historically and culturally specific locations. The interviewees included a number of related but distinctive jobs, in and across the areas of camera, sound, music editing, make-up, lighting, production design, and various production roles. All had worked professionally in film as crew at some point. They ranged from core workers, who worked pretty consistently for good pay, to peripheral workers who hung on to the dream of working in film while making a living mostly doing other things. About a third were also aspiring or practising creatives – musicians, writers, directors. They were equally men and women, all but one non-Māori,[2] and aged 22–61.

Our respondents did not necessarily share our feminist approach, or see their working lives in terms of power relations in the labour process. Our analysis

The Sociological Review, 63:S1, pp. 37–49 (2015), DOI: 10.1111/1467-954X.12239

addresses 'the tension between the different types of evidence' (Gill, 2002: 85), between the individualized accounts where gender is often unspoken or marginalized, and a bigger picture, not only of gender and cultural work, but of gendered work in general. Our discussion below focuses on exemplary data which illustrates, first, how our interviewees saw themselves as workers, and then the key ways that gender played out in their working lives.

Examples from our study: 'That's the kind of world I signed up for ...'

Once film industry workers have accepted the often very difficult conditions of film industry work, acceptance or ignorance of gender inequalities is written into the psychological contract. As one woman explained it:

> It's really like 'harden up'. You have to just deal with it ... Yeah, no rights, completely powerless ... But that's the kind of world I signed up for ... being an independent contractor, and someone can fire me at a moment's notice ... To do what you love there's big drawbacks to it ... yeah, it's what I want to do but definitely I wouldn't recommend to most people ... Working in the film industry ... it's my dream job.

By the same token, 'I'm quite happy but it's just such a boys' world, it really is ... you've just got to make it work really'. By this logic 'to do what you love' inevitably has 'drawbacks'. This is the 'dream' of creative expression, to which not all are called, and for which sacrifices must be made (Taylor, 2011). The challenge of surviving as a woman in a 'boys' world' may intensify a sense of exceptionalism which further underwrites the merit myth.

Being able to handle tough conditions on set is linked to the skills required to access work and keep it. One woman explained:

> You get jobs half on talent and experience and half on personality ... It is all about who you know and if they know you're someone that's easy to get along with and doesn't cause much of a fuss and doesn't get too stressed out and is just happy to come along and work.

In this environment, said another: 'you don't want to look like you're causing any problems because that may be detrimental to you getting some more work later on down the track'. For women being 'easy to get along with' requires further emotional labour to fit into what our respondents described as a 'male-dominated industry, always has been'. Because it is 'really really competitive and cutthroat', then to maintain your reputation you 'have to be able to join in and get along with lots of males when they're being really blokey' as one woman camera operator put it. To show that you are not the female stereotype, two women suggested, 'it is important to work hard and don't complain', and not to 'whine'.

In spite of the extra labour required for them to fit in, women could be excluded from crews 'in a sort of not really noticing or thinking about it way', as one described it, if they were not part of the social networks of male department directors. Countering inequalities, however, requires 'noticing or thinking about' them. In Acker's terms, the regulatory practices, the 'ordinary, often daily, procedures and decisions' (Acker, 2006a: 146) of the film industry perpetuate sexism and discourage speaking out. Despite the high price many women pay in order to carve out a successful career, the 'fragility of their relationship with the industry' persists (Rowlands, 2009: 131).

Examples from our study: mortgage, babies and 'opting out'

It is commonplace for researchers of gender and the creative industries to argue that the precariousness of work and the intense working conditions make it hard for women to have children and maintain personal relationships. The starting point of this 'dilemma' is that childcare and relationships are a women's problem, not an industry one (Lauzen, 2012: 315). Describing reproduction of labour in the gendered private sphere as a key underpinning of gender inequality, Acker (2006a) points out that it extends gender divisions outside work spaces to the household. One strategy is for a couple to include 'one person who's in the real world', as an informant described it, in secure work that can underwrite the film worker. Another is for both partners to work in the industry: in some cases they were able to operate as a tag team and share childcare, in others they decide together that they would not have children: 'we weren't prepared to give up what we were doing'. Some participants explained that if they were unable to take work that was offered – whether because of pregnancy, childcare or for any other reason, such as injury – they were likely to drop off the scene. Some women moved to 'real' jobs in film-related organizations once they had children, giving them access to regular hours and workplace rights that helped them to sustain parenthood in terms of both time and money. Men as well as women found it difficult to have close relationships given the huge work demands, although some found it easier if the partner was also in the industry. In these ways, precarious work based on a self-employment model moves 'business risk' from employers to the household (Randle, 2011: 151). Workers and their families bear all the personal and economic costs of parenting, which in other industries would be partly mitigated by employers through flexible work provisions, paid parental leave and on-site childcare. While 'family' issues were seen as affecting both men and women, there was a stronger emphasis on women being the ones who were most affected, and studies provide evidence of women leaving the industry at child-bearing ages (eg Sargent-Disc, 2011).

Examples from our study: gung-ho jocks and girly girls

Gender roles among technical below-the-line workers seem more stereotypical than those in 'creative' roles:

> It's still quite traditional. There are a lot of girly girls running around in make-up and I do actually still find it quite stereotypical, personally ... the crew type people – they're the people who go from job to job, rigging lights or doing make-up. They're not the people choosing jobs for creative reasons.

Here a female production designer is making a creative class distinction linked to technical roles. Contrary to the claim here, we found that nearly all the workers in our study saw themselves as 'choosing jobs for creative reasons'. However, it may be that sexist attitudes in technical roles are more traditional and overt, and possibly class-inflected. Technical crews are identified with a particularly blokey culture that has a 'jock kind of gung-ho rock and roll element to it'. A female camera assistant told us that some male technical crew made comments that 'if somebody said it in other kinds of work it would be considered to be kind of outrageous and very conservative. But somehow in the film industry it seems to be okay'. The example she gave described a female colleague who:

> …was talking to a focus puller who was male, because focus pullers often hire the camera assistant or the second camera assistant, and [the focus-puller] said that he is less likely to hire a woman because (a) he doesn't think that they'll be able to lift things all day and (b) because he thinks that you know, they'll work for a while and then they'll leave because they'll go and have babies.

While these statements might be considered discriminatory in other kinds of workplaces, where there might be a range of options for employment grievances, in freelance film work there is no such space in which complaints can be made, no practical access to unions or human resources practitioners, and a huge pressure not to complain. In this environment people with the power to hire can say whatever they like with little fear of serious challenge.

There were conflicting views among our respondents about whether different physical capacity excludes women from film industry jobs such as camera or lighting. This is a common theme in film industry studies (Skillset, 2008) and beyond, linking gendered occupations to bodies in ways that naturalize inequalities. Another kind of naturalized difference is evident in accounts of the ways that women and men do the same job. For instance, production tends to be a female-intensive occupation, with women concentrated at the lower-status, lower-paid end. This gendered distribution is described by one female producer as follows:

> Men are normally quite crap at production and women are quite good at it generally as a rule, as a stereotype I guess … It's a very female trait to want to look after people and making sure everything's organized, everything has a plan, everything has a plan B, it just suits the way women kind of think … [Male producers are] dealing with money and business and all this other stuff which is out for the kill which is a kind of male trait … Men do the, thumping the table.

The speaker here is consciously drawing on 'stereotypes', and while she affirms women's skills, her argument tends to naturalize differences which perpetuate inequalities.

Another female producer wanted to separate merit from gender, asking:

> Do I feel it's inherently sexist? No … The funny thing in this industry still, like the thing that you can never get away from is in the end, everybody wants to work on a good idea. And if that good idea comes from anywhere that's still what people want …

Managing sexism in the film industry

What might it mean to say that an industry is 'inherently sexist'? Sexism can imply situations where 'decisions are consciously directed at maintaining gender or other divisions' (Acker, 2006a: 196), and this may not be the situation in the film industry. But as Acker goes on to argue, while 'often such outcomes are unintended' (2006a: 196), there are sexist outcomes nonetheless. In spite of beliefs about merit, talent and the 'good idea', women's 'good ideas' and their work capabilities across a range of roles are less likely to be recognized and rewarded than those of men. The gendered processes of film industry work manage to produce regular inequalities between women and men in terms of pay, access to work, affirmation, support systems. This unequal outcome applies to both the 'super-creative' roles and 'below the line' crew. The key difference is that there is more overt occupational segregation 'below the line', often naturalized by references to physical abilities or other essentialized gender attributes. In this article we have emphasized the ways that sexism in the film industry is unexceptional, both in terms of traditional sexism with its blatant conservatism about gender, and in terms of 'new' sexism which does not directly speak its name, but works through excuses for inequalities and the neoliberal normalization of individual and voluntaristic modes of 'managing' inequalities (Özbilgin and Tatli, 2011).

There is a perceived discrepancy between the 'cool' and progressive world of creative work, and the discussion of labour issues such as inequality, or even the recognition of the labour process and capitalist production. There has been a widespread refusal to acknowledge inequalities: where they do exist, widespread and consistent statistical claims are combatted by lists of token women, by deep-seated belief in talent as the decider, and by a conservative approach to gender difference. As in other industries, even where there has been a history of addressing inequalities, the tide of neoliberalism has moved the emphasis from organizational and collective ways of addressing inequalities to individualistic solutions. Recent interventions to reduce inequalities have taken place at the level of state funding, rather than working through collective employment relationships. All these issues are exacerbated in New Zealand's small film industry where there is no historical base of sustainable work and legislation makes collective organizing very difficult. In a situation where there are no unions, there are few statistics that make inequalities visible, and equal opportunities policies have no traction, inequalities may well be unmanageable.

Notes

1 In her later work Acker uses the expression 'inequality regime' to indicate an intersectional approach (Acker, 2009). Here we address gender specifically, but also draw on concepts from her work on inequality regimes.
2 Our wider study included a study of indigenous Māori screen production specifically, by Ella Henry and Rachel Wolfgramm (Wolfgramm and Henry, 2013).

References

Acker, J., (2006a), 'The gender regime of Swedish banks', *Scandinavian Journal of Management*, 22: 195–209 (first published *SJM*, 1994, 10: 117–130).

Acker, J., (2006b), 'Inequality regimes: gender, class, and race in organizations', *Gender & Society*, 20 (4): 441–464.

Acker, J., (2009), 'From glass ceiling to inequality regimes', *Sociologie du Travail*, 51: 199–217.

Banks, M., (2010), 'Craft labour and creative industries', *International Journal of Cultural Policy*, 16 (3): 305–321.

Banks, M. and Milestone, K., (2011), 'Individualization, gender and cultural work', *Gender, Work & Organization*, 18 (1): 73–89.

Bebbington, D., (2002), 'Women in science, engineering and technology: a review of the issues', *Higher Education Quarterly*, 56 (4): 360–375.

BFI, (2013), 'Research and diversity', British Film Institute, available at: http://www.bfi.org.uk/about-bfi/policy-strategy/film-forever/research-diversity

Blair, H., (2001), ' "You're only as good as your last job": the labour process and labour market in the British film industry', *Work, Employment and Society*, 15 (1): 149–169.

Blair, H., Culkin, N. and Randle, K., (2003), 'From London to Los Angeles: a comparison of local labour market processes in the US and UK film industries', *International Journal of Human Resource Management*, 14 (4): 619–633.

Bridges, M., (2013), 'Why aren't there more women directors in the UK film and TV industry?', *Britflicks*, 13 September, available at: http://www.britflicks.com/blog.aspx?blogid = 394

Coe, N. M., (2000), 'On location: American capital and the local labour market in the Vancouver film industry', *International Journal of Urban and Regional Research*, 24 (1): 79–94.

Cohen, L., Duberley, J. and Mallon, M., (2004), 'Social constructionism in the study of career: accessing the parts that other approaches cannot reach', *Journal of Vocational Behavior*, 64 (3): 407–422.

Conor, B., (2011), 'Problems in "Wellywood": rethinking the politics of transnational cultural labor', *Flow*, 28 January, available at: http://flowtv.org/2011/01/problems-in-wellywood/

Eikhof, D. R. and Warhurst, C., (2013), 'The promised land? Why social inequalities are systemic in the creative industries', *Employee Relations*, 35 (5): 495–508.

Evans, M., (2008), 'PhD report for people who've helped me', available at: www.victoria.ac.nz/modernletters/about/showcase.aspx (accessed 24 April 2010).

Evans, M., (2010), 'Big Picture: could I do that?' *Wellywoodwoman (Blog)*, 27 May, available at: http://wellywoodwoman.blogspot.co.nz/2010/05/big-picture-could-i-do-that.html

Evans, M., (2012), 'A New Zealand problem, or two', *Wellywoodwoman (Blog)*, 6 November, available at: http://wellywoodwoman.blogspot.co.nz/2012/11/a-problem-or-two.html

Film Auckland, (2012), *Feature film: Infrastructure: Crew*, available at: http://www.filmauckland.com/feature-film/infrastructure/facts/Crew

French, L., (2012), *Women in the Victorian Film, Television and Related Industries*, Melbourne: RMIT (research report). Available at: http://researchbank.rmit.edu.au/eserv/rmit:160233/French.pdf

Gill, R., (2002), 'Cool, creative and egalitarian? Exploring gender in project-based new media work in Europe', *Information Communication and Society*, 5 (1): 70–89.

Gill, R., (2011), 'Sexism reloaded, or, it's time to get angry again!', *Feminist Media Studies*, 11 (01): 61–71.

Grugulis, I. and Stoyanova, D., (2012), 'Social capital and networks in film and TV: jobs for the boys?', *Organization Studies*, 33 (10): 1311–1331.

Heery, E., (2006), 'Equality bargaining: where, who, why?', *Gender, Work & Organization*, 13 (6): 522–542.

Jones, D. and Smith, K., (2005), 'Middle-earth meets New Zealand: authenticity and location in the making of *The Lord of the Rings*', *Journal of Management Studies*, 42 (5): 923–945.

Jones, D. and Torrie, R., (2009), 'Entering the Twilight Zone: the local complexities of pay and employment equity in New Zealand', *Gender, Work & Organization*, 16 (5): 559–578.

Kelan, E., (2008), 'Gender, risk and employment insecurity: the masculine breadwinner subtext', *Human Relations*, 61 (9): 1171–1202.

Lauzen, M., (2009), *The Celluloid Ceiling II: Production Design, Production Management, Sound Design, Key Grips, and Gaffers (employment figures for 2008)*, San Diego, CA: The Center for the Study of Women in Television and Film, available at: http://womenintvfilm.sdsu.edu/files/2008%20Celluloid%20Ceiling%20II.pdf

Lauzen, M., (2012), 'Where are the film directors (who happen to be women)?', *Quarterly Review of Film and Video*, 29 (4): 310–319.

Lauzen, M., (2013), *The Celluloid Ceiling: Behind-the-Scenes Employment of Women on the Top 250 Films of 2012*, San Diego, CA: Center for the Study of Women in Television and Film, San Diego State University, available at: http://womenintvfilm.sdsu.edu/files/2012_Celluloid_Ceiling_Exec_Summ.pdf

McAndrew, I. and Risak, M. E., (2012), 'Shakedown in the Shaky Isles: Union Bashing in New Zealand', *Labor Studies Journal*, 37 (1): 56–80.

MCH, (2009), *Employment in the Cultural Sector 2009*, Wellington: Ministry for Culture and Heritage, available at: http://www.mch.govt.nz/research-publications/cultural-statistics/employment-cultural-sector-2009

McRobbie, A., (2011), 'Reflections on feminism, immaterial labour and the Post-Fordist regime', *New Formations*, 70 (1): 60–76.

MED, (2012), 'Growth and dynamics of the New Zealand screen industry', Discussion paper. April, Wellington: Ministry of Economic Development, available at: http://www.med.govt.nz/about-us/publications/publications-by-topic/evaluation-of-government-programmes/Economic%20study%20of%20the%20NZ%20film%20industry.pdf

Nochlin, L., (1988), 'Why have there been no great women artists?' in *Women, Art, and Power: And Other Essays*, 145–178, New York: Harper & Row, available at: http://faculty.winthrop.edu/stockk/contemporary%20art/Nochlin%20great%20women%20artists.pdf

Nolan, E., (2004), *'Breaking through the celluloid ceiling? A study of the effectiveness of social capital in Women in film and video'*, PhD thesis, Vancouver: Simon Fraser University, available at: http://ir.lib.sfu.ca/dspace/handle/1892/8962?mode=full&submit_simple=Show+full+item+record

NZFC, (2014), *NZFC Feature Film Development Funding Information on Gender 2009–2014*, Report, September. Wellington: New Zealand Film Commission, available at: www.nzfilm.co.nz/news/feature-film-development-funding-information-on-gender-2009--2014

O'Brien, A., (2009), 'The battle is over... Yeah right!' *Onfilm*, June, http://www.archivesearch.co.nz/default.aspx?webid = ONF&articleid = 46638

Özbilgin, M. and Tatli, A., (2011), 'Mapping out the field of equality and diversity: rise of individualism and voluntarism', *Human Relations*, 64 (9): 1229–1253.

Proctor-Thomson, S. B., (2012), 'Feminist futures of cultural work: creativity, gender and diversity in the digital media sector', in M. Banks, S. Taylor and R. Gill (eds), *Theorizing Cultural Work: Transforming Labour in the Cultural and Creative Industries*, 137–148, London: Routledge.

Randle, K., (2011), 'The organization of film and television production', in M. Deuze (ed.), *Managing Media Work*, 145–153, Thousand Oaks, CA: Sage.

Rowlands, L., (2009), *'The life of freelance film production workers in the new Zealand film industry'*, Master's thesis, Palmerston North: Massey University, available at: muir.massey.ac.nz/bitstream/10179/1083/1/02whole.pdf (accessed 28 May 2010).

Rowlands, L. and Handy, J., (2012), 'An addictive environment: New Zealand film production workers' subjective experiences of project-based labour', *Human Relations*, 65 (5): 657–680.

Sargent-Disc, (2011), *Age and Gender in UK Film Industry*, http://www.sargent-disc.com/sargent-disc-uk/news-insights/insights/uk-film-industry-age-and-gender.aspx

SFI, (2012), *Gender Equality,* (Website: Towards gender equality in film production), Swedish Film Institute, available at: http://www.sfi.se/PageFiles/22839/Eng_Towards%20gender%20equality%20in%20film%20production_May2013.pdf

Shepard, D., (2000), *Reframing Women: A History of New Zealand Film*, Auckland: Harper Collins.

The Sociological Review, 63:S1, pp. 37–49 (2015), DOI: 10.1111/1467-954X.12239

Skillset, (2008), *Why Her? Factors that Have Influenced the Careers of Successful Women in Film & Television*, AFTV & Alliance Sector Skills Councils, UK, available at: http://publications.skillset.org/admin/data/why%20her/why%20her%202009.pdf

Skillset, (2012), *Women in the Creative Media Industries* (based on Creative Skillset Census 2012), available at: http://www.skillset.org/research/activity/census/article_9236_1.asp

Smith, P., Caputi, P. and Crittenden, N., (2012), 'A maze of metaphors around glass ceilings', *Gender in Management: An International Journal*, 27 (7): 436–448.

Smith, S. L., (2009), 'Gender oppression in cinematic content? A look at females on-screen & behind-the-camera in top-grossing 2007 films', *Annenberg School for Communication & Journalism, University of Southern California*, 1–28, available at: https://seejane.org/downloads/2007Films_GenderReport.pdf

Taylor, S., (2011), 'Negotiating oppositions and uncertainties: gendered conflicts in creative identity work', *Feminism and Psychology*, 21 (3): 354–371.

Tomsic, M., (2005), 'WIFT works for women: a short history on how to marry filmmaking with feminism', *Metro Magazine: Media & Education Magazine*, 145: 112–116.

Trollunteer, (2013), 'Gendered divisions of creative labour in Hollywood', (Blogpost, March), *Thesis to Journal Article Wk3 D1–2*, available at: http://www.trollunteer.org/thesis-to-journal-article-working-paper/

UK Film Council, (2003), *UK Film Council Diversity Report* (Success through diversity and inclusion), available at: http://industry.bfi.org.uk/media/pdf/3/r/Success_through_diversity_and_inclusion.pdf

WIFT NZ, (2013), 'WIFT women in film and television', available at: http://www.wiftnz.org.nz/home.aspx

Wolfgramm, R. and Henry, E., (2013). 'A relational dynamics approach to leadership based on an investigation of Māori leaders in the screen industry', International Leadership Association Oceania Conference, Aotearoa New Zealand, 22–23 April, available at http://www.nzli.co.nz/file/Conference/Papers/engaging-a-relational-leadership-approach.pdf

The Sociological Review, 63:S1, pp. 37–49 (2015), DOI: 10.1111/1467-954X.12239
© 2015 The Authors. Editorial organisation © 2015 The Editorial Board of the Sociological Review

Part 3: Flexibility and informality

Getting in, getting on, getting out? Women as career scramblers in the UK film and television industries

Leung Wing-Fai, Rosalind Gill and Keith Randle

Abstract: This article looks at the predominance of freelancing in the film and television industries as a lens to examine the persistence of gender inequalities within these fields. Previous research has indicated that women fare better in larger organizations with more stable patterns of employment, and in this article we explore why that might be the case, by focusing on the experiences of female freelancers at a moment when project-based, precarious work and informal recruitment practices are increasing in the UK film and television sector. We highlight in particular the ways in which gender inequality is mediated by age and parental status, and the impact of intersectional identities on women's ability to sustain a career in film and television.

Keywords: freelancing, film, television, informality, parenting

Introduction

The free agent scrambles, bee-like, from opportunity to opportunity without regard to boundaries. (Jones and DeFillippi, 1996: 89)

The article draws on more than 100 interviews with people in the film and television industry in the UK, and takes an intersectional approach. It focuses on the challenges posed by 'informality' in recruitment and as a means of finding work, pointing to the ways in which reputation, networking and homophily structure who gets in and gets on within these fields. It also looks at the issue of parenting, highlighting the practical difficulties of combining motherhood with a career in film or television, alongside subtle forms of discrimination that affect mothers and women more generally – highlighting particularly the ways in which not hiring women can be presented as 'rational' or 'understandable', producing what we call 'reasonable sexism'. The article further shows how an entrepreneurial ethic and an antipathy to 'whinging' mean that difficulties associated with inequality or with parenting are rarely voiced and are devolved to individuals to resolve

The Sociological Review, 63:S1, pp. 50–65 (2015), DOI: 10.1111/1467-954X.12240

themselves. In this way the article contributes to understanding how inequalities are both unmanageable and unspeakable within film and television production.

In recent years a number of terms have been coined to try to capture the ways in which working lives and career patterns are changing. Portfolio careers, project-based working and boundaryless careers are just some of the attempts to create a lexicon that speaks to what Beck (2000) has characterized as 'the Brave New World of work'. In this, short-term, discontinuous employment marked by precariousness and insecurity is 'discursively sweetened' by talk of entrepreneurialism and risk-taking, as 'cool, creative and egalitarian' work (Gill, 2002). While the people most affected by these changes have been the lowest paid workers, struggling in 'McJobs', among skilled and professional workers those in the cultural and creative industries (CCI) have been at the forefront of this trend towards 'precarization'. As Ross (2009) has argued, freelance 'creatives' have become 'new model workers' in contemporary capitalism, built upon the idea of the musician's gig: 'nice work if you can get it'.

In this article we look at the predominance of freelancing in the film and television industries as a lens to examine the persistence of gender inequalities within these fields. This article aims to examine the effects of freelance work, focusing specifically on women's employment in the UK film and television sector. Previous research has indicated that women fare better in larger organizations with more stable patterns of employment, and here we want to explore why that might be the case, by focusing on the experiences of female freelancers at a moment when project-based, precarious work is increasing in the UK film and television sector. Fewer women than men 'get in' to these industries, the way that they 'get on' is often different, and, increasingly, it seems women 'get out' of film and television after relatively short 'careers'.

The article adopts an intersectional (Brah and Phoenix, 2004; Crenshaw, 1991) ethic, which seeks to understand the connections between multiple axes of oppression and exclusion, on the understanding that these are not simply 'additive' but constitute distinct experiences and subjectivities. It examines how gender acts in conjunction with other salient personal characteristics, and as such problematizes theoretical frameworks that focus on single issues within a diversity agenda. Here we focus on intersections between gender, age and parental status. The article is informed by a broader study funded by the European Social Fund Diversity in Practice project and conducted by the Creative Industries Research & Consultancy Unit (CIRCU) at the University of Hertfordshire, UK (Randle *et al.*, 2007), which examined in detail class, race and ethnicity, and disability, in the context of film and television employment. The data comprise more than 100 semi-structured interviews conducted in 2006 with some interviewees revisited in 2011 – the latter designed to explore the effect of recent changes including the global financial crisis and associated recession and the impact of the Single Equalities Act in the UK on the film and television industry. Interviews were conducted with representatives from film and television sector bodies and broadcasters as well as practitioners in the industry and included 51 female interviewees (see Randle *et al.*, 2007 for more information about the methodology).

The Sociological Review, 63:S1, pp. 50–65 (2015), DOI: 10.1111/1467-954X.12240

This article is divided into four sections. In the first we provide a brief overview of gender inequalities in the film and television industries. We then examine typical work practices and the dominance of freelancing in film and television production. We focus on our data in the following two sections looking first at how a number of features of the film and television industry's *informality* may contribute to inequalities in the numbers, status and pay of women and men, and second at the variety of ways in which *parenting* may impact upon women's life chances in film and television. Here we attempt to move current debates beyond discussion of the practical challenges of parenting while holding down a job in these fields, to also consider the subtle kinds of *discrimination* that can affect all women – regardless of whether they are mothers – and which render children and caring responsibilities 'unspeakable' (Gill, 2014a). Finally, there is a brief conclusion.

Gender inequalities in the film and television industries

Women are under-represented in the film and television industries, particularly in key creative and decision-making roles (see Conor, Wreyford, this volume, and editors' introduction). In the USA, the celluloid ceiling report (Lauzen, 2012) which examines employment in the top 250 films each year, found that women represented only 5 per cent of directors, 14 per cent of screenwriters and just 4 per cent of cinematographers. In the UK, the figures are similar. The British Film Institute's Statistical Yearbook (2013) records that only 7.8 per cent of British films were directed by a woman and 13.4 per cent written by a woman. From the Skillset employment census of the creative media sector in 2012, women represented only 13 per cent of the camera department, 5 per cent of lighting (down from 10 per cent in 2009) and 13 per cent of sound (Creative Skillset, 2012: 15). By contrast women are concentrated and over-represented in wardrobe (73 per cent) and make-up/hairdressing (81 per cent) – fields that are well documented as the most precarious, with the highest levels of freelancing (Creative Skillset, 2012: 15).

TV production has an overall representation of women that is somewhat better (particularly in the larger terrestrial broadcasters), yet inequalities are revealed as soon as one examines questions of seniority, contractual status and pay. Women are seriously under-represented in more senior roles in television – something that is seen right across the CCI. Indeed, the Equality and Human Rights Commission's audit *Sex and Power* (2011) found that women's representation in senior positions in the field of media and culture as a whole was only 15.1 per cent. As chief executives of media companies in the FTSE 350 they represented just 6.7 per cent. It is worth noting that women in this field are significantly better qualified than their male counterparts, with a greater proportion being graduates and an even more significant difference in the numbers of women, compared to men, with higher degrees (Skillset, 2010a: 6). Moreover, women are significantly more likely to have undertaken industry-specific training. Nevertheless, women earn on average 15 per cent less than their male colleagues and are much less likely to

The Sociological Review, 63:S1, pp. 50–65 (2015), DOI: 10.1111/1467-954X.12240

be promoted or to make it into senior positions (Skillset, 2010a: 6). This marked pay inequality holds true even when other factors are adjusted (controlled for), for example, the lower age profile of women in the workforce, an issue we will turn to now.

More complex, intersectional inequalities are becoming evident in which the effects of gender are mediated by other factors including age, relationship status and parental status. In a debate about women in television (Skillset, 2010b), the Executive Director of Skillset, Kate O'Connor, noted that the TV industry was better at recruiting women than at keeping them, leading to a distorted age profile in which 70 per cent of men in the TV industry are over 35, whilst the largest proportion of women is in the 25–34 age group. One interpretation of this might be that a once male-dominated industry is now recruiting younger women, who have simply not yet had chance to 'get on' and work their way into the older age categories. However, this benign reading is not borne out by the evidence, which notes the youthful and junior profile of female industry entrants, but does *not* see them progressing in line with their male peers. In fact women are 'haemorrhaging' from the industry in their late 30s and 40s. As a study by Sargent-Disc (2011: n.p.) puts it, women's and men's experiences 'are different [...] and there is difficulty in retaining a large number of women beyond their 30s'. A participant in our research noted:

I think at senior roles [...] there's still more men than women.

The further up you go, the less chances [the employers]'ll take on you [...]

Women working in creative media are less likely than men to have dependent children living with them (23 per cent compared to 35 per cent), indicating that women may be leaving the sector after starting a family (Skillset, 2010a: 5). Perhaps reflecting the itinerant nature of an industry that requires production staff to work away from home for long periods of time, 81 per cent of film workers have no dependent children (Skillset, 2010a: 19).

During the recession that marked the period between our first and follow-up interviews, the UK's TV industry contracted dramatically, a troubling experience for all affected. However, it is notable that women lost their jobs at a rate that was six times that of men, indicating the particular and heightened vulnerability of women in the industry. In the subsequent years, women's representation improved, going from a low of 27 per cent in 2009 to 36 per cent in 2012 (Creative Skillset, 2012) but the job losses cast a long psychological shadow in making women in the industry feel more 'disposable' than their male counterparts. All this indicates the complexity of understanding the reasons for women's continued under-representation, and their status as what Oakley (2013) has described as 'absentee workers', those people 'lost' to employment in the cultural and media industries by dint of their gender, class or ethnic origins.

Freelance work in the UK film and television industries

Film and television have been described as 'different industries with some important similarities and overlaps in their production and labour processes' (Randle, 2011: 145). In both cases the production process is frequently project-based with a set of common stages: pre-production (conception, design and planning), production, post-production (editing, adding music tracks and special effects) followed by broadcast (television) or exhibition (film). Individuals may move between these sectors, especially those involved in the production and post-production stages of a project. This is perhaps most obvious where the products are similar, for example in TV drama and feature film productions requiring crews made up of a range of common technical occupations (such as camera, hair and make-up, and lighting).

One of the shared experiences of growing numbers of people working in the film and television industries is of precariousness and job insecurity. This is especially the case in those occupations involved in production and post-production and less so in, for example, broadcasting where long-term employment within large broadcasting corporations is more common. An important development in the organization of film and television has been the fragmentation which has resulted in an 'hourglass' shape where a relatively large number of people are employed (more often permanently) by a small number of sizeable TV broadcasters, satellite and cable companies or film majors, while an equally large number of others are employed by numerous small or micro businesses (Randle, 2011).

Increasingly workers in these fields, especially, but by no means limited to, those employed in the bottom half of the 'hourglass', are freelancers and work on short contracts that are counted in days or weeks rather than months. Indeed film and television workers – like other workers in the CCI – have become the poster children of 'precarity', iconic exemplars of a group that lives individualized 'risk biographies' in which all the uncertainties and costs are borne by them rather than by employers or the state; they are what Neff (2012) pertinently dubs 'venture labour'. As we discuss below, this mode of living requires constant attentiveness and vigilance to the possibility of future work, and heightened forms of network sociality (Wittel, 2001). It is, for many, a precarious existence, with many of our interviewees expressing anxiety about the flow of work, or about becoming sick and thus being unable to work.

The film industry has a long history as a project-based enterprise, marked by high levels of freelancing. Skillset reported that 90 per cent of film production workers were freelancers (House of Lords Select Committee on Communications, 2010: 264). Skillset's research also shows that on average respondents had worked on three feature films in the previous twelve months. The majority of respondents had also worked on some other kind of audio-visual production (often TV or advertising). The project-based nature of the majority of employment means that even established workers experience periods out of work (Skillset/UKFC, 2008: 16).

The Sociological Review, 63:S1, pp. 50–65 (2015), DOI: 10.1111/1467-954X.12240

Changes in the competitive and regulative conditions of UK television during the 1990s have also engendered the dramatic increase in freelancing among the television workforce. The Communication Act 2003 made it mandatory for public sector broadcasters (PSBs) to commission 25 per cent of their non-news programmes from independent production companies. The BBC pledged another 25 per cent to be open to external competition under its commissioning slate entitled Window of Creative Competition (WOCC) (Ofcom, 2006: 9). The PSBs have achieved their quotas, resulting in the reduction of in-house commissioning and growth in the market share of the independent sector by 5 per cent to 46 per cent in the five years from 2005 (Ofcom, 2010: 142). The reliance on freelancers varies considerably by subsectors of the television industry; over two-fifths (44 per cent) of the independent production workforce are freelance, but this drops to 19 per cent in terrestrial broadcast and 11 per cent in cable and satellite TV (Skillset, 2011: 4), further contributing to the 'hourglass' shape of employment structure we have discussed.

With the reduction in spending by PSBs and the decline of terrestrial television, there is likely to be further impact on project-based, freelance working in the UK television sector. Research conducted for the Broadcast Training & Skills Regulator, showed that many freelancers worked relatively little (CIRCU, 2008). A total of 120 freelancers in London and 46 in Scotland completed questionnaires during two events. Nearly half (46 per cent) in London worked fewer than 100 days a year. Roughly two-thirds of freelancers (66 per cent) from London and Scotland worked fewer than 200 days during the previous year. This means that they were unemployed for about 12 weeks per year. Therefore, many freelancers are likely to feel the financial impact of the periods of unemployment. Even though project-based work has been a long-standing feature of the film industry in the UK, the casualization of television has made this common to both sectors (Grugulis and Stoyanova, 2010).

With the deregulation of the television industry and the growth of the independent sector (Grugulis and Stoyanova, 2010), the responsibility for training shifted from the broadcaster to the individual, as this interviewee explains:

> [Until] 20 years ago, the BBC employed and trained everybody in the technical areas. That doesn't happen anymore. And whilst independent access and the freeing up of television have been good in many ways, there is always a downside to everything.

The high cost of training may pose an obstacle for some people aspiring to enter the sector. Training for the different roles within the sector is usually through formal training courses, degree education or on-the-job learning. There are no set paths into the industries. Work experience, working for free and low-paid jobs at the beginning of media careers are common routes through which people enter the sector (see Randle and Culkin, 2009 for an account of similar arrangements in the US industry). Unpaid work experience may contravene National Minimum Wage requirements where an employment relationship is considered to exist and some employers may be acting illegally (something that has been the topic of much discussion, see Regan, Shade and Jacobson, this volume). The lack of financial support for training can lead to exclusion on the grounds of social class, geographical location, disability and economic marginality. As the sector is dominated by graduates, the increasing costs of completing a degree in the UK make this a potentially exclusionary route. Training for some technical grades is still gender biased as they are traditionally male occupations and women may not be encouraged to pursue these careers. In the next section we look in more detail at the informality of the sector, exploring how this may impact upon gender inequalities.

Informality and unmanageable inequalities within film and television

The most distinctive feature of recruitment in the sector is its informal, word of mouth nature, as film and television productions come under time and resources pressure. Working under time pressure is a particular feature of employment in the sector; a project may get the 'green light' on a Friday and have to crew up for the following Monday to begin shooting. As a result, freelancers have to constantly pitch for work, using a variety of methods. Personal recommendations are seen to ensure quality; workers in the sector only recommend those they can trust (see Wreyford, this volume).

It is important to note that unlike many other sectors, recruitment in the film and television industries is deregulated, informal and often ad hoc. It is often not a company or broadcaster who performs the function of hiring and firing on a daily basis. In some of the technical departments such as camera or lighting, the heads of department choose the crew. For example, a Director of Photography may choose the gaffer who will then be in charge of the electricians. Producers may be consulted if there is non-availability of the usual crew members and contacts. Equally, recommendations from colleagues may be sought. This practice produces 'semi-permanent groups' that move from job to job (Blair, 2000). The majority of those in the film production workforce (87 per cent) were recruited to their latest project through word of mouth, including 23 per cent directly by the producer or director, 40 per cent by the head of department or supervisor and 20 per cent recommended by an individual or company that they had worked with before. Only 1 per cent was recruited through job advertisement (Skillset, 2010c: 10). This interviewee from camera crew sums up the practice:

> Looking for work [...] no matter how well you're doing, the fact that you shot that great film last year isn't going to help you. You've still got to find your next job. It is a cliché [....] you're only as good as your last job. It's a lot of energy [...] if you haven't got the drive, you're not going to get there. There's a lot easier jobs to do.

Informal recruitment practices dominate. While an up-to-date résumé is vital and film and television are increasingly graduate entry industries, a résumé and a degree are necessary but not sufficient. These are 'reputation economies' in which people are hired on the soft judgements of insiders about whether they are trustworthy, reliable and good to work with. Networks and contacts are the main means of gaining employment, which forms a barrier for fresh and diverse talent from under-represented groups, as many may not have access to social events and opportunities. As some of our female interviewees pointed out, networking is a time-consuming and demanding requirement of freelancing: 'you need to maintain very strong links and networks with people to get the jobs', said one senior and very experienced TV researcher. The spaces for networking – particularly pubs – could also form challenging environments for women, and the requirement for 'compulsory sociality' (Gregg, 2006) after already long working days posed problems for everyone with caring responsibilities. One interviewee, a female, disabled film-maker from a regional city, had decided to give up a film career as she explains in a follow-up interview in 2011:

> It's hard for everybody but it's compounded with other things. I can't do the networking, going to film festivals, the being-there. So my decision not to be a filmmaker anymore is to do with diversity, disability and inclusion issues. I don't sit comfortably in the sector because of disability, and also as a woman, a single parent. I can't compete on the terms that this sector requires.

Another issue is the tendency towards homophily: the practice of insiders recruiting in their own image, or selecting candidates with whom they feel they have an easy rapport. Working relationships in the industry are forged on the basis of trust, which generally entails working with those one has worked with previously, or accepting a recommendation from such a person. This is a particular danger in (but not limited to) the very large number of small firms without formal recruitment procedures, HR functions or equal opportunities policies and monitoring and in those occupations where vacancies are not formally advertised. This could make it challenging for many women to break into such close-knit groups if the jobs have been dominated by men to date. As a consequence, male practitioners may be able to build up a longer work history than their female counterparts. Exclusionary patterns of hiring could, in this sense, emerge unconsciously, the outcome not of explicit sexism but of a network of trust relationships based on affect and tacit judgements such as 'he's a good bloke'. As one female camera operator put it:

> I do think that if the majority of people who are making the decisions are men, they feel more comfortable with their own, and that's come out a lot. The peer on peer thing, and the stories that they relate to.

Conversely, one of our female interviewees (working in film accounting) in 2011 reported that she had worked almost consistently, except for four months enforced unemployment in early 2010 when many of her contemporaries were in the same situation, irrespective of their backgrounds. Networking has been crucial in her career:

> The same people employ me as did before, so although my network of peers has expanded, I tend to be working for the same employers. For my part any decisions around work have been about my personal preferences: Do I like the people I am working with?

Many interviewees observe that the differences in behaviour between men and women have also contributed to the gender imbalance. A female assistant producer expressed the view that men are more confident in selling themselves, while fear of failure hinders the career progression of many women. Some female interviewees suggested that they might not have come across as confidently as the men they were competing against in job interviews. This could have a detrimental effect on their careers as in the freelance world one has to constantly attend job interviews and prove oneself. Yet this self-promotion might be felt to conflict with notions of appropriate feminine behaviour (see also Scharff in this volume). As one female assistant producer told us:

> The nature of freelancing is that: [...] this is because of the way the interview works, you have to always prove yourself on your jobs. You always have to prove to your next employer [...] to give you a chance, and that can be difficult and I think it's especially difficult for women.

Taken together, these features of the network culture and reputation economies of film and television often serve to disadvantage women. There are strong parallels here with Thanki and Jeffreys' discussion of challenges affecting working class and BAME individuals in the media:

> The particularly strong dependence upon informal networking and freelancing still present a number of specific obstacles and barriers to working class people and particularly those from minority ethnic backgrounds. Together these create a web of indirect racism that is dense enough to 'push' many of these professionals to quit as the audio-visual industries are predominantly middle-class and their senior posts are still largely run by a largely white 'old boy' Oxbridge network. (Thanki and Jeffreys, 2007: 114)

This is echoed by Randle *et al.* (forthcoming) who refer to a 'web of reciprocity' in film and television employment, leading to a 'resilient, self-perpetuating habitus' which excludes those without certain cultural and social capital and results in the continual replication of a white, male and middle-class industry. Legislation designed to promote and protect gender (and race) equality has a long history in Britain. Equal Opportunity and Equal Pay legislation was passed in the 1970s and, as in many European countries, is backed up by various statutory instruments and bodies at the national as well as European level – most recently the establishment of the Equalities and Human Rights Commission. Yet this raft of legal measures fails to make much impact upon employment in the media and other creative fields. It does not touch or engage with informal practices relating to recruitment and pay, or other enduring inequalities, particularly those reflected in the growing number of small and medium-sized companies in production and post-production. It is often difficult to trace evidence of discrimination in informal recruitment practices and even when such evidence can be found, individuals seeking work in 'reputation economies' may be reluctant to file formal legal challenges.

One entrenched problem is that the legislation is taken up predominantly in the very largest organizations, while increasingly the media world is dominated by small production companies or temporary project-based enterprises in which management is enacted informally – with little or no regard for the relevant equal opportunities laws, let alone dedicated schemes to support under-represented groups. Eikhof and Warhurst (2013) go so far as to put the project-based model of production at the heart of what they see as systemic inequalities in the creative industries. Even when equality and diversity policies are in place, they rarely translate into practice. Reviewing this in the audio-visual industries Holgate and McKay (2009) note that even statements of 'good intentions' such as 'working towards equality' or 'this organisation welcomes applications from all sections of the community' have all but disappeared. In film, television and most other cultural and creative industries, people gain and lose jobs in a way that is largely outside the formal apparatuses put in place to protect equality of opportunity. What we see in these fields are what Jones and Pringle (this volume) call 'unmanageable inequalities' – unmanageable because they exist outwith all the measures designed to deal with them. Our research supports a growing appreciation that informal hiring practices and lack of transparency in appointing and promoting staff is the enemy of equality and diversity.

Parenting and gender inequalities within film and television

Wreyford (2013: 1) argues: 'It is difficult to talk about women and work without talking about childcare. The same is not true of men and work and this is still one of the most obvious difficulties to be managed by working women, even those who choose not to have children'. This brings to the fore one of the dilemmas for feminist analysts in addressing the role that parenting plays in perpetuating gender inequalities: on the one hand, one needs to recognize the continued reality that caring for children is largely undertaken by women, yet on the other, by doing so, one risks re-cementing the relationship between women and children and perpetuating the very gender inequality one wants to critique. This section considers what interviewees had to say about how family responsibilities impacted on their careers, but considers these to be social conventions and thus not essential but open to transformation. We need to remain attentive to the question of why parenting does not negatively impact on men's careers in film and television in the way it does on women's – and guard against this becoming an unquestioned assumption, because it is precisely in the realm of taken-for-grantedness that sexism becomes invisible and naturalized. We seek to draw distinctions between two analytically distinct sets of issues – first the difficulties of balancing creative work and childcare, and secondly the discrimination faced by women because of assumptions about their parental status – or indeed their potential to become mothers.

Many of our research participants – both men and women – assumed an automatic connection between gender and childcare, taking for granted the idea that parenting is primarily women's responsibility. This male interviewee is typically 'sympathetic' in highlighting this as 'difficult' for women:

I think women have a lot of difficulty with working freelance because of childcare issues, family care issues [...] it's not helpful to their careers.

Respondents mentioned a number of different issues – some common across all fields of work, others particular to film and television – such as long hours, very short notice of jobs, and bulimic (Pratt, 2000) patterns of work with intense periods of working around the clock, followed by weeks or months with very little work at all. These interviewees explain:

I think [...] there's a presentee-ism, there's the hours that you work and [...] being available 24/7, which when you have a family, inevitably many women just find it's too much.

I still think it's an issue, the unfriendly hours, especially if you've got kids around, because we'll routinely have to get up at 4 o'clock in the morning, go out and work a 12 hour day and then get back at 10 o'clock at night.

Some women with children explained the impossibility of finding appropriate childcare for these kinds of hours or working patterns, for example the lack of nurseries for night shift workers or the difficulty of hiring a nanny because of the unpredictability of the flow of work. In this sense findings here echo those of Skillset, which asserts 'it has been impossible to avoid the hypothesis that women have been leaving the industry because of difficulty reconciling a career in the creative industries with raising a family' (2010a: 2). Several female interviewees anticipated dropping out of the industry or trying to take up more permanent roles when they start a family. This young female TV researcher, for instance, discusses how she anticipates her own career path in television:

Television's great while you're young and it's exciting and all the rest of it, but I'm also very family orientated [...] and I do want to eventually get married and have my 2.4 children [...] it's not a career for women with children, I don't think.

Even the most successful, high profile, female film-makers in the UK, such as Antonia Bird and Gurinder Chadha, comment on children as a barrier for women in the film industry (quoted in Kellaway, 2007):

Chadha: I don't think I would be where I am today if I had had children earlier or had a mortgage. I was living in a rent-controlled apartment until three years ago. If I'd had a huge mortgage and I'd had to service the needs of a family, I wouldn't be where I am.

Bird: I definitely wouldn't be where I am today if I'd had children.

One consequence of this is that the industry still lacks female role models in the upper echelons who have successfully balanced career and family life. One of our interviewees observes:

It's noticeable that women [at the top of in the industry] are not married or have not had children, a lot of them. And does that say, in order to get on, you can't have children?

Distinct from the actual practical challenges of maintaining a career in film or television alongside parenting were the difficulties that women faced in

The Sociological Review, 63:S1, pp. 50–65 (2015), DOI: 10.1111/1467-954X.12240

overcoming sexist attitudes about the possibility that they might have children. These could take many forms and clearly affect all women, including those who do not become mothers. Common was the assumption that the possibility of young women having children could make it more 'rational' in any given situation to hire a man, because he would be less likely to leave or to take time off. Relatedly, women attempting to find work later on in their careers after taking time off to have a child or children could also be subject to this disadvantage, which would again almost always be glossed as 'reasonable' or 'understandable' – in the manner of 'benevolent' sexism (Glick and Fiske, 1996) or 'new sexism' (Gill, 1993, 2014b). As one of our interviewees, in a key hiring position, put it

> You put two CVs blind together, one of them will understandably have years more experience than the other because the woman has lost five, six years.

A different kind of sexism can be seen in the assumption that having children in some way 'taints' or absorbs a woman's creative energy or will to succeed. One of our interviewees reports a conversation she had with a commissioning editor in which he said,

> I just think [...] a woman of a certain age who's got kids [...] the hunger isn't there anymore, so they'll do you a good enough job but they won't die and fight for the programme.

This sudden diminution of professional hunger or fight is not attributed to men when they become parents, highlighting its one-sidedness and the way it works selectively to justify the exclusion of women. Many interviewees suggest that successful female professionals put their personal life on hold to pursue their careers because gaps in the career affect the freelancer's portfolio. '*Knowing when* requires understanding the timing of career choices, to stay or leave, to push forward or pull back' (Jones and DeFillippi, 1996: 99, italic original), but this also means prioritizing work over any family considerations. For these reasons, those who have children often do not talk about them for fear of it affecting their careers. In this sense having or wanting children could become unspeakable, prompting situations in which pregnancies were hidden and references to one's children avoided, or in which female workers went back to work soon after giving birth, in order not to have any interruption in their career biographies. The costs of this are borne heavily – and often without support – by women, who often feel that they must not talk about these issues. As one interviewee commented, the issues of lack of childcare or proper leave are rarely raised as women do not want to draw attention to these for fear of being labelled a problem, or someone who whinges. In this way, maternity and caring responsibilities become individualized and privatized 'problems' for women to deal with on their own. This is paralleled more broadly by the ethic of 'getting on with it', not 'moaning' or 'whinging' – in case this made one seem difficult (see also Jones and Pringle this volume). In these ways, women in the industry were silenced and had to become 'responsibilized' entrepreneurial subjects who took on and carried all the costs, risks and challenges of being working parents alone.

Discussion

In this article we have examined the lives of freelancers working in the film and television industries, as these industries become increasingly fragmented and casualized. Our interviews demonstrated that freelancing can be challenging for many people, with struggles about endemic job insecurity, anxiety about the flow of work, one's ability to meet financial obligations and stay afloat in a desired career. Here, though, we have sought in particular to understand the role that freelancing may play in exacerbating persistent gender inequalities in film and television. Our analysis is focused upon two broad themes – the informality that characterizes the hiring for and securing of jobs in creative media, and the distinct challenges of parenting while working in these fields. Our interviewees highlighted particular challenges that women face in relation to the normalized practices of finding work – challenges that relate to breaking into male-dominated fields, to promoting oneself, and to joining or building the networks that are crucial to securing work. Other aspects of the work, including long hours, unpredictable and bulimic working patterns, and a culture of presenteeism could also pose particular challenges for women with caring responsibilities.

Jones and DeFillippi argue that in the USA, 'the boundaryless career system challenges its participants to improvise their home and hearth around the unpredictable vicissitudes of frenetic project activity and involuntary unemployment' and for many film professionals 'family life had been deferred, denied, or at least compromised during their careers' (1996: 93, 94). The informality of film and television employment has a major impact on practitioners, especially women who are often adversely affected by the precarious nature of freelance employment and a male- and network-dominated work place. Work patterns, childcare, money and freelance culture affect women practitioners' decisions to have children or not and whether they are able to sustain a film or media career as parents. While parenting and childcare do not need to be the exclusive responsibility of women, it is striking in our research that few, if any, interviewees discussed this in relation to men, reinforcing assumptions about the gendering of responsibility for childcare. In the UK context, our findings lend support to research from Skillset that highlights motherhood – but not fatherhood – as a key factor in understanding the persistence of gender inequalities in film and television.

However, alongside the practical difficulties associated with being a mother in tandem with working in film or television, we have also highlighted the sexism that women face in relation to potential parenthood. This could affect all women regardless of whether they were – or wished to become – mothers, and found no parallel among men. This widespread sexism is based around the assumption that, given male and female candidates with equal CVs, it would be 'rational' or 'understandable' to hire the man. This form of apparently 'reasonable' sexism is difficult for women to address or challenge, both because of its deep roots and the lack of any apparatus to manage it within the informal casualized world of film and television project networks (see Jones and Pringle, this volume). It is

The Sociological Review, 63:S1, pp. 50–65 (2015), DOI: 10.1111/1467-954X.12240
© 2015 The Authors. Editorial organisation © 2015 The Editorial Board of the Sociological Review

further underscored by a culture of silence which makes it very difficult for women to speak out about such issues, since to talk about children or childcare in these environments is potentially to call into question one's commitment to work, or even to be labelled 'difficult'. This highlights the ways in which new, subtle forms of sexism interact with a neoliberal work culture that calls on individuals to be autonomous, entrepreneurial subjects who prioritize work above all else and have an unwritten contract to be mobile, to be flexible, and to take private responsibility for anything that might impede their availability to be on the job 24/7.

Gender is clearly not the only factor influencing media careers. Class, race, age, disability and even geography have profound impacts, sometimes in surprising ways. For example, one disabled female film researcher discussed how it was the fact that she could not (for financial and childcare reasons) live in London that had the biggest impact on her chances within the industry, and not her gender or disability:

> Because I have a young family and I live in [a regional city], and there weren't the opportunities to get enough work basically [...] as a freelancer, you've got to be in the nub, you've always got to be networking and keep yourself known to get those offers of work, and I just couldn't be in the nub because I didn't live in London.

This article has focused on gender while being attentive to the ways in which other intersecting identities are key. It has highlighted in particular the ways in which gender inequality is mediated by age and parental status, while also paying attention to the importance of place and class in the ability to sustain a career in film and television.

Women do 'get in' to film and television, but they still rarely 'get on' as well as their male peers, despite superior qualifications and considerable talent. Women are career 'scramblers' in these fields but set against the more positive associations Jones and DeFillippi (1996) attribute to the 'opportunities' available to the free agent, the term seems more appropriate here to indicate 'without a secure hold'. This is demonstrated by their disproportionate exodus during the recent recession, when women were forced to 'get out' at six times the rate of men (O'Connor, 2010). We hope to have shown some of the factors that contribute to this, and that also – paradoxically – make this very inequality both unmanageable and unspeakable for many women working within these fields.

References

Beck, U., (2000), *The Brave New World of Work*, Cambridge: Polity Press.

Blair, H., (2000), 'Working in film: employment in a project-based sector', *Personnel Review*, 30 (2): 170–185.

Brah, A. and Phoenix, A., (2004), 'Ain't I a woman? Revisiting intersectionality', *Journal of International Women's Studies*, 5 (3): 75–86.

British Film Institute, (2013), *BFI Statistical Yearbook 2013*, London.

CIRCU, (2008), Report on the Training Needs of Freelancers, for Broadcast Training & Skills Regulator.

The Sociological Review, 63:S1, pp. 50–65 (2015), DOI: 10.1111/1467-954X.12240

Creative Skillset, (2012), *Employment Census of the Creative Media Industries*, London.

Crenshaw, K., (1991), 'Mapping the margins: intersectionality, identity politics, and violence against women of color', *Stanford Law Review*, 43 (6): 1241–1299.

Eikhof, D. and Warhurst, C., (2013), 'The promised land? Why social inequalities are systemic in the creative industries', *Employee Relations*, 35 (5): 495–508.

Equality and Human Rights Commission, (2011), *Sex and Power 2011: Who Runs Britain?* Leeds: Centre for Women and Democracy.

Gill, R., (1993), 'Justifying injustice: broadcasters' accounts of inequality in radio', in E. Burman and I. Parker (eds), *Discourse Analytic Research: Readings and Repertoires of Texts in Action*, 75–93, London: Routledge.

Gill, R., (2002), 'Cool, creative and egalitarian? Exploring gender in project-based new media work in Europe', *Information, Communication and Society*, 5 (1): 70–89.

Gill, R., (2014a), 'An ideological dilemma: the resurgence of sexism and the disappearance of "sexism"', in C. Antaki and S. Condor (eds), *Rhetoric, Ideology and Social Psychology: Essays in Honour of Michael Billig*, 109–121, London: Routledge.

Gill, R., (2014b), 'Unspeakable inequalities: postfeminism, entrepreneurial subjectivity and the repudiation of sexism among cultural workers', *Social Politics*, first published online 24 July.

Glick, P. and Fiske, S., (1996), 'The ambivalent sexism inventory: differentiating hostile and benevolent sexism', *Journal of Personality and Social Psychology*, 70 (3): 491–512.

Gregg, M., (2006), 'On Friday night drinks: neoliberalism's compulsory friends', paper presented at the UnAustralia Conference of the Cultural Studies Association of Australasia.

Grugulis, I. and Stoyanova, D., (2010), ' "I don't know where you learn them": skills in film and TV', in A. McKinlay and C. Smith (eds), *Creative Labour*, 135–155, Basingstoke: Palgrave Macmillan.

Holgate, J. and McKay, S., (2009), 'Equal opportunities policies: how effective are they in increasing diversity in the audio-visual industries' freelance labour market?', *Media, Culture and Society*, 31 (1): 151–163.

House of Lords Select Committee on Communications, (2010), *The British Film and Television Industries – Decline or Opportunity? Volume II: Evidence*, London: House of Lords.

Jones, C. and DeFillippi, R. J., (1996), 'Back to the future in film: combining industry and self-knowledge to meet the career challenges of the 21st century', *Academy of Management Executive*, 10 (4): 89–103.

Kellaway, K., (2007), 'Celluloid ceiling? Ask the experts', *The Observer*, 4 March.

Lauzen, M., (2012), *The Celluloid Ceiling: Behind-the-Scenes Employment of Women on the Top 250 Films of 2012*, San Diego: Center for the Study of Women in Television & Film.

Neff, G., (2012), *Venture Labor: Work and the Burden of Risk in Innovative Industries*, Boston, MA: MIT Press.

Oakley, K., (2013), 'Absentee workers: representation and participation in the cultural industries', in M. Banks, R. Gill and S. Taylor (eds), *Theorizing Cultural Work: Labour, Continuity and Change in the Cultural Industries*, 56–67, London: Routledge.

O'Connor, K., (2010), 'Speech to Women in TV Debate', BAFTA, London, 17 March, available at: http://www.bafta.org/access-all-areas/women-working-in-tv-is-it-a-young-girls-game,1048,BA.html

Ofcom, (2006), *Review of Television Production Sector Consultation Document*, London: Ofcom.

Ofcom, (2010), *The Communications Market 2010. 2. TV and Audio-Visual*. London: Ofcom.

Pratt, A., (2000), 'New media the new economy and new spaces', *Geoforum*, 31 (4): 425–436.

Randle, K., (2011), 'The organisation of film and television production', in M. Deuze (ed.), *Managing Media Work*, Los Angeles: Sage.

Randle, K. and Culkin, N., (2009), 'Getting in and getting on in Hollywood: freelance careers in an uncertain industry', in A. McKinlay and C. Smith (eds), *Creative Labour*, 93–115, London: Palgrave Macmillan.

Randle, K., Forson, C. and Calveley, M., (forthcoming), 'Towards a Bourdieusian analysis of the social composition of the UK film and television workforce', *Work, Employment and Society*.

The Sociological Review, 63:S1, pp. 50–65 (2015), DOI: 10.1111/1467-954X.12240
© 2015 The Authors. Editorial organisation © 2015 The Editorial Board of the Sociological Review

Randle, K., Leung, W. and Kurian, J., (2007), *Creating Difference: Overcoming Barriers to Diversity in UK Film & Television Employment*, Report to European Social Fund.

Ross, A., (2009), *Nice Work if You Can Get It: Life and Labor in Precarious Times*, New York: New York University Press.

Sargent-Disc, (2011), *Age and Gender in UK Film Industry*, available at: http://www.sargent-disc.com/sargent-disc-uk/news-insights/insights/uk-film-industry-age-and-gender.aspx

Skillset, (2010a), *Women in the Creative Media Industries*, London: Skillset.

Skillset, (2010b), *Women Working in Television*, London: Skillset, available at: http://guru.bafta.org/women-working-television-debate

Skillset, (2010c), *Film Sector – Labour Market Intelligence Digest*, London: Skillset.

Skillset, (2011), *Television Sector – Labour Market Intelligence Profile*, London: Skillset.

Skillset/UKFC, (2008), *Feature Film Production Workforce Survey Report 2008*, London: Skillset/UKFC.

Thanki, A. and Jeffreys, S., (2007), 'Who are the fairest? Ethnic segmentation in London's media production', *Work Organisation, Labour and Globalisation*, 1 (1): 108–118.

Wittel, A., (2001), 'Towards a network sociality', *Theory Culture and Society*, 18 (6): 51–76.

Wreyford, N., (2013), 'The real cost of childcare: motherhood and project-based creative labour in the UK film industry', *Studies in the Maternal*, 5 (2), available at: http://www.mamsie.bbk.ac.uk/documents/Wreyford_SiM_5(2)2013.pdf

Please quote the article DOI when citing SR content, including monographs. Article DOIs and "How to Cite" information can be found alongside the online version of each article within Wiley Online Library. All articles published within the SR (including monograph content) are included within the ISI Journal Citation Reports® Social Science Citation Index.

Labile labour – gender, flexibility and creative work

George Morgan and Pariece Nelligan

Abstract: The growth of the new economy and creative work has posed a range of challenges for young workers in the West. Creativity has come to signify something more than simply performing symbolic and knowledge work. To be creative is now also to exhibit an entrepreneurial savviness and a readiness to endure the vagaries of precarious work and the scrutiny of creative gatekeepers. In this paper, based on research in Australia amongst creative aspirants, we suggest that young men from working-class backgrounds, who are steeped in the traditions of communities of practice, are less able than young women to endure the rigours of the creative career. They are disinclined to 'sell themselves' and their skills, in churning creative labour markets, preferring the stable and cooperative forms of the work group to the individualistic and competitive structures of the new economy.

Keywords: masculinities, community of practice, aspirant, creativity, working class

Introduction

There is now a substantial literature on creative work (Adkins, 2000, 2004; Banks, 2010; Conor, 2013; Gill, 2002, 2010; Haukka *et al.*, 2010; Haukka, 2011; Hesmondhalgh and Baker, 2011; Luckman, 2012, 2013; McRobbie, 2002a, 2002b, 2013; Ross, 2009), much of which recognizes the complex challenges associated with making a living and building a career in fields where work is often in short supply, project based, allocated by word-of-mouth informal networks, and where workers feel under constant threat from changes in technology and fashion.[1] Some theorists (Adkins, 2000; Banks and Milestone, 2011; Gill, 2002, 2009) have suggested that this volatile environment throws up tripwires, particularly for women, even going so far as to observe that the structures of the creative economy produces a 're-traditionalisation' of gender roles (Adkins, 1999, 2000). For example, creative industry workers typically experience bouts of intense work followed by slow periods (what Gill and Pratt, 2008, call 'bulimic' work patterns). For women who are primary carers or who shoulder an equal burden of domestic labour, these arrangements are far from ideal. In fields

The Sociological Review, 63:S1, pp. 66–83 (2015), DOI: 10.1111/1467-954X.12241
© 2015 The Authors. Editorial organisation © 2015 The Editorial Board of the Sociological Review. Published by John Wiley & Sons Ltd, 9600 Garsington Road, Oxford OX4 2DQ, UK and 350 Main Street, Malden, MA 02148, USA

involving non-traditional work relations – subcontracting, 'permalancing' and casual employment – those responsibilities can prevent women from earning a regular and sufficient income. Furthermore, the informal recruitment processes that predominate in many creative fields can work against women who, in more formalized and bureaucratically regulated workplaces, can call on the protections of gender equity/anti-discrimination regulations.

We recognize these obstacles but our aim in this paper is to explore the disjunctions between the demands of creative careers and a particular kind of working class masculinity. Despite the virtual disappearance of stable blue-collar employment in much of the Western world there are values and habits associated with what we might call Fordist masculinity that endure in residual forms. These are embodied in specific forms of practice and values: of solidarity, informal/mimetic learning practices, and a general hostility to the scrutiny and evaluation of those external to workplace communities of practice. The challenges facing young men in the new economy have been recognized by many of those researching youth transitions (eg Kenway *et al.*, 2006; McDowell, 2000; Nixon, 2006) and particularly the challenges they face in gaining entry to labour markets that require affective or emotional labour, dealing with customers and performing many of the roles associated with the service and caring professions. We argue, following Cohen (1999), that there are certain cultural codes, connected to work and working life that structure working-class masculinity and that have inertia: they don't die with the social and economic arrangements that underpinned them. Rather they survive in residual form in places other than the factory floors in which masculine values and solidarities were traditionally cultivated. These include the workshops and studios in education institutions where artistic, musical, media, design skills are taught and the places of informal learning – garages and workshops in back gardens. So these working-class masculine codes continue to be transmitted inter-generationally and can also be reconstituted in 'new economy' workplaces, even though based on a particular blue-collar class memory. Importantly these codes shape vocational identities in ways that may not be compatible with the demands of creative work. So our research suggests that in order to understand the 'creative career', the fortunes of those who embark on this career and their ability to endure its vicissitudes, it is necessary to go beyond the conventional frame for understanding creative work and to consider a broader range of influences on occupational socialization (Hesmondhalgh and Baker, 2011). Semi-structured biographical narrative interviews allowed us to look to various sites of informal pedagogy (familial, communal) as well as the ways communities of practice were constituted through cultural enthusiasms, in order to understand the experiences of the creative worker.

In what follows we will look at gender and the rigours of establishing the creative career. Our research is based on life history interviews with 80 young creatives[2] with the great majority of the sample from working-class, minority backgrounds (in a society where those from non-English speaking backgrounds perform most low-paid work, Ho and Alcorso, 2004). We present five brief case studies illustrating some classed and gendered aspects of creative careers. Unlike most research on creative work that focuses on those who are already established in their fields, our project has focused on aspirants: those who have yet to make a reasonable (and, for some, any) living from creative work. We interviewed both students/trainees, those in the early stages of their careers and a few who have abandoned their ambitions in the fields of film/video, music production and design. All were acutely aware that their vocational fortunes depend as much on chance, and their ability to adapt to contingency, as on their talents.

To survive in turbulent labour markets most creative aspirants must become what we term *labile labour*: mobile, spontaneous, malleable, and capable of being aroused by new vocational possibilities. They must also present as eager and ambitious, but, paradoxically, this ambition must be diffuse. These dispositions can be contrasted with those of Taylorist labour: stable, dependable and inert, the factory hands amenable to managerial direction. Specifically, the qualities required of the new worker include, first, an ability to view skills as abstract and transferable, rather than as grounded, singular and non-negotiable. Under conditions of new capitalism, of rapid technological and stylistic change and innovation, the permutations of working life are less foreseeable. As Rose argues, contemporary workers should 'engage in skilling, reskilling, enhancement of credentials and preparation for a life of incessant job seeking: Life is to become a continuous economic capitalization of the self' (Rose, 1999: 161). Secondly, the labile worker must bring individualistic and competitive inclinations to working life, a readiness to improvise and 'rebrand' in response to this change and innovation. In Adkins and Lury's terms, the new worker is involved in an ongoing project of reflexivity and recalibration:

> A self-transforming subject – who can constantly adapt his or her performance of a self-identity and who can claim the effects of that performance of self-identity to define their own goals (to fill in the blanks along the way) – is figured as the ideal subject of the employment contract. (1999: 601)

Thirdly, the new worker must be capable of recognizing and being excited by serendipitous opportunities, wherever and whenever they arise, through friendship, family and community networks as well as vocational contacts (Gill, 2010; Taylor and Littleton, 2012). Fourthly the new worker must be prepared to endure the scrutiny and arbitrary judgements of gatekeepers in those occupations where work is usually allocated informally. To challenge the legitimacy, credentials and caprice of those exercising this judgement is to mark oneself as unworthy.

Our work complements the findings of Haukka (2011) who, with colleagues, conducted a major survey-based study of creative aspirants in Australia. This research identified the complex challenges faced by those who graduate from creative training courses but struggle to find work in the fields for which they have trained, particularly creative arts and media studies graduates. In situations of precarious employment/ underemployment, creative aspirants find it difficult to find sources of mentorship/ communities of practice to stimulate the development of new skills and provide information on work opportunities. Haukka (2011) also found that creative industry employers were dissatisfied with the skills

The Sociological Review, 63:S1, pp. 66–83 (2015), DOI: 10.1111/1467-954X.12241
© 2015 The Authors. Editorial organisation © 2015 The Editorial Board of the Sociological Review

of graduates[3] and that employees were dissatisfied with their employers' under-utilization of their creative skills. While valuable, however, quantitative research such as this is limited in its capacity to illuminate the ways that troubled 'creative transitions' are lived. Qualitative data, like that presented here, can better illuminate the sorts of worker-subjects who are produced by the experience of precarity and labour market churning (Taylor and Littleton, 2008). We hypothesize that the capacity to endure these pressures is socially patterned, and that working-class men are ill suited to perform the particular disciplines required of workers in creative labour markets. While only five case studies are presented below, they suggest a larger social pattern in which the inheritance of a 'classed masculinity' may operate as a brake on vocational aspirations in post-industrial settings.

Narratives of creative disenchantment

Biographical narrative accounts of working life are valuable sociological resources when read symptomatically, to uncover the deeper forces governing experience. Such accounts are complexly layered and can be read at different levels (Mishler, 1999; Riessman, 2008; Wengraf, 2001), not simply in order to chart unfolding lives, and document chains of causation as presented by interviewees, but also to problematize these common sense accounts and uncover the larger influences of social structure and culture that may not be superficially apparent. Life history narrative analysis allows for intensive scrutiny of, and the production of new perspectives on, social phenomena, such as quantitative data may fail to yield. This is not to deny the importance of representativeness, but to suggest that this form of research will frequently point to the need for further research, both qualitative and quantitative, to confirm this representativeness. As Watson argues:

> life histories represent 'instances' of social processes and thereby illuminate the way such processes emerge from particular structural relations. Each case study stands on its own; an additional case study or two cannot confirm the 'validity' of patterns which emerge in the first case study. Instead, the value of additional case studies is their potential to reveal more of the complexity of social processes, to illustrate how those 'socio-structural relations' emerge under a different set of conditions. (Watson, 1994: 27)

Taylor and Littleton's (2008, 2012) study of art and design graduates and their ability to adapt to financial pressures and fragmented careers perhaps most closely parallels our own work. We are particularly interested in creative workers' abilities to adapt and narrate their careers in post-modern terms, to articulate a sense of agency and biographical unity, as Sennett recognizes:

> The labours of the modern, flexible workplace pose quite a different challenge to the task of narrating one's work: how can one create a sense of personal continuity in a labour market in which work-histories are erratic and discontinuous rather than routine and determinate? (2001: 183)

Our data reveals that youthful creative dreams frequently give way to a sober reckoning with the prospect and reality of failure, poverty and insecurity. These experiences can challenge creative aspirants' values and sense of self, especially those from socially disadvantaged backgrounds who lack sources of familial and communal advice and direction. The myths of meritocracy are shattered as creative aspirants come to realize that they are often judged in ways that have nothing to do with their skills, and that in order to succeed they will have to change, for example the way they speak, dress and present themselves in order to meet with the approval of those who allocate work. The individualist and entrepreneurial ethos prevailing in the new economy can challenge the collectivist values and practices through which many have learned their creative skills and have come to understand the social character of their work (McRobbie, 2002b; Taylor and Littleton, 2008). Furthermore, aspirants encounter the pressure to dissemble, to negotiate creative ambitions and to tailor and 'spin' their skills to the market: to become the labile labour required by post-modern capitalism. Most have to postpone their cherished creativity and meander through the vague, shifting pathways of creative careers that bear little resemblance to the ways such careers are represented in official discourse (Morgan and Wood, 2014). Taylor and Littleton wrote that their art and design interviewees were diffident about formulating clear goals or even speaking about their vocational futures at all: 'the reluctance to set goals might follow from the pattern that there was an inherent contradiction between being creative and planning systematically' (2012: 62).

In reckoning with the sorts of compromises required of them, aspirants have to decide what is non-negotiable or intractable about their vocational identities. It is here we see the influence of what Cohen calls narrative codes, or grids that shape the biographical tales:

> Each generalised form of labour and learning has its own special kind of social routine organising certain, largely unconscious, frames of mind and body into specific dispositions of skill and competence, which in turn are associated with particular kinds of identity work. (1999: 130)

He contrasts the code of apprenticeship with that of career, and identifies the former with a mode of masculinity now in decline. The apprenticeship system had historical routes in the pre-modern guild and trade system, but was central to Fordist production. The particular social and corporeal relations associated with skilled trades/craft work involve the use of 'implements of labour [that] were often thought of as a kind of prosthetic extension of bodily skill, moulded by customary usages of handicraft' (1999: 132). Tradesmen and craftsmen, the aristocrats of labour, were a breed apart from unskilled labourers and exercised what Cohen calls a 'specialised dexterity' (1999: 132) in working raw materials with tools. Importantly access to this 'patrimony of skill … always entailed an apprenticeship'. This involved becoming submerged in a community of practice – often achieved through father-son recruitment – in which learning occurred through observation and emulation (Lave and Wenger, 1991; Wenger, 1998). But this is not simply a narrative of skill but also one of the social relations in which those skills are

The Sociological Review, 63:S1, pp. 66–83 (2015), DOI: 10.1111/1467-954X.12241

developed. Hollands refers to this as 'cultural apprenticeship' and describes how this helped to develop 'a peculiarly masculine shop-floor culture' (1990: 103). The history of mass production involved a steady erosion of the solidarity and industrial strength of trades and crafts. Taylorist management confronted the established rhythms of skilled labour, the power that communities of practice exerted over production. Semi-skilled, repetitive and routine labour came to replace skilled work and eventually digital skills superseded manual labour as the main sources of employment.

The consequence is that the narrative codes associated with manual labour including apprenticeship – as an accomplishment of a particular form of recognition and accreditation of self – were never particularly easy to represent. Indeed, they relied for their power on informality and privileging the vernacular: and contempt for the interference of managers and accredited experts. The taciturn workingman is venerated in some aspects of popular culture and nostalgic representations of traditional working life (for example the representations of declining working-class communities in films like *Brassed Off* and *Billy Elliot*), but his story is not easily told. The archetypal blue-collar worker is mute and awkward, unused to manners and formality, suspicious of authority and credentials. Such patterns can be learned and reproduced across generations. Those steeped in these cultures find it difficult to reinvent themselves when the material conditions on which communities of manual labour are dissolved.

All of this complicates youth transitions (Stokes and Wyn, 2007) particularly for young working-class men. In his classic research, nearly forty years ago, into this cohort Willis (1977, 1979) observed that working-class schoolboys, the 'lads', developed cultures of resistance based on rejecting academic expectations as effete and feminine, and evolved their own 'hard' subcultures of implacable masculinity. Indifferent to the consequences of breaking the rules, they valued loyalty to the subculture over institutional imperatives, and ended up inevitably in low-paid factory jobs. Willis's work stressed the agency of the youth and not simply the ways they were officially excluded. The older ethnographies of working-class men, secure in their jobs and occupational identities, now appear dated (Kriegler, 1980; Metcalfe, 1988; Williams, 1981; Willis, 1979) as the restructuring of Western capitalism, rising unemployment, disinvestment in old industries, has meant that Willis's lads are less likely to follow their fathers into factories, mines or agricultural labour, less likely to work with their hands and less able to find stable employment. As Watson *et al.* show (2003), labour market 'churning' means that many young people will have more jobs by aged thirty than their parents had throughout their working lives. Inherited role models have limited utility in the skittish environment of the new economy.

In recent times Western societies have sought to increase education retention rates to deal with the structural fact of endemic youth unemployment: raising the leaving age; developing child-centred pedagogies; broadening the curriculum to include more vocational and creative options, to provide alternatives to traditional academic subjects. So those who would otherwise have endured the fate of Willis's lads are more likely to remain at school and in the post-school system longer. However, they are also likely to study outside the traditional academic curriculum, and to find their way into the places in which learning is less formalized and more closely resembles the community of practice: the art rooms, computer labs and workshops where the practical curricula are taught.

Patterns of communal learning and mentorship were long important for working-class men. Those from poor backgrounds, of various ethnicities, have traditionally relied on older men to recruit and initiate them to the world of work (Pahl, 1984; Shields, 1992). It is important to acknowledge that the patriarchal character of these recruitment practices, with which employers colluded, guaranteed that women were excluded from better-paid trades and confined to low-paid 'unskilled' occupations. In addition they were expected to perform domestic labour (Cockburn, 1983). However, the new economy has disorganized both gender relations and templates of inter-generational masculinity, undermining the sense of self-worth for both mentors and initiates (McDowell, 2000, 2003; Nixon, 2006). Historically working men developed their skills on-the-job in stable workplace communities. These communities are now much less common. However, the sites in which men learn skills from each other are not restricted to places of employment. Indeed the manual work dispositions of many young men are formed through spending time in groups of men who participate in making and fixing things in spaces like sheds and garages. These informal communities of practice (Lave and Wenger, 1991; Wenger, 1998) continue to form part of masculine growing-up experiences, even if there are fewer jobs that draw on the skills they have learned. These are both domestic/familial but can also form around community organizations (Light and Nash, 2006). As Parker (2006) observes in his study of young male trainees at professional football clubs, the collective rituals and practices associated with apprenticeship – initiation, banter, criteria of esteem – are not only practised on the shop floor but are transferable to new workplace settings.

Residual masculinities and new work patterns

The five case studies presented below[4] are three young men and two young women from relatively modest backgrounds. While Douglas, Tony and Hayley had more conventional suburban upbringings, Jake and Theresa had more exposure to bohemian culture. However, what is most important is to identify the ways gender affects what is negotiable and what is not, about vocational identities. As we will see, the young women are generally able to assimilate some of the pressures and turbulence of the unfolding creative career. While these case studies are by no means definitive, they appear to be representative of a larger social pattern in which the capacity to adapt to the flux and uncertainty of post-modern working life is shaped by the residual codes and values of gender and class.

Douglas, design and dissimulation

Douglas rebelled at school.[5] He exemplified what Connell termed 'protest masculinity' (Connell, 1996) and he failed to matriculate. Lucky to get a trade apprenticeship as a sheet metal worker, he spent four years exposed to factory floor culture. He 'hated every minute of it' but was driven by his mother to complete despite knowing that this was not what he 'wanted to do in life'. With hindsight, he makes a virtue out of perseverance. Now, as a student in a design course at technical college, he values the skills he obtained during his apprenticeship.

> [L]ooking back on it now I learnt a lot of skills … I can make stuff and it is awesome. I didn't like it because of the environment, I like making stuff, I still tinker and kind of like just doing stuff around the house and making things, like I make jewellery at home just on the side and sell that, and it helps me heaps here, like I am ten steps ahead of everyone else because I have the knowledge of making stuff.

Douglas has laboured to transpose his skills, from industrial to post-industrial setting. He retains a sense of craftsmanship, however. The economic or industry imperative, in other words, has not yet taken over. Consequently he struggles to reconcile the sorts of self-reconstruction required if he is to become a successful designer in a highly competitive and precarious field.

Douglas's design education covers not just skills training, but provides a broader cultural initiation to the field and the social and cultural skills that are required to succeed in it. Like many of our interviewees he spoke of being given a primer in the importance of getting to know and becoming memorable to cultural brokers – studio and gallery operators, agents, dealers. He quickly became aware of the hierarchical character of design where very few become auteurs and most remain on the exploited edges of industry. He is forced to reckon with the injunction to market himself, to network, to develop a personal brand or style. These things do not come naturally to Douglas because he has a tendency to pour scorn on pompous, phoney and self-aggrandizing forms of behaviour. His straightforward, down-to-earth disposition is at odds with the design world that requires an ability to dissimulate.

> They are wanker designers and I didn't know this at the start, but yeah I don't reckon I could act like they are, not most of them. Just the ones that you see in the media you know what I mean … But I have already decided that I am not going to lose my integrity if I do make it because, you know what I am talking about, black turtle-necks and the glasses?

Here Douglas refers to a vocation expectation that he is still seeking to fathom, in which branding and performance – what Nickson *et al.* (2003) call aesthetic skills – are more important than the skills you possess, the quality of your work. For those, like Douglas, who arrive in the hyper-real, entrepreneurial field of design, and who have very little experience of creative work, and few family and community narratives to draw on, or advice to guide them, the realization that they will be judged on how cool they are, rather than how good their work is, is bewildering and salutary. If he responds to these pressures to dissimulate, he loses his integrity. The idea of the authentic masculine self, that refuses to perform to the crowd, to strangers and outsiders, runs very deep for Douglas and for others who we interviewed (see Bourgois, 1995). We can see how his years as an apprentice led him to embrace a no-nonsense working-class persona, something that is functional to the factory floor, but which is anathema to the world of the new economy: ' ... nothing wrong with blue collar work at all like a lot of my mates are tradesmen but I just want something more I guess, and something into design, like I fell into design'.

Here Douglas describes the biographical project of straddling the old and the new economy. Sheet metal work represents old labour, manual trade skills central to industrial workplaces, but with the decline in demand for those skills, as metal processing work goes offshore, he seeks to recalibrate. This appears in the narrative as being the product of choice ('I just want something more') but is also strategic, part of a larger biographical project to avoid redundancy as old work gives way to new.

Tony and the artisanal yearning

Tony comes from a poor immigrant family. His parents worked as commercial cleaners and discouraged his ambition to become a film editor ('is this job going to pay the bills? Is it going to give you a pay packet?'). Nevertheless his single-mindedness leads him to devote much of his young adult life to training courses which have yielded very little paid work. So his inspiration comes from learning from the seasoned professionals who taught him (although are probably unable to make a living themselves from editing). He describes the pedagogical process in terms of an artisanal apprenticeship:

> I guess in as far as finding a mentor, one of our editing teachers, he'll come into our suites individually and give constructive feedback, and I think we admire him a lot because he's more old school, doing it for years, respected in the industry, you know, editors that are competent enough to use the computer they edit on but that's not where they learnt their craft from. I think that's the trend, people are under the impression that to be an editor, it's about learning to use the software very well but they don't really know much about the craft of editing [and] maybe it's not necessarily their own fault because you have to go to a school that have teachers that are working editors or retired editors who can teach the old, traditional way, and it's more about technology now.

In emphasizing the virtues of his teacher/mentor's experience on old equipment Tony seeks to conserve the idea of editing as a craft, not simply a technical function. New technologies guarantee standardization but remove judgement, craft skill, and the imperfections that can make cultural products quirky and interesting. This attitude was also very much apparent within a group of (largely male) music production students we interviewed. Although they were impressed with the state-of-the-art equipment available to them at their technical college, they also had a deep respect for those raised on 'old school' techniques. Tony also embraces the idea that the work should combine both craft and artistic skills:

> [you can learn] on the job but the sorts of thing you can't learn has to come from yourself, having that emotion and intuition of telling stories and that came natural to me. That's what it's really about ... you do it on a subconscious level.

The Sociological Review, 63:S1, pp. 66–83 (2015), DOI: 10.1111/1467-954X.12241

His aspirations reflect the reaction to Taylorism, the critique of alienated work, by recuperating the aesthetic dimension, but also a desire to conserve the artisanal element of slow accretion of craft skills learned through observation and trial-and-error hands-on practice.

Regrettably, his training has produced few opportunities. He volunteered in a production house but this experience left him intensely disillusioned:

> I was just doing bits and pieces of stuff that other people weren't doing. And pretty much the owner, I worked as his camera assistant, you know did some other things here and there, learnt a couple of things but then I thought, how much more can you learn when all you do is the same thing over again? How do you exactly make the move from working in these small production houses doing corporate stuff, where all you're doing is trans-coding or tape loader or something like that, or you're the guy who dabbles in everything – I'm the editor, I'm the photoshop guy, I'm the after-effects guy, the colourist, sound designer whatever else. Make lunch, bring coffee – well everyone's gotta do that in the beginning – um, how do you make the move to the real big stuff. Should I be taking the road where I start working in these small production houses, where all they seem to do is focus on cranking out cheap, corporate stuff? That's boring, banal and then you may learn to be more of a technical person but creatively you're doomed, you just die in there.

Tony is far from being the flexible subject of the creative industries. His investment in the craft artist identity is deep-rooted and indivisible. Not willing to 'rebrand' or transfer skills superficially, nor improvise for the sake it, he would prefer to salvage whatever creative integrity he can by not 'cranking out cheap corporate stuff'. He accepts the short-term need to multi-skill and to work around corporate imperatives but only as a means to achieving some greater creative autonomy later on. It is apparent that he is unlikely to earn a living from his creative work, and that, like many he will only be able to practise his creative skills on amateur projects.

Jake and the lost community of practice

By contrast with Tony, Jake has been successful in finding craft work in the film industry, in a specialized niche: designing and producing animatronic puppets for fantasy, science fiction, children's films.[6] Growing up in a small rural town, but with a strong artistic/counter cultural community, Jake played in a successful band as a teenager, and spent some time on a school work-experience programme with a man who made latex model puppets for the film industry. This sparked his interest because the craft, specialized, project-based work seemed to combine new and old skills: employing the same technology as mechanized cars that he played with as a child, and the design skills that he learned in a well-resourced school workshop. Jake had fond memories of his teachers and especially those who taught him in informal settings, in his music and design/technology classes. It became clear that it was not only the pleasure at both mechanical and aesthetic free play, that he experienced in these settings but also the cultures of informal learning and the communities of practice that he found in the classroom.

Additionally Jake spoke of spending time with his father, a bus driver, fixing cars and motorbikes, doing mechanical things in the garage.

Later on, while living and working in a mundane job in Sydney, he got a break when he learned 'that the creature department on [a feature film project] needed a runner'. So he called and got the job. This allowed him to hang around the edges of the work group of model makers and eventually to be accepted and learn their techniques. Eventually he was able to set up his own business but the work has always been project based, highly specialized and intermittent. As a freelancer in the early stages of his career, he makes a reasonable living (unlike most of our interviewees) from his puppet-making work but nevertheless voiced regret at the individualistic and competitive structures that the film industry imposes on his trade. We asked him about his attitude to his peers:

> I wouldn't want to be competition, I just want to work with them, for them … I've put so many hours into people's stuff before and get no gratitude and I watch them do it to other people … yeah, there's a lot of people that do that, take that angle but then they're constantly trying to get stuff out of you and you help them, like I still will help them. I don't know why I do but I do…

He gives freely but often without reciprocation ('like I still will help them. I don't know why but I do') but is frustrated with those whose selfish guarding of knowledge disrupts the community of practice:

> Yeah, I'm lucky I've had a lot of help from so many different people, that's the most important thing, and I help those people out heaps, like the guys I work for, I help them with stuff where most people would charge them. They give me materials sometimes and I help them do other things … [and] I appreciate it when people help me and a lot people I work with don't, and they're the sort of people I have zero time for, that's just pathetic…

This illustrates the residual influence of the culture of craft collaboration. Jake has successfully made the transition from old to new labour, has added specialized aesthetic skills to both mechanical and digital knowledge. He has found craft artist work in the film industry (Banks, 2010), but is unhappy about the individualist structures of the relations of production. By relating nostalgic narratives about the informal teaching and learning of his youth, he shows a yearning for the relations of mutual support in which trade skills were traditionally practised.

Hayley and the eye for the main chance

Hayley grew up poor in the western suburbs of Sydney:

> … always had hand-me-downs, bikes and clothes … never had lunch money, got a [school] lunch order on my birthday, still take a packed lunch everywhere and I think hard before buying something and I'd get pocket money and save it …

When she left school she worked in shops and offices. Hayley spoke of not feeling family pressure in relation to her work choices. Rather she was encouraged to find her calling, 'I've always gone with the flow and mum's always just been,

The Sociological Review, 63:S1, pp. 66–83 (2015), DOI: 10.1111/1467-954X.12241

"do whatever you like, whatever makes you happy, it'll work out"'. She exemplifies the qualities of the new worker: eagerness but with tractable ambition and a singular and all-consuming commitment to work (Gregg, 2011):

> what I put my mind to I do well because I'm really determined … whatever I apply myself to and as long as you set your mind to it, it will happen and there's an addiction to success … It's just I've never really known what I wanted to do, still don't know, even now, so totally fell into it … But for me to get that far I've had to push really hard and for me to go further I need to push harder … your life becomes your work and you can't do this career without it taking over your life …

She sees her skills are transferable, and her career is structured according to industry rather than craft imperatives. Being 'determined' suggests a willingness to improvise, to recalibrate her ambitions and occupational identity in pursuit of 'success', and importantly, to build her networks, which are looser forms of association than communities of practice. Her media career began in the creative arts and communications course through which she found her way into broadcast television. As one of a group of student interns at GMT television, she saw it as necessary to stand out from the crowd, to be noticed, rather than treating her peers as a community of practice:

> I remember when I walked through the doors at GMT I was like, I am not leaving here … I would always keep away from all the other students because I just wanted to be on my own so the people there, it wasn't the group from uni it was always just Hayley they were talking to and stuff … and just because I'm a bit chatty and friendly with people and I'll often talk my ideas through with people there … [And] I'm good at calling people and getting through to the right people …

Hayley was recognized by those with the power to offer work opportunities, where the others were not, although these were always short term and part time. However, she seeks to make a virtue out of her precarious circumstances (Morgan *et al.*, 2013), internalizing the creative economy discourse that sees vocational restlessness as guaranteeing renewal. Like many of the young women we interviewed, but rarely the men, Hayley embraces a sense of fatalism about the direction of her working life, resisting the temptation to try to engineer outcomes: 'I think in terms of one year, I just don't really think further than that so I'm trying to relax and not be such a controlling person, tell myself that everything falls into place … '.

Like several other young women aspirants that we interviewed, Hayley is happy to surrender to the judgement of the creative gatekeepers, and this fatalism allows her to steel herself against the inevitable rejections that are part of the creative career. Under the code of apprenticeship, by contrast, the community of practice is the primary source for legitimatizing skill and conferring vocational esteem, and the arbitrary judgement of outsiders regarded with contempt. Another young woman interviewee described the experience of being 'discovered' and being offered a job in the music industry, after a chance encounter with a customer while she was working in a clothing store in an upmarket part of

Sydney. 'This was my chance to shine' she said, in terms reminiscent of the language of those who audition their creative talents – from cooking, to designing, modelling and various performing arts – on reality television programmes.

Theresa's magical realism

Theresa, around thirty, grew up in a northern New South Wales town 'on an old hippy commune really' and her class background is difficult to specify. Like several others in our sample, she had an artist bohemian father who subsidized his unpaid creative endeavours with low-wage labour and the family was relatively poor. She moved to the city to study sound engineering but did not enjoy the technical demands, dropped out and, at the suggestion of her sister, turned her interests to film. Her break came after she overheard a conversation between fellow customers in a café, one of whom was lamenting their inability to find a styling assistant for a film shoot:

> I heard this girl beside me going oh my god, I've got this shoot and I need a styling assistant and I can't find one anywhere, and I looked over [and said] excuse me, I just heard you mention that and I'm a styling assistant so I got a contact and straight on the job ...

Not particularly bound to a fixed creative vocation, Theresa is able to recognize and take advantage of diverse opportunities and the serendipitous moments that often define the creative career narrative. Later she became a location scout. Working for low pay for a film production company she saw the opportunity to move sideways:

> ... I was actually out scouting one day and I was knocking on a door to look for some house for a commercial and this lady answered and I said hi I'm a location scout blah, blah, blah and she said 'oh my god I've just moved here from England and I've started up my own location company and you know, I'm looking for someone blah, blah, blah and she said what do you charge', I knew the other scouts at the other place were getting like $300 a day so I told her $300 a day, I can't believe the words came out of my mouth, like I got this air of confidence about myself and she said do you want to meet up, I'd love to have you come work for me ...

She speaks of her life as littered with incidents of happenstance and, like Hayley, rationalizes this in the language of fatalism and teleology: nothing has meaning until the final unravelling is clear and what happens is 'meant to be'. Such a Zen-like disposition allows her to weather the vagaries of the creative career, and to break with the idea of a fixed idea of creative skill or talent:

> I think I'm just a big believer in the way that energy works; you put energy out there and it comes back, like there's no way that it doesn't. I just don't believe that if you're out there doing things whether you're getting paid or not, if you're just out there doing things, things will happen, they just have to. I've always just believed that.

Like Hayley, Theresa is a much more supple vocational subject than the young men we discuss above, one who is able to reshape herself in response to the

The Sociological Review, 63:S1, pp. 66–83 (2015), DOI: 10.1111/1467-954X.12241

random interpellations of the volatile creative labour markets. It is this more diffuse notion of art and calling that equips her to become a 'slashie' (stylist – slash – location scout etc.), a term the popular media now uses to describe inner-urban multi-skilled young adults.

Conclusion

Creative industry biographies typically follow a pattern of enchantment and disenchantment (McRobbie, 2002a, 2002b). When asked to recount the origins of their creative interests most interviewees described youthful sub/cultural enthusiasms and many referred to inherited traits, talents or interests (eg by having musical or artistic parents), or the stimulation and encouragement they received in places of informal learning – both inside and outside school. Only later are they conscripted to the ideas of the creative industry and creative career (Morgan and Nelligan, 2012). While training or gaining early experience, perhaps as interns or through scraps of paid work, most discover that they are expected to tread water for years before they can make a living doing genuinely creative work. This proves to be a sobering corrective to their artistic idealism, and can appear to many to profane the very sacred, personal and self-revelatory impetus of their early cultural practice. Some are able to adapt while many feel a sense of betrayal. While thirty or forty years ago most youthful creativity rarely strayed beyond amateurism, today the idea of the creative economy has encouraged more young people to develop vocational aspirations. A large proportion of these people will have their career dreams dashed.

The case studies presented here suggest that there is a gender and class dimension to the creative industry subject, that the grounded cultures of learning and labour are not easily translatable into the forms of presentation of self that are required in the new economy. A larger study, involving both qualitative and quantitative methods, might be needed to confirm these results. Others have written of brittle masculinity, of the difficulties experienced by men of certain backgrounds in assimilating to the terrain of new work. Our argument is that there is an inertia associated with the habits of working life; that certain collective forms and habits are communicated inter-generationally. In the postmodern workplace, characterized by short-term and unorthodox employment arrangements, stable communities of practice no longer exist. While these might be improvised and convened around particular projects, they are ephemeral, and participants are forced into competitive and individualistic forms. By contrast with the 'disembedded subjects' of reflexive modernity (Beck *et al.*, 1994), many of the young men in our research sample are encumbered by residual cultural baggage that works against the achievement of a successful creative career. We have seen how both Tony and Jake value the slow learning and unconditional sharing of skills that exist in communities of practice at sites of formal and informal learning. Douglas expresses his aversion to the flamboyant performativity that is demanded of auteur success in the highly competitive field of design. This statement of distaste for networking with strangers, and touting their credentials at times and places outside working hours, exemplified general patterns evident in our research. However, Douglas recognized that such performance was necessary for professional advancement. Additionally, our male interviewees from disadvantaged backgrounds commonly expressed diffidence towards the pressures to diversify their skills and ambitions in ways elicited by the volatile structures of the creative industries. Their entry point was, and remains, the particular creative skill and they are lukewarm towards the more nebulous idea of transferable aesthetic skills. The two young women we presented here described themselves as more versatile and responsive to the possibility of becoming the protégée, to being recognized, discovered and to placing their fortunes in the hands of those who act as creative brokers/gatekeepers. While there are other obstacles to women achieving success in creative fields, as we acknowledged at the outset, our argument is that, with limited communal exposure to the code of career, young working-class men carry particular forms of cultural baggage that prevent them thriving in the unstable environment of the creative industries. This is not by any means to suggest that workplace solidarity is the sole province of men. However, there are collective values and habits associated with the masculine trade and apprenticeship traditions that are incompatible with post-modern capitalism, where working lives are often fluid, and success based on individualism and enterprise. In biographical narrative testimony these dissonances bubble to the surface. They are apparent in the many interviewees' sober reflections on creative training courses, and early industry experience describing the collision of values and circumstances, why *who I am* does not dovetail neatly with *who I wish to become*.

Notes

1 We would like to acknowledge the assistance of our colleagues at the University of Western Sydney's Institute for Culture and Society, and in particular Julian Wood, Greg Noble and Sherene Idriss.
2 The sample is drawn from two separate but related/cognate studies: that conducted as part of Nelligan's doctoral thesis and the Australian Research Council project 'Just-in-Time Self: Young Men Skill and Narratives of Aspiration in the New Economy' (Greg Noble as second named Chief Investigator).
3 Although it should be noted that employers will commonly lament the shortcomings of skills training in state-provided education in order to evade responsibility for providing this themselves (for a larger history of employer relinquishment of skills training see Watson *et al.*, 2003).
4 Pseudonyms have been used for all interviewees.
5 Interview conducted by Julian Wood.
6 Banks (2010) has argued that craft labour has been under-represented in the literature on creative work, as researchers focus on artistic labour instead.

References

Adkins, L., (1999), 'Community and economy: a re-traditionalisation of gender', *Theory, Culture & Society*, 16 (1): 119–141.

The Sociological Review, 63:S1, pp. 66–83 (2015), DOI: 10.1111/1467-954X.12241

Adkins, L., (2000), 'Objects of innovation: post-occupational reflexivity and re-traditionalisations of gender', in S. Ahmed, J. Kilby, C. Lury, M. McNeil and B. Skeggs (eds), *Transformations: Thinking through Feminism*, 259–272, London: Routledge.

Adkins, L., (2004), 'Reflexivity: freedom or habit of gender?' *Sociological Review*, 20 (6): 21–42.

Adkins, L. and Lury, C., (1999), 'The labour of identity: performing identities, performing economies', *Economy and Society*, 28: 598–614.

Banks, M., (2010), 'Craft labour and creative industries', *International Journal of Cultural Policy*, 16 (3): 305–321.

Banks, M. and Milestone, K., (2011), 'Individualization, gender and cultural work', *Gender, Work and Organization*, 18 (1): 73–89.

Beck, U., Giddens, A. and Lash, S., (1994), *Reflexive Modernization: Politics, Tradition and Aesthetics in the Modern Social Order*, Cambridge: Polity Press.

Bourgois, P., (1995), *In Search of Respect: Selling Crack in El Barrio*, Cambridge: Cambridge University Press.

Cockburn, C., (1983), *Brothers*, London: Pluto Press.

Cohen, P., (1999), 'Apprenticeship a la mode? Some reflections on learning as cultural labour', in P. Ainley and H. Rainbird (eds), *Apprenticeship: Towards a New Paradigm of Learning*, 129–147, London: Kogan Page.

Connell, R. W., (1996), 'New directions in gender theory, masculinity research and gender politics', *Ethnos: Journal of Anthropology*, 61 (3–4): 157–176.

Conor, B., (2013), 'Hired hands, liars, schmucks: histories of screenwriting work and workers contemporary screen production', in M. Banks, R. Gill and S. Taylor (eds), *Theorizing Cultural Work: Labour, Continuity and Change in the Cultural and Creative Industries*, 44–55, London: Routledge.

Gill, R., (2002), 'Cool, creative and egalitarian? Exploring gender in project-based new media work', *Information, Communication and Society*, 5 (1): 70–89.

Gill, R., (2009), 'Creative biographies in new media: social innovation in web work', in P. Jeffcutt and A. Pratt (eds), *Creativity and Innovation*, 1–20, London and New York: Routledge.

Gill, R., (2010), '"Life is a pitch": managing the self in new media work', in M. Deuze (ed.), *Managing Media Work*, 249–262, London: Sage.

Gill, R. and Pratt, A., (2008), 'In the social factory? Immaterial labour, precariousness and cultural work', *Theory Culture & Society*, 25 (7–8): 1–30.

Gregg, M., (2011), *Work's Intimacy*, Cambridge: Polity Press.

Haukka, S., Hearn, G. N., Brow, J. and Cunningham, S. D., (2010), *From Education to Work in Australia's Creative Digital Industries : Comparing the Opinions and Practices of Employers and Aspiring Creatives*, Brisbane, Queensland: QUT; Australian Research Council; Institute for Creative Industries and Innovation.

Haukka, S., (2011), 'Education-to-work transitions of aspiring creatives', *Cultural Trends*, 20 (1): 41–64.

Hesmondalgh, D. and Baker, S., (2011), *Creative Labour: Media Work in Three Cultural Industries*, Milton Park, NY: Routledge.

Ho, C. and Alcorso, C., (2004), 'Migrants and employment: challenging the success story', *Journal of Sociology*, 40 (3): 237–259.

Hollands, R., (1990), *The Long Transition: Class, Culture and Youth Training*, London: Macmillan.

Kenway, J., Kraack, A. and Hickey-Moody, A., (2006), *Masculinity beyond the Metropolis*, Basingstoke: Palgrave Macmillan.

Kriegler, R., (1980), *Working for the Company: Work and Control in the Whyalla Shipyard*, Melbourne: Oxford University Press.

Lave, J. and Wenger, E., (1991), *Situated Learning: Legitimate Peripheral Participation*, Cambridge: Cambridge University Press.

Light, R. and Nash, M., (2006), 'Learning and identity in overlapping communities of practice: surf club, school and sports club', *The Australian Educational Researcher*, 33 (1): 75–94.

Luckman, S., (2012), *Locating Cultural Work: The Politics and Poetics of Rural, Regional and Remote Creativity*, Basingstoke: Palgrave Macmillan.

Luckman, S., (2013), 'Precarious labour then and now: the British arts and crafts movement and creative work re-visited', in M. Banks, R. Gill and S. Taylor (eds), *Theorizing Cultural Work: Labour, Continuity and Change in the Cultural and Creative Industries*, 19–29, London: Routledge.

McDowell, L., (2000), 'Learning to serve? Employment aspirations and attitudes of young working-class men in an era of labour market restructuring', *Gender, Place and Culture*, 7 (4): 389–416.

McDowell, L., (2003), *Redundant Masculinities? Employment Change and White Working Class Youth*, Oxford: Blackwell.

McRobbie, A., (2002a), 'From Holloway to Hollywood: happiness at work in the new cultural economy', in P. du Gay and M. Pryke (eds), *Cultural Economy: Cultural Analysis and Contemporary Life*, 97–114, London: Sage Publications.

McRobbie, A., (2002b), 'Clubs to companies: notes on the decline of political culture in speeded up creative worlds', *Cultural Studies*, 16 (4): 516–531.

McRobbie, A., (2013), *Be Creative: Making a Living in the New Culture Industries*, London: Sage.

Metcalfe, A., (1988), *For Freedom and Dignity: Historical Agency and Class Structures in the Coalfields*, Sydney: A&U.

Mishler, E. G., (1999), *Storylines: Craftartists' Narratives of Identity*, Cambridge, MA: Harvard University Press.

Morgan, G. and Nelligan, P., (2012), 'Taking the bait: minority youth in Australia, creative skills and precarious work', in E. Armano and A. Murgia (eds), *Maps of Precariousness*, 32–50, Bologna: I libri di Emil.

Morgan, G. and Wood, J., (2014), 'Creative accommodations: the fractured transitions and precarious lives of young musicians', *Journal of Cultural Economy*, 7 (1): 64–78.

Morgan, G., Wood, J. and Nelligan, P., (2013), 'Beyond the vocational fragments: creative work, precarious labour and the idea of "flexploitation"', *Economic and Labour Relations Review*, 24 (3): 397–415.

Nickson, D., Warhurst, C., Cullen, A. M. and Watt, A., (2003), 'Bringing in the excluded? Aesthetic labour, skills and training in the new economy', *Journal of Education and Work*, 16 (2): 185–203.

Nixon, D., (2006), '"I just like working with my hands": employment aspirations and the meaning of work for low-skilled unemployed men in Britain's service sector', *Journal of Education and Work*, 19 (2): 201–217.

Pahl, R., (1984), *Divisions of Labour*, Oxford: Basil Blackwell.

Parker, A., (2006), 'Lifelong learning to labour: apprenticeship, masculinity, and communities of practice', *British Education Research Journal*, 32 (5): 687–701.

Riessman, C., (2008), *Narrative Methods for the Human Sciences*, London: Sage.

Rose, N., (1999), *Governing the Soul*, London: Free Association Books.

Ross, A., (2009), *Nice Work if You Can Get It*, New York: New York University Press.

Sennett, R., (2001), 'Street and office: two sources of identity', in W. Hutton and A. Giddens (eds), *On the Edge: Living with Global Capitalism*, 175–190, London: Vintage.

Shields, J., (1992), 'Craftsmen in the making: the memory and meaning of apprenticeship in Sydney between the Great War and the Great Depression', in J. Shields (ed.), *All our Labours: Oral Histories of Working Life in Twentieth Century Sydney*, 86–122, Sydney: UNSW Press.

Stokes, H. and Wyn, J., (2007), 'Constructing identities and making careers: young people's perspectives on work and learning', *International Journal of Lifelong Education*, 26 (5): 495–511.

Taylor, S. and Littleton, K., (2008), 'Art work or money: conflicts in the construction of a creative identity', *The Sociological Review*, 56 (2): 275–292.

Taylor, S. and Littleton, K., (2012), *Contemporary Identities of Creativity and Creative Work*, Aldershot: Ashgate.

Watson, I., (1994), 'Class memory: an alternative approach to class identity', *Labour History*, 67: 23–41.

Watson, I., Buchanan, J., Campbell, I. and Briggs, C., (2003), *Fragmented Futures: New Challenges in Working Life*, Sydney: Federation Press.

Wenger, E., (1998), *Communities of Practice*, Cambridge: Cambridge University Press.

The Sociological Review, 63:S1, pp. 66–83 (2015), DOI: 10.1111/1467-954X.12241

Wengraf, T., (2001), *Qualitative Research Interviewing: Biographic Narrative and Semi-structured Methods*, London: Sage.

Williams, C., (1981), *Open Cut: The Working Class in an Australian Mining Town*, Sydney: Allen and Unwin.

Willis, P., (1977), *Learning to Labour: How Working Class Kids Get Working Class Jobs*, Farnborough: Saxon House.

Willis, P., (1979), 'Shop floor culture, masculinity and the wage form', in J. Clarke, C. Critcher and R. Johnson (eds), *Working Class Culture: Studies in History and Theory*, 185–198, London: Hutchinson.

Please quote the article DOI when citing SR content, including monographs. Article DOIs and "How to Cite" information can be found alongside the online version of each article within Wiley Online Library. All articles published within the SR (including monograph content) are included within the ISI Journal Citation Reports® Social Science Citation Index.

Birds of a feather: informal recruitment practices and gendered outcomes for screenwriting work in the UK film industry

Natalie Wreyford

Abstract: The film industry offers an exemplary case study for examining the recruitment processes to which the 'socialized worker' (Gill and Pratt, 2008) is subject. Even among the creative industries, film is exceptional in its reliance on networking and word of mouth as its primary – and in many cases only – tool for recruitment and for identifying the 'right' candidate for the job (Blair, 2000a). Increasingly there is evidence that reliance on personal networks and informal employment practices has different outcomes for men and women (Grugulis and Stoyanova, 2012). Hiring on short-term contracts in a context of ambiguity, risk and uncertainty, necessitates reliance on social networks and informal subjective criteria, with outcomes that reinforce the status quo (Bielby and Bielby, 1999). Fenstermaker, West and Zimmerman argue that to overcome gender inequality 'we will need to understand the mechanisms by which it is sustained in institutional social arrangements' (Fenstermaker *et al.*, 2002: 38). This article will unpack how recruitment procedures that rely on 'connections' and 'affinities of habitus' (Bourdieu, 1984: 151) can contribute to the way that gender inequality is sustained for screenwriters.

Keywords: film industry, recruitment, networking, informality, risk

Introduction

A substantial amount of data is available to illustrate just how few films have women in key creative positions, and how little the situation is changing (see Conor in this collection for a full and up-to-date account). Critical sociological studies of work in creative industries have revealed the perpetuation of inequalities of opportunity along gender lines. Notable scholars have explored some of the reasons for these inequalities, (eg Scharff, this collection) on classical musicians (Gill, 2002) on new media workers and on radio DJs (Gill, 2000), but in creative labour studies 'surprisingly little attention has been paid in sociology to the means of, and barriers to entry' (Hesmondhalgh, 2007: 71). This article makes a contribution to the research on gender inequality in creative professions

The Sociological Review, 63:S1, pp. 84–96 (2015), DOI: 10.1111/1467-954X.12242
© 2015 The Author. Editorial organisation © 2015 The Editorial Board of the Sociological Review. Published by John Wiley & Sons Ltd, 9600 Garsington Road, Oxford OX4 2DQ, UK and 350 Main Street, Malden, MA 02148, USA

by exploring the dynamics of informal, networked recruitment processes. It is informed by key thinking from the fields of creative industries, cultural studies and gender and work, and introduces new empirical data from interviews with screenwriters and employers of screenwriters, to examine how inequality of opportunity is sustained through structural and subjective mechanisms that are not held accountable through equal opportunities policies (Bielby, 2009; see Jones and Pringle, this collection).

Informal, socialized recruitment processes in project-based labour markets

The film industry is not a new creative industry, but it offers a case study for how 'insecure, casualized or irregular labour' (Gill and Pratt, 2008: 2) has widely replaced integrated, factory-style industrial production for workers in cultural industries (see, for example, Christopherson, 2008; Florida, 2004). Most film workers fit a 'flexible specialization' model (Christopherson and Storper, 1988; Storper and Christopherson, 1987) – that is, they are employed on a freelance basis, applying their own particular specialization across a range of projects and often across different media. A career in film, in as much as it can still be called that, shares the new characteristics of other creative labour. It is precarious, discontinuous, and the labour is 'deterritorialized, dispersed and decentralized' (Gill and Pratt, 2008: 7) and the 'factory' 'disseminated out into society as a whole' (Gill and Pratt, 2008: 6). The insecurity and anxiety produced by the unpredictable nature of project-based employment means that workers must be in a continuous process of looking for work (Randle and Culkin, 2009). In the film industry the need to be constantly 'networking' is an accepted part of the job.

Skillset's report on the status of women in the creative industries in the UK found that representation was highest in sectors with larger employers in which more stable, permanent employment models are common, such as terrestrial television (48 per cent), broadcast radio (47 per cent), cinema exhibition (43 per cent), and book publishing (61 per cent) (Skillset, 2010). Permanent employment might be more attractive for workers with childcare responsibilities (see Wreyford, 2013, for a more detailed review of the effects of childcare responsibilities on female creative workers) because motherhood has been shown to have a detrimental effect on networking. Campbell demonstrates how 'women with young children have more restricted network range, and lower network composition', but finds no correlating disparity for men who start a family (Campbell, 1988: 193). Since mothers are still required to allocate more time to domestic responsibilities than fathers, or men and women without children (Hochschild, 1983; Renzulli *et al.*, 2000), they also have less time for other activities. However, motherhood does not provide the complete explanation (see Gill, 2014). Bielby and Baron have also demonstrated that 'autonomous employers operating small firms need no explicit rationale for excluding female workers; they can unilaterally exercise their preference for an all-male network' (Bielby and Baron, 1984: 38). How can we account for such discriminatory practices?

Structural factors, which suggest how the opportunities available to an individual may be limited by their social position and background, are the favoured explanation in studies of gender and networking (eg Ibarra, 1992; McGuire, 2000). Since networking 'is primarily a social activity' (Cromie and Birley, 1992: 242) it is therefore likely to be highly influenced by the status and social position of the person doing the networking. This argument is most persuasive when considering the limited numbers of women and black, Asian and minority ethnic individuals (BAME) in more senior, decision-making roles. For screenwriters, the equivalent would be a film's producers. Screenwriters are most frequently commissioned (employed) by producers, the majority of whom are men (75 per cent of producers and 85 per cent of executive producers of the 250 highest grossing films in 2013 were men (Lauzen, 2014)).

Academic research on finding employment using personal networks in the film labour markets in the UK and USA has tended to focus on the physical production phase of the industries, (Blair, 2000b; Blair, 2003; Blair *et al.*, 2001; Christopherson, 2008; Christopherson and Storper, 1988; Grugulis and Stoyanova, 2012). Some of the observations and conclusions of this work are not easily translated to roles outside the specialized world of the production community. For instance, Blair's (2000a) formulation of the 'semi-permanent work group' – a team of individuals who move between jobs as a unit with only the most senior member responsible for procuring work – applies to film production departments but similar protective enclaves are not available for screenwriters. To understand more precisely the wider mechanisms of informal recruitment and its ramifications for key creative workers such as screenwriters, it is necessary to turn to the research on networking in other fields, including those where personnel are recruited in a more formal manner through job advertisements and by Human Resource departments. The usefulness of this literature is clear, since even within formal employment structures it has been shown that informal networks play a powerful role in upholding gender inequality (McGuire, 2002). McGuire's interviewees – over a thousand financial services employees – confirm that informal networks are the place where the real power and opportunities are. Some are even disparaging of those who rely on the formal processes. As one interviewee reported: 'He said that vice presidents routinely exchanged such favors and that only "losers" went to human resources (ie used a formal procedure) to try to obtain promotions' (McGuire, 2002: 318). It is therefore important to understand exactly how informal recruitment works to ensure different outcomes for women.

In her study of new media workers, Gill reports that some of her interviewees found networking to be 'a form of gendered exclusion – the activities of an "old boys" network' (2002: 82). She cites one woman as longing for a return to a more formal and transparent job market and refers to Franks' observation about the Hansard Commission: 'The clubbier the culture, the less likely women are to make the top' (1999: 52). In my research, the employers were keen to disavow – unprompted – that such mechanisms exist in the film industry. The most frequent way they did this was by referring to the very visible women in senior positions

The Sociological Review, 63:S1, pp. 84–96 (2015), DOI: 10.1111/1467-954X.12242
© 2015 The Author. Editorial organisation © 2015 The Editorial Board of the Sociological Review

in the three largest, publicly funded film financing entities – the BBC, Film Four and the BFI.

> There was a time, not so long ago when it was pointed out to me that major areas of film finance in the UK were being run by women. (Rob, male employer)

Indeed, there is recent evidence that these women may have played a part in the support of female creative workers (Steele, 2013). However, they all report to male bosses, and none was in a position to fully finance a film. Indeed their potential private finance partners are most frequently men:

> I notice that distributors are very male. They're all male. (Gillian, female employer)

> I mean, to be fair, all three of the financiers were men. (Jo, female employer)

Moreover, even when women hold senior positions, McGuire's (2002) research reveals that women receive less instrumental help from their network members, whereas BAME men were only discriminated against due to structural disadvantage, that is, when they obtained positions with more status, they received the same amount of help from their networks as white men do. The rest of this article will seek to establish how accepted discourses limit opportunities for female screenwriters, even in an apparently egalitarian creative industry (Gill, 2002) such as UK film production and finance, where overt sexism is rarely deemed acceptable behaviour.

The study

The data I introduce here are part of a larger research project consisting of 40 semi-structured interviews with screenwriters and their employers that is attempting to identify reasons for the continued scarcity of female screenwriters in the UK film industry. Women screenwriters made up just 16.1 per cent of all the writers of UK independent films released in 2010–2012 (Steele, 2013) and only 10 per cent of the writers of the 250 top grossing films in 2013 (Lauzen, 2014). The employers range from individual producers working as sole traders, to the senior personnel of large production companies, distribution companies, public financiers and broadcasters. The screenwriters had, at the time of our interviews, experience ranging from no produced features to more than twelve feature film credits. My sample included 34 white and six non-white participants, and was weighted to include a higher percentage of females (23 out of 40) than is found in the UK film industry generally. All of the employers were based in London, reflecting the predominance of the film industry in the south-east. The screenwriters, however, were scattered across the UK and even further afield, demonstrating perhaps some of the potential flexibility of the profession. All the participants' identities are protected by the use of pseudonyms. In my analysis of these interviews, I examine the subjective methods of assessment to which screenwriters are exposed and draw on discourse analysis (Potter and Wetherell, 1987; Taylor and Littleton, 2006; Wetherell, 1998) to unpack how industry-wide discourses

The Sociological Review, 63:S1, pp. 84–96 (2015), DOI: 10.1111/1467-954X.12242
© 2015 The Author. Editorial organisation © 2015 The Editorial Board of the Sociological Review

work to uphold gender inequalities. I will demonstrate that these discourses have become legitimized as 'best practice' by both screenwriters and their potential employers and highlight the function of the discourses, which go beyond talk to limit opportunities in the UK film labour market.

A dominant discourse can be identified in the talk of my participants, in which a contacts culture is downplayed in favour of meritocratic and market-led decision-making processes. However, this is contradicted by another prevalent discourse that reveals the importance of personal connections. I will give examples of recurring patterns in the talk of my participants that contest the key film industry discourse of democratic meritocracy, and demonstrate how, in a context of high risk and uncertainty, employers use risk reduction strategies in their recruitment processes such as a reliance on personal contacts or the opinions of trusted or powerful individuals. I will further argue that the same high-risk environment has been shown to encourage reliance on homophily as shorthand for trust, and examine how these two strategies combine to limit individual opportunity and uphold gender inequality.

Understanding the gendered outcomes of informal recruitment practices

A dominant discourse shared by employers and screenwriters and used to account for the unpredictability of career opportunities is the idea of the film industry as a meritocracy and the notion that 'talent will out'. This phrase refers to the commonly held belief that if you have any talent or ability you will inevitably be recognized by the film industry and a successful career will follow:

> ...there's a side of me that also feels very irritated by people who say there should be more women, there should be 50/50, because for me it has to be ultimately based on merit. (Eloise, female employer)

This was also often related to the view that the selection of projects and screenwriters is based on 'what the market wants', that is, what sells:

> I don't think there will ever be a really self-conscious 'oh we really, really need to be favouring...' you know, I don't think we'll get to a point, because there's a commercial imperative, so I don't think there will ever be a place of active, positive discrimination. (Nick, male employer)

However, some of the screenwriters did express opinions that suggested they did not believe good work was always recognized:

> ...there is no point in railing against the people that make these decisions because a lot of people don't, wouldn't, know a good screenplay from a bar of soap to be totally honest. (Catherine, female screenwriter)

As can be seen in the quotes above from Nick and Eloise, this discourse of meritocracy is also used to justify not taking action to redress inequalities.

Another repeated discourse attributed to apparently neutral market forces was the desire for 'experienced' writers, with a demonstrable track record. This preference supports Faulkner and Anderson's (1987) argument that cumulative disadvantage may be the reason for continued gender inequality in the film industry. With women not being employed in key roles in sufficient numbers they have less experience and credits when the next opportunity comes along. However, this does not explain why employers talked about the contradictory and apparently endless search for 'new talent', or 'the next big thing' ('that sort of slight wrestling match between those bigger names who I'd ideally like to get to but they're always invariably unavailable for a really long time, and discoveries that you might find' – Vanessa, female employer). Somehow this search for the new keeps turning up writers who fit the existing mould of white, middle- or upper-class men. To understand this, I will now explore how two key discourses of risk reduction and trust in the talk of employers of screenwriters can uphold gender inequality.

Risk reduction

Here I will explore in more detail how certain discourses that occur in accounts from screenwriters and their employers function to present exclusionary practices as benign, and as a 'logical' and 'rational' response to the high risk of making an expensive creative product. In this way, discrimination and inequality are reinforced by mechanisms that are accepted as good business practice, leaving little room for any requirement to improve the industry's equal opportunity record. Creative work takes place in a context of high risk where the financial cost of the product must be paid out while profit is still uncertain (McKinlay and Smith, 2009). Each product is a unique, speculative endeavour in which the usual supply/demand dynamic is reversed and there is huge uncertainty about whether anyone will actually buy the product (see Hesmondhalgh, 2007, for a full discussion on how cultural industry companies respond to the perceived difficulties of making a profit). My interviewees repeatedly described a common solution that film producers can utilize, in order to attempt to attract investors to the risky prospect of a new film: employing key creative personnel who are known in the industry and have a track record. However, the difficulty in assessing an individual's contribution to the success of past projects (Bielby, 2009) creates two distinct recruitment practices that were frequently referenced by my research participants. The first of these methods is to identify screenwriters who are trusted by recognized authorities, most commonly either individuals with recourse to significant film finance, or producers with prominent success:

> ...I heard this person that everybody respects loves this new writer, so it can only mean that they're great. (Eloise, female employer)

> We've got good relationships with Working Title,[1] so we talk to them, ask their advice, who they think is good. (Colin, male employer)

The other practice repeatedly referred to by the research participants is a reliance on people they already know, which resonates with Rogers's (2007) findings that 50 per cent of writers of British films had a previous working relationship and 42 per cent had a personal relationship with the producer, director or production company responsible for their hiring. This most commonly occurs when screenwriters who have been identified by the previous method are unavailable or unattainable, but is also significantly observable in the discussions of those employers who fall into the previous category of recognized authorities, for example:

> But you know a lot of our work comes from relationships that exist. (Yvonne, female employer)

> In the first instance … there will be a handful and it really only is a handful of you know, really tried and tested writers that we've generally got pre-existing relationships with, have worked with before and have probably produced films with, you know, people that we know, people that we trust. They will make their way onto the list in pole position and then we will comb through the lists and try and find someone who might have written in that genre before, might have some experience, might be of an age where it would make sense and then we'll look at TV writers, sort of new and interesting voices and so we'll put some sort of new or leftfield ideas on – and then we'll generally just go to [Male Screenwriter] [laughs] or [Male Screenwriter]. (Nick, male employer)

Identifying these two related discourses reveals that screenwriters need to be in a personal or professional relationship with one of the key financiers or successful production companies to stand the best chance of being hired in the film industry. The employers who spoke to me showed little if any embarrassment about the reliance of the industry on 'who you know', which suggests the practice is both accepted and legitimized, and indicates that – in this world – contacts are extremely important:

> It's a small, incestuous world. (Vanessa, female employer)

> It's a guy I've know for a long time. (Eloise, female employer)

> I think we've been a little bit reliant on people finding us or being recommended and us going to a fairly small pool of usual suspects. (Jo, female employer)

It's even proposed as a productive way to manage a potentially vast pool of interested candidates by small companies with limited resources. This is not a new concept, nor one particular to the film industry:

> The problem facing the employer is not to get in touch with the largest number of potential applicants; rather it is to find a few applicants promising enough to be worth the investment of thorough investigation. (Rees, 1966)

Attributing responsibility to risk-averse financiers who want a writer with a track record, and the subjective nature of creativity and creative relationships, it is easy for employers to believe they are 'gender blind'. However, 'blind' auditions opened up symphony orchestras to female musicians (Goldin and Rouse, 1997), so evaluation of creativity is not always as objective as it may appear to be. How can screenwriters form these key relationships with one of a small number of influential people? More specifically for the purposes of this article, how does this reliance on the friendship and favour of selected individuals become gendered?

Trust and homophily

When asked what they looked for in a potential screenwriter, the employers who I interviewed almost universally answered: trust. This was something the experienced screenwriters also appeared to be aware of:

> I think they need security because it's a terrifying thing to hire somebody really young on a wing and a prayer. (Jo, female screenwriter)

The employers do not demonstrate a desire to embrace the vulnerability and risk that is associated with trust as a distinct concept (Mayer *et al.*, 1995) as indeed it is precisely these difficulties that they hope to overcome by finding a screenwriter whom they feel they can trust. The concept of trust in their discourses is closer to the notions with which it is commonly conflated: co-operation, confidence and predictability (Mayer *et al.*, 1995). Confidence and predictability fostered through familiarity were apparent in the participants' understanding of trust:

> You've got to be able to trust that person. (Natasha, female screenwriter)

> ... we kind of knew each other very well and we'd spent a lot of time together developing the project so she trusted me. (Jo, female employer)

However, women and people of working class or BAME background are not given equal access to employment in the UK film and television industries precisely because they are *not* trusted by the industry establishment who are still most frequently white, middle- and upper-class men (Grugulis and Stoyanova, 2012). Kanter's groundbreaking study of gender at work, *Men and Women of the Corporation*, argues that in 'conditions of uncertainty' people fall back on social similarity as a basis for trust (1977: 49). Every film is a unique product and must be marketed to potential audiences as such. Veteran screenwriter William Goldman (1983) famously said of the film industry 'Nobody knows anything', referring to the impossibility of predicting the success of creative work. There is a great deal of uncertainty about which films will find an audience sufficient to make a profit, and most films never do. At the point of screenplay commission, this uncertainty is at its greatest. The conditions prevail for those involved to want to work with others who are most like them, who are more likely to share cultural references and to pull together around decisions.

> Making a film is really hard, and so if you set out on the journey with somebody who you just don't quite get on with ... (Vanessa, female employer)

A reliance on homophily provides the employers with the desired conditions to trust those that they are employing, but a lack of awareness of its contribution to their recruitment processes masks the way such subjectivity upholds the inequality of gender, race and class in key creative positions.

As defined by Ibarra (1993), homophily is the extent to which two individuals in a network are similar and can be understood as the tendency for people to want to associate with those they feel they are most like. 'Interpersonal similarity increases ease of communication, improves predictability of behaviour, and fosters relationships of trust and reciprocity' (Ibarra, 1993: 61). People's networks have a strong tendency to contain others who are similar along multiple dimensions including gender, age, ethnicity and sexuality (Blau, 1994). This supports the evidence that networking is an activity that excludes (Christopherson, 2009; Grugulis and Stoyanova, 2012). Burt argues that 'network closure facilitates sanctions that make it less risky for people in the network to trust one another' (Burt, 2002: 154). Famously, the film industry relies on such small networks and such high barriers to entry that it is often necessary to have a relative to kick-start your career. Nepotism is a widely tolerated practice in the film industry (Blair, 2009; Blair *et al.*, 2001; Blair *et al.*, 2003; Francke, 1994; Grugulis and Stoyanova, 2012; Randle, 2010; Skillset, 2009), clearly recognizable through shared surnames and potentially creating a very small talent pool:

> ...my dad works in film, and my uncle and my godfather. (Kate, female employer)

One male employer listed his grandfather, father, uncles, cousin and 'other relatives' as all working in the industry.

Women need additional advocacy to foster trust in potential employers (Burt, 2002). Ibarra (1992) demonstrates that women are less likely to be friends with those who can help their careers. Networking for work is a relatively unconscious act where job information is often passed on through social process rather than purposefully designed occasions (Blair, 2009; Granovetter, 1995). Many of the research participants talked about the mutual backgrounds, long-term relationships and shared social circles of those they work with:

> ...sometimes you meet a writer socially between drafts. (Frank, male employer)

> [Male Producer] and [Male Screenwriter] are very good friends. (Vanessa, female employer)

> [Good screenwriters are] I guess the kind of people you want to sit in a pub with for six hours. (Kate, female employer)

My sample, which was artificially weighted to create a gender balance not reflected in the reality of the film industry, contained discussions of female homophily as well as male, eg:

> ...we don't have a similar background or anything but the fact that we both have a female sensibility... (Jo, female employer)

The Sociological Review, 63:S1, pp. 84–96 (2015), DOI: 10.1111/1467-954X.12242
© 2015 The Author. Editorial organisation © 2015 The Editorial Board of the Sociological Review

But with men continuing to far outnumber women as producers, executive producers and directors of films (Lauzen, 2014), the reality is likely to be much more biased. Indeed the prevalence of women employing women in my sample suggests that those who are working are finding a large percentage of opportunities through other women and perhaps are not so trusted by men:

> I've only worked with one male director. (Natasha, female screenwriter)

> All three of my feature films were directed by women. All three produced by women. (Catherine, female screenwriter)

Conclusion

My research supports Bielby's claim that, in the film industry, 'high levels of risk and uncertainty' turn stereotyping and discrimination 'into everyday business practices' (2009: 239). It is an attempt to challenge the symbolic violence (Bourdieu and Wacquant, 1992) of discourses of 'meritocracy' so prevalent and embedded in the creative industries that they are accepted and seen as legitimate even by those who benefit least from them. By studying feature films screenwriters it is possible to identify mechanisms that work to uphold gender and other inequalities through informal recruitment practices, even when those processes are not conscious or deliberate by those taking part. The results potentially have wider application in other creative professions, and indeed in other labour markets, where more formal recruitment systems have been repeatedly shown to operate as façades for parallel and powerful informal recruitment practices that are the key to the best and most lucrative jobs (Granovetter, 1995). In this article I have contributed to the research on gendered outcomes of informal recruitment. I have demonstrated that where conditions of high risk and uncertainty prevail, individuals use risk reduction strategies in their recruitment processes such as a reliance on the opinions of trusted or powerful individuals. Those individuals in turn reduce their own perceived risk by working with screenwriters who are known to them either professionally or personally. When an individual's credits or experience cannot be relied upon, the employers turn to homophily to facilitate trust. While white, middle- to upper-class men still dominate decision-making positions in the film industry, this in turn upholds the status quo and these powerful men are able to draw on the established discourses discussed here to present exclusionary practices as logical, understandable and indeed, good business practice. One of the questions raised by my findings is why we still see others of a different gender, ethnicity, class, age, sexuality or indeed physical ability as so different that we find it difficult to trust them?

Note

1 Working Title is arguably the UK's most successful production company. See their credits here: http://www.imdb.com/company/co0057311/

References

Bielby, D. D., (2009), 'Gender inequality in culture industries: women and men writers in film and television', *Sociologie Du Travail*, 51: 237–252.

Bielby, W. T. and Baron, J. N., (1984), 'A woman's place is with other women: sex segregation within organizations', in B. Reskin (ed.), *Sex Segregation in the Workplace: Trends, Explanations, Remedies*, 27–55, Washington DC: National Academy Press.

Bielby, W. T. and Bielby, D. D., (1999), 'Organizational mediation of project-based labor markets: talent agencies and the careers of screenwriters', *American Sociological Review*, 64 (1): 64–85.

Blair, H., (2000a), 'Active networking: the role of networks and hierarchy in the operation of the labour market in the British film industry', *Management Research News*, 23: 20–21.

Blair, H., (2000b), '"You're only as good as your last job": the relationship between labour market and labour process in the British film industry', *Work and Employment*, 15 (1): 149–169.

Blair, H., (2003), 'Winning and losing in flexible labour markets: the formation and operation of networks of interdependence in the UK film industry', *Sociology*, 37 (4): 677–694.

Blair, H., (2009), 'Active networking: action, social structure and the process of networking', in A. S. C. McKinlay (ed.), *Creative Labour: Working in the Creative Industries*, London: Palgrave Macmillan.

Blair, H., Culkin, N. and Randle, K., (2001), 'From Hollywood to Borehamwood: exploring nepotism and networking in US and UK freelance film careers', Business School Working Papers, UHBS 2001–6, Film Industry Research Group Paper, 7, University of Hertfordshire.

Blair, H., Culkin, N. and Randle, K., (2003), 'From London to Los Angeles: a comparison of local labour market processes in the US and UK film industries', *International Journal of Human Resource Management*, 14 (4): 619–633.

Blau, P. M., (1994), *Structural Contexts of Opportunities*, Chicago: University of Chicago Press.

Bourdieu, P., (1984), *Distinction: A Social Critique of the Judgement of Taste*, Cambridge, MA: Harvard University Press.

Bourdieu, P. and Wacquant, L. J. D., (1992), *An Invitation to Reflexive Sociology*, Chicago: University of Chicago Press.

Burt, R. S., (2002), 'The social capital of structural holes', in M. Guillen, R. Collins and P. England (eds), *The New Economic Sociology: Developments in an Emerging Field*, New York: Russell Sage Foundation.

Campbell, K. E., (1988), 'Gender differences in job-related networks', *Work and Occupations*, 15 (2): 179–200.

Christopherson, S., (2008), 'Beyond the self-expressive creative worker an industry perspective on entertainment media', *Theory, Culture & Society*, 25 (7–8): 73–95.

Christopherson, S., (2009), 'Working in the creative economy: risk, adaptation, and the persistence of exclusionary networks', in A. McKinlay and C. Smith (eds), *Creative Labour: Working in the Creative Industries*, London: Palgrave Macmillan.

Christopherson, S. and Storper, M., (1988), 'Effects of flexible specialization on industrial politics and the labor market: the motion picture industry', *Industrial and Labour Relations Review*, 42 (3): 331–347.

Cromie, S. and Birley, S., (1992), 'Networking by female business owners in Northern Ireland', *Journal of Business Venturing*, 7 (3): 237–251.

Faulkner, R. R. and Anderson, A. B., (1987), 'Short-term projects and emergent careers: evidence from Hollywood', *American Journal of Sociology*, 92 (4): 879–909.

Fenstermaker, S., West, C. and Zimmerman, D. H., (2002), 'Gender inequality: new conceptual terrain', in S. Fenstermaker and C. West (eds), *Doing Gender, Doing Difference: Inequality, Power, and Institutional Change*, New York: Routledge.

Florida, R., (2004), *The Rise of the Creative Class and How it's Transforming Work, Leisure, Community and Everyday Life*, New York: Basic Books.

Francke, L., (1994), *Script Girls: Women Screenwriters in Hollywood*, London: British Film Institute.

Franks, S., (1999), *Having None of It: Women, Men and the Future of Work*, London: Granta.

The Sociological Review, 63:S1, pp. 84–96 (2015), DOI: 10.1111/1467-954X.12242

Gill, R., (2000), 'Justifying injustice: broadcasters' accounts of inequality in radio', in E. Burman and I. Parker (eds), *Discourse Analytic Research: Readings and Repertoires of Texts in Action*, 75–93, London: Routledge.

Gill, R., (2002), 'Cool, creative and egalitarian? Exploring gender in project-based new media work in Europe', *Information, Communication & Society*, 5 (1): 70–89.

Gill, R., (2014) 'Unspeakable inequalities: postfeminism, entrepreneurial subjectivity, and the repudiation of sexism among cultural workers', *Social Politics* doi: 10.1093/sp/jxu016. First published online: 24 July 2014.

Gill, R. and Pratt, A., (2008), 'In the social factory? Immaterial labour, precariousness and cultural work', *Theory, Culture & Society*, 25 (7–8): 1–30.

Goldin, C., and Rouse, C., (1997), 'Orchestrating inequality: the impact of "blind" auditions on female musicians', NBER Working Paper No. 5903, available at: http://www.nber.org/papers/w5903.

Goldman, W., (1983), *Adventures in the Screen Trade: A Personal View of Hollywood*, Great Britain: Macdonald & Co.

Granovetter, M. S., (1995), *Getting a Job: A Study of Contacts and Careers*, Chicago: University of Chicago Press.

Grugulis, I. and Stoyanova, D. (2012), 'Social capital and networks in film and TV: jobs for the boys?' *The British Sociological Association Annual Conference 2012: Sociology in an Age of Austerity*.

Hesmondhalgh, D., (2007), *The Cultural Industries*, 2nd edn, London: Sage.

Hochschild, A. R., (1983), 'The second shift: working parents and the revolution at home', in A. Skolnick and J. Skolnick (eds), *Family in Transition*, Boston, MA: Allyn and Bacon.

Ibarra, H., (1992), 'Homophily and differential returns: sex differences in network structure and access in an advertising firm', *Administrative Science Quarterly*, 37 (3): 422–447.

Ibarra, H., (1993), 'Personal networks of women and minorities in management: a conceptual framework', *Academy of Management Review*, 18 (1): 56–87.

Kanter, R. M., (1977), *Men and Women of the Corporation*, New York: Basic Books.

Lauzen, M., (2014), 'The celluloid ceiling: behind-the-scenes employment of women on the top 250 films of 2013', available at: http://Womenintvfilm.Sdsu.Edu/Files/2013_Celluloid_Ceiling_Report.Pdf.

Mayer, R. C., Davis, J. H. and Schoorman, F. D., (1995), 'An integrative model of organizational trust', *Academy of Management Review*, 20 (3): 709–734.

McGuire, G. M., (2000), 'Gender, race, ethnicity, and networks', *Work and Occupations*, 27 (4): 500–523.

McGuire, G. M., (2002), 'Gender, race and the shadow structure: a study of informal networks and inequality in a work organization', *Gender & Society*, 16 (3): 303–322.

McKinlay, A. and Smith, C., (2009), *Creative Labour: Working in the Creative Industries*, London: Palgrave Macmillan.

Potter, J. and Wetherell, M., (1987), *Discourse and Social Psychology: Beyond Attitudes and Behaviour*, London: Sage Publications.

Randle, K., (2010), 'The organization of film and television production', in M. Deuze (ed.), *Managing Media Work*, 145–154, London: Sage Publications.

Randle, K. and Culkin, N., (2009), 'Getting in and getting on in Hollywood: freelance careers in an uncertain industry', in A. McKinlay and C. Smith (eds), *Creative Labour*, 93–115, London: Palgrave Macmillan.

Rees, A., (1966), 'Information networks in labor markets', *The American Economic Review*, 56 (1–2): 559–566.

Renzulli, L. A., Aldrich, H. and Moody, J., (2000), 'Family matters: gender, networks, and entrepreneurial outcomes', *Social Forces*, 79 (2): 523–546.

Rogers, S., (2007), 'Writing British films – who writes British films and how they are recruited', *Report for UK Film Council*, University of London: Royal Holloway College.

Skillset, (2009), 'Why her? Report: Factors that have influenced successful women in film and TV', available at: http://www.Creativeskillset.Org/Film/Industry/Article_7432_1.Asp.

Skillset, (2010), 'Women in the creative media industries', available at: http://www.Creativeskillset.Org/Uploads/Pdf/Asset_15343.Pdf?3.

Steele, D., (2013), 'Succes de plume? Female screenwriters and directors of UK films, 2010–2012', available at: http://www.Bfi.Org.Uk/Sites/Bfi.Org.Uk/Files/Downloads/Bfi-Report-On-Female-Writers-And-Directors-Of-Uk-Films-2013--11.Pdf.

Storper, M. and Christopherson, S., (1987), 'Flexible specialization and regional industrial agglomerations: the case of the US motion picture industry', *Annals of the Association of American Geographers*, 77 (1): 104–117.

Taylor, S. and Littleton, K., (2006), 'Biographies in talk: a narrative-discursive research approach', *Qualitative Sociology Review*, 2 (1): 22–38.

Wetherell, M., (1998), 'Positioning and interpretative repertoires: conversation analysis and post-structuralism in dialogue', *Discourse & Society*, 9 (3): 387–412.

Wreyford, N., (2013), 'The real cost of childcare: motherhood and flexible creative labour in the UK film industry', *Studies in the Maternal*, 5 (2), available at: http://www.mamsie.bbk.ac.uk/documents/Wreyford_SiM_5(2)2013.pdf

The Sociological Review, 63:S1, pp. 84–96 (2015), DOI: 10.1111/1467-954X.12242
© 2015 The Author. Editorial organisation © 2015 The Editorial Board of the Sociological Review

Part 4: Image-making and representation

Blowing your own trumpet: exploring the gendered dynamics of self-promotion in the classical music profession

Christina Scharff

Abstract: This chapter explores the gendered dynamics of self-promotion by drawing on 64 in-depth interviews with female, classically trained musicians in London and Berlin. As in other sectors in the cultural industries, the ability to self-promote is considered key to finding employment. However, many research participants were reluctant to engage in self-promotion. First, it was associated with pushy behaviour that conflicts with normative expectations that women are modest. Second, self-promotion was regarded as a commercial activity and positioned as unartistic. Taking into account that women have been constructed as the artist's Other, engagement in self-promotion may threaten their already tenuous status as artists. Lastly, the notion of selling yourself may evoke the spectre of prostitution due to the sexualization of female musicians and the fact that it is mainly women who sell their bodies. As I will show, these gendered dynamics do not mean that female musicians are unable to pursue self-promotion, but that they engage in a range of discursive strategies to negotiate and secure their identities as female artists.

Keywords: classical musicians, self-promotion, entrepreneur, discursive strategy

Introduction

In September 2013, Marin Alsop became the first woman to conduct the prestigious Last Night of the Proms in London. Several days before the event, the conductor Vasily Petrenko provoked outrage by stating that orchestras 'react better when they have a man in front of them' and that 'a cute girl on a podium means that musicians think about other things' (Higgins, 2013). While he subsequently revised his remarks, his comments bespoke the prevalence of sexism and heteronormative assumptions in Western classical music. Indeed, out of the 58 conductors at the Proms in 2013, only five were women and only two – Marin Aslop and Xian Zhang – conducted on the main stage at early evening Proms (Maddocks, 2013).

The Sociological Review, 63:S1, pp. 97–112 (2015), DOI: 10.1111/1467-954X.12243
© 2015 The Author. Editorial organisation © 2015 The Editorial Board of the Sociological Review. Published by John Wiley & Sons Ltd, 9600 Garsington Road, Oxford OX4 2DQ, UK and 350 Main Street, Malden, MA 02148, USA

Reflecting wider trends in the cultural industries (Skillset, 2010; this volume), sexism and intersecting racial and classed inequalities persist in the classical music sector. Women and ethnic minority groups continue to be under-represented in prestigious orchestras (Goldin and Rouse, 2000; Yoshihara, 2007). While East Asians constitute a considerable presence in the world of classical music, other non-European groups remain largely invisible (HEFCE, 2002; Yoshihara, 2007) and the costly investments required to train as a musician mean that there are classed barriers to entering the profession (Yoshihara, 2007). These contemporary inequalities resonate with older ones. As historical research has demonstrated (Green, 1997; Johnson-Hill, 2014; Kok, 2014), female musicians, working-class and minority-ethnic players were marginalized from the classical music profession in various ways in the past. According to Green's (1997: 65) research on the history of women's musical practices, affirmations of femininity risked 'reducing the seriousness with which women's instrumental music-making is taken', which is an issue that I will explore in more detail below. Similarly, Johnson-Hill (2014) has demonstrated that Victorian music education set in place the very ideologies of social status, class and race associated with classical music-making that still pervade musical practice in Britain and the Commonwealth to this day. The grade exam boards and music conservatoires which were established in the late 19th century continue to shape the musical lives of young musicians today, thereby reinforcing existing inequalities, as Bull's (2015) research on contemporary youth music education demonstrates.

Also in parallel with the broader field of creative labour, work in the classical music sector is casualized. As several studies have shown (Bennett, 2008; Cottrell, 2004; Gembris and Langner, 2005; Yoshihara, 2007), classical musicians tend to be wholly or partly self-employed and frequently have multiple jobs ranging from teaching to performing. Low pay and the scarcity of full-time and permanent employment make it a necessity for them to pursue different lines of work (Bennett, 2007). As a report by the Musicians' Union (2012) has demonstrated, many musicians have portfolio careers, which are marked by low incomes (less than £20,000 a year for 56 per cent of those surveyed), uncertainty, and lack of workplace benefits such as pensions. Only 10 per cent of surveyed musicians were full-time salaried employees, half reported not having regular employment whatsoever, and 60 per cent stated that they had worked for free in the past 12 months.

In addition to the casualized nature of employment and the under-representation of musicians from diverse backgrounds, there are further parallels between work in the classical music sector and other cultural industries. Both are marked by newer forms of inequalities which relate to the informal nature of creative labour and a prevailing ethos of entrepreneurialism (Gill, 2002, 2014). Entrepreneurialism, in this context, is understood in Foucauldian terms and refers to a process where the 'schema of *enterprise* is presented as a model not only for the conduct of economic activity, but for the totality of human action' (Gordon, 1987: 314). Cultural work is increasingly (though not exclusively) governed by

The Sociological Review, 63:S1, pp. 97–112 (2015), DOI: 10.1111/1467-954X.12243

the values of entrepreneurialism (Banks, 2007) and the field of classical music is not exempt from this trend (Bennett, 2007). Giving career advice in her book *Beyond Talent: Creating a Successful Career in Music*, Beeching encourages musicians to '[t]hink like an entrepreneur' (2010: 11) and states that '[t]hrough your attitude and actions, you can determine your luck and success' (2010: 2). This shift towards entrepreneurialism means that the worker:

> must be enterprising about making herself enterprising: becoming in effect a micro-cosmic business; developing a strategy, marketing herself, developing 'products', establishing herself as a brand, understanding the market (for herself) and so on. (Storey *et al.*, 2005: 1036)

If workers are businesses that have to be marketed, they have to promote themselves. 'Promoting the self, then, refers to processes in which different forms of marketing and branding are combined with 'advancing the self' in one way or another' (Mäkinen, 2012: 16). Or, to use Rudman's definition (1998: 629), self-promotion includes 'pointing with pride to one's accomplishments, speaking directly about one's strengths and talents, and making internal rather than external attributions for achievements'. Self-promotion constitutes a central aspect of the entrepreneurial work ethos, yet the gendered politics of self-promotion have not been examined in great detail (but see Mäkinen, 2012, on self-promotion in the context of coaching). By exploring some of these gendered dynamics, I aim to deepen our understanding of newer forms of inequality. More specifically, I follow Gill's (2014) call for the need to explore the exclusions that are linked to the entrepreneurial work ethos prevalent in the cultural industries.

Based on in-depth interviews with female, classically trained musicians, this chapter explores the gendered dynamics of self-promotion in the context of the classical music profession. After a short discussion of the methodological orientation of my study, the first section will demonstrate that research participants readily took on board entrepreneurial discourses by describing their work and themselves as products that had to be sold. When asked how they felt about self-promotion, most stated that they disliked it. As the subsequent sections will show, self-promotion presents gendered difficulties that female musicians have to navigate. These dilemmas relate to normative expectations that women are modest; the construction of self-promotion as unartistic and the way this intersects with women's positioning as the artist's Other; and the association of women who sell themselves with prostitution.

In presenting this analysis, the chapter will open up further areas of investigation that relate to the need for intersectional analyses to trace and understand the exclusionary dynamics of self-promotion; the dilemmas around performing particular gendered identities in this context; and the economization of subjectivity. I will thus conclude by arguing for the importance of critical research on self-promotion, particularly in the wider context of an increasing entrepreneurial ethos in classical music and the cultural industries in general.

The Sociological Review, 63:S1, pp. 97–112 (2015), DOI: 10.1111/1467-954X.12243

The study

The data presented here is part of a larger research project on the classical music profession with a particular focus on the subjective experiences of precarious and entrepreneurial labour, inequalities in the workforce, and the ways in which work is affected by its urban context. In order to obtain individuals' subjective accounts, I conducted 64 semi-structured in-depth interviews.[1] The interviews took place in Berlin and London (32 in each city) in an attempt to explore the participants' 'structure of feeling' in two creative cities. All research participants were female and at an early stage in their career. Most were in their late twenties/early thirties and thus fell in the category of 'young women'. As feminist research has demonstrated, young women have been positioned as ideal entrepreneurial subjects in policy, media and public discourse in recent years (McRobbie, 2009). As cultural workers and young women, they are thus twice positioned as entrepreneurial subjects. By focusing on individuals who may be the quintessence of entrepreneurialism, the project makes a timely contribution to research on newer forms of inequalities in creative labour, and in particular those that pertain to the entrepreneurial work ethos.

I spoke to musicians who played a range of instruments (string, woodwind, brass, piano, organ, percussion), as well as singers, conductors, opera directors and composers. While based in London or Berlin, the research participants came from a range of countries and, reflecting the under-representation of working-class as well as black and minority ethnic players, most identified as white and middle class.[2] In order to identify recurring discursive patterns in the talk of the participants, and to analyse the rhetorical function that they fulfil, I drew on discourse analysis (Potter and Wetherell, 1987; Taylor and Littleton, 2012). As I hope to demonstrate, this form of analysis offers useful analytical tools to trace how self-promotion and gendered dynamics are negotiated in talk about creative labour.

Being a product

Resonating with the findings of wider research on cultural workers (Storey *et al.*, 2005), many research participants described their work as a product or commodity:

> I look at myself as a business and a product [. . .] It's hard because it's such an emotional personal thing to be a singer, but it is business. Everything is a business. It may be, you know, all of the arts, the opera houses, are charity-run, but ... You know, I'm a commodity. (Alice)

> What people want from you is for you to deliver a readily sellable product, you see how bad I actually call myself: a product. My God. But that's what it is. People want you to be a ready product that sells. (Isabella)

The Sociological Review, 63:S1, pp. 97–112 (2015), DOI: 10.1111/1467-954X.12243

> I think it would not hurt to have some sort of information about how to run a business. How to run a freelance business, with yourself as the product, which is what we are. (Lauren)

In the context of freelance work in particular, participants emphasized that 'you have to be really proactive in selling yourself' (Rose) 'because no one would know you existed' (Linda). Through this talk, research participants construct their work and selves as products that have to be sold.

Some participants, such as Isabella, critically reflected on this approach to work by stating 'You see how bad I actually call myself' and others reacted to it with humour:

> I mean you are running your own business, in your name […]. And you have to very much think of it as a business, and if your business isn't doing very well, then you need to do something about it. For whatever reason – sack some staff or something [both laugh]. (Kelly)

Although Kelly and Isabella made humorous and self-reflexive statements, the participants' relationship to their work and self is indicative of an economization of subjectivity. It is not only one's work that is a product to be sold to others (Edwards and Wajcman, 2005), but also one's self (McNay, 2009). Indeed, various aspects of the self were commodified, including racial differences. Discussing her experiences as a black singer, Susan stated:

> Like I think 'Should I straighten my hair, should I, you know, blend in?' But then the idea isn't to blend in, it's to stand out, because there's so many singers that I've got to have something – I suppose you'd call it a USP, wouldn't you – a unique selling point [laughs].

In a similar way to Isabella and Kelly, Susan makes this claim with more than a hint of irony as expressed by her laughter. Nevertheless, racial difference is presented as a potential selling point in a competitive market environment, which reflects wider trends where difference is commodified and diversity primarily regarded as an economic value (Proctor-Thomson, 2013).

While the musicians readily and frequently used entrepreneurial rhetoric, many emphasized that they disliked selling themselves. Some of these statements were unprompted, as in Amanda's case:

> And then there is also things like you know, these days working life of a musician it's also, it's meant to be you sell yourself and you promote yourself and you do this on Facebook, and I just hate all that. I hate it with a really, really passion. I just – I always say why can't I just play? So I really, really dislike that part of it.

When asked how they felt about self-promotion, several research participants used similar, affect-laden language:

> *Author*: And how do you feel about going out there and asking people to support a particular project, this kind of marketing yourself – I guess it is a bit like that. How do you like that, how do you feel about doing that?

> *Holly*: I really don't like it. I really really really don't like it.

Echoing Holly, Amy described self-promotion as 'repulsive' and Susan as 'cringe worthy'. Emilia admitted that she does not 'find it easy at all' and three other participants felt 'uncomfortable' with promoting their work. Claiming that she sometimes spends 80 per cent of her time on promotional activities, Christine stated 'I would definitely rather not do it if I didn't have to'.

There were some exceptions with a few participants expressing more positive attitudes towards self-promotion. Talking about updating her website, a composer stated:

> Generally, if I am just adding concerts and things, or adding some sound clips to the website, it's quite like – like I said, I think it is nice to put yourself out there and kind of be proud of what you do. (Carolyn)

And as other discourse analysts have shown (Potter and Wetherell, 1987), research participants sometimes change their attitudes during an interview when they discuss the same issue in a different discursive context. Christine also worked as a composer and I cited her statement above that she 'would definitely rather not' promote her work. She subsequently described her feelings about promoting a new composition in different ways:

> You know, you have to kind of be – show your peacock feathers, you know, sort of fan out your tail a bit. And I think instead of trying to think 'I have got to constantly prove myself' I try to think of it in more of a fun way than that. And often people – you know, it can be fun, actually, because if people reply and they say 'I really love that bit of music', that's great, you know, that gives you a bit of a boost really.

By thinking of self-promotion 'in more of a fun way', Christine discusses the practice in positive terms and subsequently adopts a more affirmative attitude. Whilst attitudes towards self-promotion were overwhelmingly negative, these statements demonstrate that they were not predetermined and could shift over time.

Performing modesty and femininity

Interestingly, several research participants emphasized that they found it easy to promote *other* people's work. Alice stated: 'If it was someone else, no problem. I could sell sand to the Egyptians [...] But it's really hard to sell yourself'. Alice's (rather offensive statement) demonstrates that she did not feel she lacked the necessary skills, but that she struggled to promote her *own* achievements. Talking about her experiences of working part-time for a cultural organization, Liz said that she was very good at marketing 'but that wasn't really about myself, and that's where it becomes difficult'. This finding resonates with Moss-Racusin and Rudman's (2010) study on attitudes towards self-promotion. They found that female participants struggled to promote their own work in comparison to male participants, but that these gender differences disappeared when women acted on behalf of a peer. As Moss-Racusin and Rudman (2010: 187) point out,

The Sociological Review, 63:S1, pp. 97–112 (2015), DOI: 10.1111/1467-954X.12243

'self-promotion is problematic for women because it violates female prescriptions to be helpful, supportive and other-oriented'. In the context of creative work, Taylor (2011: 367) similarly showed that the selfishness demanded by creative working conflicts 'with long-established gendered positionings of women as other-oriented, attending to the needs of others and heeding their preferences'.

In support of these findings, several research participants pointed out that self-promotion might come more easily to men. Alice continued her statement on her difficulties with self-promotion:

> Sometimes I think it's harder for women. Girls aren't – we aren't as good at that sort of thing, men are much better at being cut-throat and straight to the point, whereas [...] I'll zigzag until I get to where I want to go.

Similarly, Christine said that self-promotion was:

> Something that you have to do, you have to do it, so I think certainly being a confident person really does help, and you know, confidence in itself is important as well, definitely. Which I think sometimes can come to men easier than it comes to women.

In these statements, Alice and Christine orient to their positionings as women to discuss their difficulties with self-promotion and to point out that confidence is key. But, as Eve's statement demonstrates, acting confidently might not provide an easy solution for women:

> If you are confident in any way people will think that's a bit aggressive or whatever, you shouldn't act like this, and – again, I don't know whether that's a personal thing or whether people would say that because they wouldn't expect a woman to act like that.

Like Alice and Christine, Eve orients to her positioning as a woman but also points to gendered expectations about women's display of confidence.

Indeed, several studies have shown that women who self-promote violate gender prescriptions to be modest (Moss-Racusin and Rudman, 2010; Rudman, 1998; Williams *et al.*, 2012). While self-confident demeanour might be helpful in the context of self-promotion, gendered expectations that women are modest mean that they may reject such behaviour. According to Nora:

> It just doesn't come naturally to me, certainly, to just try and shout out about my work or say 'I am really proud of this work, I'd really love for you to come and see it'. I mean it just smacks of self-promotion and sort of lack of modesty.

By emphasizing her natural predispositions, Nora orients to gendered expectations that women are modest. She subsequently rejects self-promotion and instead opts to perform modesty.

In negotiating the contradictory requests to engage in self-promotion on the one hand and come across as modest on the other, female musicians perform not only modesty, but also femininity (Butler, 1993; Scharff, 2012). In other words, I do not read their statements as indicative of a 'feminine essence' that naturally predisposes women to be modest. Instead, my premise is that modesty and femininity are performatively constituted, as in Nora's claim that shouting out about her work does not come to her 'naturally'. Similarly, Jane performs femininity in her talk about self-promotion:

> I feel a bit awkward doing that I suppose, yeah, I don't like to be pushy. But I'll try and do it in a nice way, just being friendly and chatting to network with people and meet people, so – more trying to make friends with people rather than appear too pushy [...]. Perhaps I would have got further quicker in my career if I had been a bit more proactive and a bit pushier, but I guess I am not *naturally* like that, and I think that is the best way to be I suppose, to get further with your career – certainly people I know that are a bit more pushy, proactive, do get more work. I guess it's a personality thing, and I'm not *naturally* like that.

Like Nora, Jane evokes naturalness in negotiating self-promotion. She rejects pushy behaviour by repeatedly emphasizing that she is not 'naturally' like that. The reiterative nature of her statement highlights its performative function, because performatives rely on reiteration to succeed (Butler, 1993).

Resonating with Jane's statement, several participants did not want to be pushy and instead wanted to do self-promotion 'nicely' and 'politely' (Janine). Indeed, a few participants mentioned that engaging in self-promotion was a tight balancing act. According to Sophie and Saaga, self-promotion is:

> Kind of difficult cause sometimes you don't want to be saying you're fabulous because then you sound like an idiot and no one will work with you but then at the same time if you say 'I'm not very good at that' then people will believe that you're not very good at that. So it's quite a fine line. (Sophie)

> Talking to another musician about yourself, what you do, is much more difficult [than talking to audience members] because you can't be general, you have to be very like, pushy, without seeming pushy. (Saaga)

These statements demonstrate the fine line between being confident and being pushy. They indicate that female musicians do not find it impossible to promote their work, but that they engage in a lot of boundary work to delineate acceptable forms of self-promotion. Indeed, the interviews can be read as discursive sites where such boundary work is undertaken and femininity performed. Such a reading suggests that the accounts provided in the interviews figure as another instance where gender is done.

In addition to gender, racial background and language skills intersected with the musicians' confidence in promoting their work (see also Williams *et al.*, 2012). As Kira stated:

> I know many good and really great pianists, but they can't sell themselves well. So I'm not saying that I am good at it, but – yeah, I am Japanese, I have spent eight years, nine years here and my German is a catastrophe and it's really, really difficult to be on the phone. And then I'm also not good at spelling. But yes, I'm trying it a bit, so that I can play a bit.

Kira also performs modesty in her statement by saying that she is not very good at selling herself. At the same time, her remarks point to the fact that self-promotion relies on a range of skills – such as language skills – that may not be equally accessible to all. Liz also referred to her ethnic background in discussing her feelings towards self-promotion:

> But I have a real problem with pushing myself out there in a publicity sense, which is I think largely connected to my dad who brought me up to think that you shouldn't say, go around saying how good you are – and almost feel ashamed of myself for doing that. Which is partly cultural, because he is Indian, there's a different sense of what's proper and not proper.

As with my analysis of femininity as performance, ethnicity is performed in Kira's and Liz's statements. Both participants evoke their ethnic background in negotiating their discomfort with self-promotion. These extracts demonstrate that self-promotion, which is part of the wider entrepreneurial ethos, posed particular dilemmas that were linked to ethnic background and language ability, but also to gender. The requirement to promote one's work challenges gendered norms that women are modest. Frequently, female musicians negotiate this fine line by rejecting pushy behaviour and doing niceness and femininity instead.

Art, commerce and femininity

In further discussion of their feelings towards self-promotion, several musicians expressed a 'strong desire for what you do to just speak for itself' (Amanda). The rejection of self-promotion was frequently justified by drawing on the commonly used discourse that art and commercial activities are incompatible. While this discourse does not hold absolutely (Taylor and Littleton, 2008), Yoshihara's (2007: 6–7) ethnographic study on Asian and Asian-American musicians has shown that '[c]lassical musicians, Asians or not, continue to proudly cherish their anti-commercialist, anti-materialist, art-for-art's sake ideals'.

In this vein, Sonja stated that self-marketing 'really has very little to do with art'. Several participants echoed her claim by drawing a distinction between musical and artistic skills on the one hand, and entrepreneurial and business skills on the other. In discussing the relationship between music making and business, Zola said:

> I don't think that it [art] belongs to any kind of business. It's such a creative thing, it's a personal thing. I feel like it shouldn't have anything to do with business. But also of course it does have to have something to do with business so we can earn some money and make a living, but I just […] I dislike it. Because it does include a lot of bragging about what you can do, what you are capable of, what you have done, and […] I want my work to speak for itself, but sadly that is not how the business works.

Similarly referring to different mind-sets, Linda claimed that:

> It's quite hard to do both – you know, the creative playing stuff and then having the business mind. It's quite hard to do them both well, I suppose. There are obviously musicians who do that, but then – and there are so many people who are, they are either really good at business, but you know, fairly average musicians, and there are

amazing musicians who just have no business mind and therefore can't quite get to where they sort of should be.

These negotiations of the relationship between creative and business skills highlight the musicians' positioning at the axis point 'between the forces of art and commerce' (Banks, 2007: 8). In drawing a distinction between artistic and commercial activities, Sonja, Zola and Linda evoke an 'aura of specialness' where musicians, and other cultural workers, 'revolt against instrumental rationality, market relations and industrial capitalism' (Toynbee, 2013: 93). By claiming specialness, the research participants discursively secure their status as artists. In this context, the distinction between art and commerce fulfils a constitutive function and affirms the participants' artistic identities.

Although the distinction between art and commerce helped the participants to establish themselves as artists, the very same distinction also had its perils. Arguably, the art-commerce axis constitutes a fraught terrain for female artists because of their historical positioning as the artist's Other. As Taylor and Littleton (2012: 36) pointedly argue, '[t]he Romantic image of the artist is almost invariably that of a man' (see also Conor, 2014 for an excellent discussion of these dynamics in the context of screenwriting). If self-promotion is associated with commerce and not art, and if women are always-already positioned as the artist's Other, the engagement of female musicians in entrepreneurial activities might threaten their credibility and status as artists.

Isabella's discussion of the difficulties of being a female artist captures these tensions well:

> I mean we know everything is now about marketing, in any profession [...] Unfortunately, talking from an art point view, it cheapens it. Because I do not want to be a product; I want to be an artist. I am not interested in, you know, the way I look, okay, well I like to look good, but that is outside from my art, that is me being a girl. But it really cheapens you when they are trying to sell it, your art, through the way you look, or whatever, and, okay I do not mind, but I do not want to be portrayed as one of those girls who just look good and cannot do it, because that is not why I work so hard. And I absolutely would not want to do it that way, but unfortunately, everything happens this way right now.

Isabella's negotiations of her appearance and femininity, and the way these are lived out in the wider cultural economy, merit closer analysis elsewhere. Key to such an analysis would be an intersectional framework which traces the racialized, classed and age-specific versions of femininity required to succeed in the classical music profession. As feminist research suggests (eg Fahs, 2012), such conventions are likely to assume white, middle-class, heterosexual and young subjects, thereby producing a range of exclusions that female musicians may have to negotiate.

What I would like to highlight here is Isabella's struggle to promote her work without jeopardizing her status as an artist. She engages in a lot of discursive work to establish her positioning as a female artist in spite of her good looks. By splitting her appearance and femininity from her art ('that is outside from my art, that is me being a girl'), Isabella attempts to distance herself from commercial preoccupations in order to affirm her status as an artist. Female musicians' struggles to be regarded as artists also emerged from other statements. Eve recounted her experiences of being a female student at a brass department:

> People always called us together, 'Oh, they are the two woman [brass players]'. I just wanted to break up that – just really push and be thought of as a musician, rather than as the token woman in the department.

By distancing herself from being the 'token woman in the department', and claiming the identity of a 'musician' instead, Eve attempts to occupy the positioning of an artist, one that is less fraught than that of a woman brass player.

In contexts where there are few women, such as in brass departments, it does, however, seem difficult to escape being positioned as female. Sasha, who played in an all-female brass ensemble, stated that they had to devise an innovative marketing strategy because they 'did not want to be typecast as women that sort of played [brass instruments], we wanted to do something more'. Lauren alludes to a similar dilemma when voicing her misgivings about self-promotion. Having stated that she just wants to play the piano, she went on to say:

> And I will do that in a place and a way where I am appreciated for my skills, I don't have to sell myself, because I am kooky or female or weird or different, you know? I wanna be good at what I'm doing, that's it.

These statements indicate that it is difficult for female musicians to promote their work in ways that affirm, rather than threaten, their positioning as artists. This means that practices of self-promotion may challenge the musicians' gendered identities not only because they involve modes of behaviour that are cast as unfeminine. Through the association of self-promotion with commercial practices that are regarded as non-artistic, self-promotion may also threaten female musicians' already tenuous status as artists.

The spectre of prostitution

When discussing their work, a few research participants alluded to prostitution. More specifically, the term prostitution came up in relation to musicians doing types of musical work they disliked. Kara observed:

> We want to make art, but often you're just being a prostitute, basically, I think that makes it difficult. I don't know many musicians that say, 'I'm going to teach today, all day! Yes! I'm looking forward to it!' [...] I think a lot of musicians just want to practice their instrument and play nice music, but that's just not life.

Astrid also referred to prostitution when reflecting on her experiences of freelancing as a singer. In this case, she had performed with a band that played popular music:

> I really liked playing with them, but it was still, it had an aura of – for example, at the end of one evening, a man approached me and was like 'How much do you cost?' And

I thought 'No, really?' [laughs]. No, and I mean it does not happen to you at every gig, but somehow you easily get into a position – I think that it's clear to everybody who is involved that it's a form of prostitution, somehow, in one way or another, I had the feeling.

Kara and Astrid do not explicitly portray prostitution as a gendered phenomenon. Indeed, their statements disarticulate (McRobbie, 2009; Scharff, 2012) the gendered dimension of prostitution by talking about 'musicians' in general and using indefinite pronouns such as 'everybody'.

A closer look at the interviews does suggest, however, that female musicians negotiate specifically gendered and sexualized connotations when selling themselves. Reflecting on the various aspects of her freelance work, Kim stated:

I mean I do Bollywood gigs, which is quite different from doing orchestral – I mean lots of orchestral musicians or freelance musicians do play for weddings and things like that. And I do that as well as in normal quartets but also Bollywood music, and there I am dressing up in either a sari or this or that. But I'm not doing it all the time, and I'm not selling my body, as it were, in that way.

As Kim's emphasis on 'not selling her body' indicates, the notion of selling yourself can take on sexual meanings. Discussing female musicians' self-presentation, Jeanette wondered:

How do you present yourself as a woman on stage? And when you look at the covers [of CDs] – they all sit there with a cleavage and you can see their G-strings shine through and they sell themselves somehow, yes, and I find that unprofessional. So yes, there, the woman gets degraded to being a sex object. And I really don't like that.

Jeanette's statement establishes links between sexy self-presentation, self-selling and women being degraded to sex objects. The sexual connotations of women selling themselves may make it more difficult for female musicians to engage in self-promotion. Discussing her experiences of playing in commercial women's bands, Sonja pointed out that 'you then sell yourself as a woman, commercially, and I find that very, very difficult'. While she did not explore her reasons for finding it difficult, I want to suggest that the notion of 'selling yourself' is not gender-neutral. On a global level, it is mainly women who sell their bodies, and many do so in the context of sex work (Outshoorn, 2004).

Although there were only a few participants like Jeanette who overtly established a link between self-selling and sexualization, there were numerous passages in the data where the sexualization of female musicians was indirectly evoked and negotiated. In relation to female players' success, for example, there was gossip that 'they had slept their way to the top' (Elena). As Yoshihara (2007: 110) has found, there are frequent rumours 'about famous female musicians having sexual relations with powerful conductors or managers who helped them launch their careers'. These rumours are gendered as it is mainly women's success that is represented, and devalued, in these ways. Reflecting on her conduct in an orchestra she was trialling with, Judith pointed out that she tried to be nice, but not too nice, because 'I would hate to feel that I only got the job because people fancy me or because they think this could happen or whatever'. Ricarda, who was exceptional in that she held a permanent position in a prestigious orchestra, reported that she sometimes made pre-emptive jokes about having a sexual relationship with the male conductor:

> Sometimes I try and say it myself to kind of prevent anyone from trying [to make a joke]. I sort of talk about how I, you know, how 'Well, you know me and [name of male conductor], I mean, how else do you think I got this job'?

In these statements, Judith and Ricarda orient to their positioning as females and actively seek to pre-empt rumours that their success is based on sexual relationships. Even though these statements are not directly related to prostitution, they highlight one of numerous instances where female musicians are sexualized. Against the backdrop of the sexualization of female players and the gendered nature of prostitution, the notion that female musicians sell themselves may evoke the spectre of prostitution. Arguably, female musicians have to perform an additional layer of identity work when engaging in self-promotion. At stake are not only their gender and artistic identities, but also the recognition of their skills that can easily get devalued through rumours that they sleep with powerful men.

Conclusions

Reflecting the entrepreneurial ethos of the cultural industries, many musicians described themselves as products that had to be sold. At the same time, they disliked the practice of selling themselves. This chapter has shed light on three gendered dynamics that help explain female musicians' reluctance to engage in self-promotion. First, self-promotion is associated with pushy behaviour that conflicts with normative expectations that women are nice and modest, and gives rise to dilemmas in the performance of femininity. Second, self-promotion is regarded as a commercial activity and positioned as unartistic. Taking into account that women have been constructed as the artist's Other, engagement in self-promotion may threaten their already tenuous status as artists. Lastly, the notion of selling yourself may evoke the spectre of prostitution due to the sexualization of female musicians and the fact that it is mainly women who sell their bodies. As I have demonstrated, these gendered dynamics do not mean that female musicians are unable to pursue self-promotion, but that they engage in a range of discursive strategies to negotiate and secure their identities as female artists.

By way of conclusion, I would like to highlight three lines of inquiry that arise from my analysis. First, and as I have discussed briefly in relation to appearance norms, there is a need for an intersectional framework that also explores how class background and age (see Williams *et al.*, 2012) affect workers' ability to promote themselves. While my analysis has traced some of the intersections between gender and race in the context of self-promotion, future research will benefit from frameworks that also explore how age and class-background affect these dynamics. Second, my analysis raises wider questions about the relationship between gender and discourse, both in relation to men's negotiations of self-promotion, and also the ways in which women and men actually perform self-promotion in the context of powerful gender norms. What are the problems that may confront individuals if they do gender 'wrong'? And does engagement in self-promotion, and its opposite, self-deprecation, have the same effects on male and female workers? Third and last, this chapter has documented an economization of subjectivity where the self, and not 'just' one's work, becomes part of an entrepreneurial logic. In the data presented here, this logic became most visible in the participants' statements about being a product that has to be sold and marketed. This insight raises important questions about the ways in which the economization of the self is registered, negotiated and lived out at a psychosocial level, and the exclusionary dynamics that this may involve.

Acknowledgements

I would like to thank the Economic and Social Research Council for funding this research (Grant reference: ES/K008765/1). I would also like to thank the editors, Bridget Conor, Rosalind Gill and Stephanie Taylor for their insightful comments on earlier drafts of this article and for publishing this important special issue and edited collection. Lastly, I am grateful that Bruna Seu suggested the title 'Blowing your own trumpet'.

Notes

1 All participants had the right to withdraw from the research at any time. Their anonymity is protected through the use of pseudonyms and the omission of any information that may identify them to others. Therefore, I only provide demographic data if it is necessary to make sense of individual statements.
2 In my sample, 44 musicians identified as middle class, 7 as working class, and 2 as lower middle class; 11 were not sure how to describe their socio-economic background, which resonates with broader arguments that popular awareness of class seems to be waning. Four described their racial background as mixed race, 56 as white, 1 as black, 1 as Asian and 2 as East Asian.

References

Banks, M., (2007), *The Politics of Cultural Work*, Basingstoke: Palgrave Macmillan.
Beeching, A., (2010), *Beyond Talent: Creating a Successful Career in Music*, Oxford: Oxford University Press.
Bennett, D., (2007), 'Utopia for music performance graduates: is it achievable, and how should it be defined?', *British Journal of Music Education*, 42 (2): 179–189.
Bennett, D. E., (2008), *Understanding the Classical Music Profession: The Past, the Present and Strategies for the Future*, Aldershot: Ashgate.
Bull, A., (2015), *The Musical Body: How Gender and Class Are Reproduced among Young People Playing Classical Music in England*, PhD thesis, Goldsmiths, University of London.
Butler, J., (1993), *Bodies that Matter: On the Discursive Limits of 'Sex'*, London: Routledge.

The Sociological Review, 63:S1, pp. 97–112 (2015), DOI: 10.1111/1467-954X.12243

Conor, B., (2014), *Screenwriting: Creative Work and Professional Practice*, London: Routledge.

Cottrell, S., (2004), *Professional Music-Making in London: Ethnography and Experience*, Farnham: Ashgate.

Edwards, P. and Wajcman, J., (2005), *The Politics of Working Life*, Oxford: Oxford University Press.

Fahs, B., (2012), 'Breaking body hair boundaries: classroom exercises for challenging social constructions of the body and sexuality', *Feminism & Psychology*, 22 (4): 482–506.

Gembris, H. and Langner, D., (2005), *Von der Musikhochschule auf den Arbeitsmarkt: Erfahrungen von Absolventen, Arbeitsmarktexperten und Hochschullehrern*, Augsburg: Wißner-Verlag.

Gill, R., (2002), 'Cool, creative and egalitarian? Exploring gender in project-based new media work in Europe', *Information, Communication & Society*, 5 (1): 70–89.

Gill, R., (2014), 'Unspeakable inequalities: post feminism, entrepreneurial subjectivity, and the repudiation of sexism among cultural workers', *Social Politics*, 21 (4): 509–528.

Goldin, C. and Rouse, C., (2000), 'Orchestrating impartiality: the impact of 'blind' auditions on female musicians', *The American Economic Review*, 90 (4): 715–741.

Gordon, C., (1987), 'The soul of the citizen: Max Weber and Michel Foucault on rationality and government', in S. Lash and S. Whimster (eds), *Max Weber, Rationality and Modernity*, 293–316, London: Allan and Unwin.

Green, L., (1997), *Music, Gender, Education*, Cambridge: Cambridge University Press.

HEFCE, (2002), 'Creating a land with music: the work, education, and training of professional musicians in the 21st century', available at: http://www.youthmusic.org.uk/assets/files/HEFCEreport1.pdf.

Higgins, C., (2013), 'Male conductors are better for orchestras, says Vasily Petrenko', *The Guardian*, 2 September, available at: http://www.theguardian.com/music/2013/sep/02/male-conductors-better-orchestras-vasily-petrenko.

Johnson-Hill, E., (2014), 'Imperial surveillance: the origins of power formation in Victorian music education', paper presented at the conference *Classical Music: Critical Challenges*, 17 October, King's College London.

Kok, R-M., (2014), 'Culture and (in)justice', paper presented at the conference *Classical Music: Critical Challenges*, 17 October, King's College London.

Maddocks, F., (2013), 'Marin Alsop, conductor of Last Night of the Proms, on sexism in classical music', *The Guardian*, 6 September, available at: http://www.theguardian.com/music/2013/sep/06/marin-alsop-proms-classical-sexist.

Mäkinen, K., (2012), *Becoming Valuable Selves: Self-Promotion, Gender and Individuality in Late Capitalism*, Tampere: Tampere University Press.

McNay, L. (2009), 'Self as enterprise: dilemmas of control and resistance in Foucault's *The Birth of Biopolitics*', *Theory, Culture & Society*, 26 (6): 55–77.

McRobbie, A., (2009), *The Aftermath of Feminism: Gender, Culture and social Change*, London: Sage.

Moss-Racusin, C. A. and Rudman, L. A., (2010), 'Disruptions in women's self-promotion: the backlash avoidance model', *Psychology of Women Quarterly*, 34 (2): 186–202.

Musicians' Union, (2012), *The Working Musician*, commissioned by the Musicians' Union. Researched and produced by DHA Communications.

Outshoorn, J. (ed.), (2004), *The Politics of Prostitution: Women's Movements, Democratic States and the Globalisation of Sex Commerce*, Cambridge: Cambridge University Press.

Potter, J. and Wetherell, M., (1987). *Discourse and Social Psychology: Beyond Attitudes and Behaviour*, London: Sage.

Proctor-Thomson, S. B., (2013), 'Feminist futures of cultural work: creativity, gender and diversity in the digital media sector', in M. Banks, S. Taylor and R. Gill (eds), *Theorizing Cultural Work: Labour, Continuity and Change in the Creative Industries*, 137–148, London: Routledge.

Rudman, L. A., (1998), 'Self-promotion as a risk factor for women: the costs and benefits of counter-stereotypical impression management', *Journal of Personality and Social Psychology*, 74 (3): 629–645.

Scharff, C., (2012), *Repudiating Feminism: Young Women in a Neoliberal World*, Farnham: Ashgate.

Skillset, (2010), *Women in the Creative Media Industries*, available at: http://www.ewawomen.com/uploads/files/surveyskillset.pdf.

Storey, J., Salaman, G. and Platman, K., (2005), 'Living with enterprise in an enterprise economy: freelance and contract workers in the media', *Human Relations*, 58 (8): 1033–1054.

Taylor, S., (2011), 'Negotiating oppositions and uncertainties: gendered conflicts in creative identity work', *Feminism and Psychology*, 21 (3): 354–371.

Taylor, S. and Littleton, K., (2008), 'Art work or money: conflicts in the construction of a creative identity', *The Sociological Review*, 56 (2): 275–292.

Taylor, S. and Littleton, K., (2012), *Contemporary Identities of Creativity and Creative Work*, Farnham: Ashgate.

Toynbee, J., (2013), 'How special? Cultural work, copyright, politics', in M. Banks, S. Taylor and R. Gill (eds), *Theorizing Cultural Work: Labour, Continuity and Change in the Creative Industries*, 85–98, London: Routledge.

Williams, C. L., Muller, C. and Kilanski, C., (2012), 'Gendered organizations in the new economy', *Gender & Society*, 26 (4): 549–573.

Yoshihara, M., (2007), *Musicians from a Different Shore: Asians and Asian Americans in Classical Music*, Philadelphia: Temple University Press.

The Sociological Review, 63:S1, pp. 97–112 (2015), DOI: 10.1111/1467-954X.12243

'Egotist', 'masochist', 'supplicant': Charlie and Donald Kaufman and the gendered screenwriter as creative worker

Bridget Conor

Abstract: This article offers a gendered reading of the screenwriter as creative worker in the context of the unequal socio-economy of screenwriting work. A number of ideal subject positions for the screenwriter are evoked in screenwriting manuals, pedagogies and representations of writers themselves, in particular, the 'egotist', the 'masochist' and the 'supplicant'. These subjects are masculine in orientation although rarely acknowledged in gendered terms. The article draws on findings from a three-year study of British screenwriters but for the purposes of this volume, focuses on on-screen portrayals of screenwriting work. In particular, the analysis looks at the film *Adaptation* (2002) and the ways in which the film and its characters embody these subject positions. Not only are these ideal types circulated and recirculated in discourse about screenwriting as creative work but they are constitutive of screenwriting as a profession and a representative sphere.

Keywords: screenwriting, masculinities, sex-typing, inequalities, profession

Introduction

In the introduction to the published edition of the *Being John Malkovich* screenplay (2000) Charlie Kaufman offers his advice to other budding screenwriters who admire his work and harbour dreams of producing a film script of similar originality and vision. Kaufman seemingly scuppers those aspirations with an existential riff on his authoritative position as conceiver of the film, as 'screenwriter'. He offers little practical advice but rather presents a parodic vision of the screenwriter as a neurotic, isolated and tortured individual. He laments, 'I have nothing cute or sparkling or insightful to say. I am a miserable lonely person who has no charming anecdotes' (Kaufman, 2000). He reworks some of the well-worn aphorisms that pepper 'how-to' screenwriting manuals to emphasize the assumed torment of his own ego:

The Sociological Review, 63:S1, pp. 113–127 (2015), DOI: 10.1111/1467-954X.12244
© 2015 The Author. Editorial organisation © 2015 The Editorial Board of the Sociological Review. Published by John Wiley & Sons Ltd, 9600 Garsington Road, Oxford OX4 2DQ, UK and 350 Main Street, Malden, MA 02148, USA

> If there's anything I can say about screenwriting in this introduction it's that you need to write what you know. And I don't know anything. I don't understand a damn second of my life. I exist in a fog of confusion and anxiety and clutching jealousy and loneliness.

Kaufman also enthusiastically punctures the familiar puffed-up myth of individual creative drive and the moment of 'inspiration':

> What can I tell you about the screenwriting process as I know it? Just maybe that you're alone in this. Take your inspiration where you find it. I don't even know what that means. Inspiration? What the hell is inspiration anyway? You just sit there and wait. That's all I do. I sit and wait. I don't even know for what. For it to get better? What is it? You tell me. You write an introduction and send it to me.

Yet Kaufman embodies that puffed-up myth even at the same time as he attempts to dispel it. He is now one of the most well-known screenwriters in the mainstream screen production industry. His screenplays are hailed as groundbreaking and highly idiosyncratic works that upend all the traditional conventions of the feature film medium that screenwriting manuals endlessly repeat. He is now a writer-director, commanding huge sums for his original scripts and able to attract large, eager audiences when he speaks about his films. Kaufman has also become renowned for his commentary on the screenwriter as a creative individual, particularly in his film *Adaptation* (2002), in which a screenwriter called Charlie Kaufman struggles to adapt a non-fiction book into a screenplay. In the film the multi-stranded plot ranges between characters, locations and time periods, from dramatized scenes from and about the non-fiction book, to scenes involving Charlie and his twin brother Donald (also an aspiring screenwriter[1]) discussing the merits of screenwriting guru Robert McKee's 'Story' seminar.[2]

Adaptation, released in 2002 with a budget of US$19 million, went on to gross US$32,801,173 worldwide.[3] The film was nominated for four Academy Awards and won one (for best supporting actor Chris Cooper) and Charlie Kaufman won the BAFTA for best adapted screenplay in 2003. The film was declared one of the best films of the 2000s by critics such as Roger Ebert and in publications such as *Sight and Sound*: 'It is the revenge of the writer', wrote Henry Bean in his *Sight and Sound* review.[4] *Adaptation* has also had a robust critical afterlife, meaning that although the film is now almost 15 years old, it is often prominent in screenwriting pedagogy and popular critique. It currently has a 91 per cent approval rating on the popular film review websites *Rotten Tomatoes* and *Metacritic* (on which the film earns a score of 83: 'universal acclaim').[5] More pointedly, the film continues to be used routinely in the teaching of screenwriting. It is cited in screenwriting manuals as a film and a screenplay that provides numerous lessons: about both how to learn the 'rules' of screenwriting and how to break them; how to formulate a non-linear narrative; and how to expand the possibilities of the form itself. Thus it remains a touchstone for those who teach and study screenwriting. More than this, and as the first part of this article will demonstrate, it is a particularly potent representation of screenwriting work, rather than exclusively the outcome of that work.[6]

The Sociological Review, 63:S1, pp. 113–127 (2015), DOI: 10.1111/1467-954X.12244

The research project on which this article draws was an in-depth interdisciplinary study of screenwriting as creative labour conducted mainly in London. It involved 17 interviews with screenwriters, producers and other professionals adjacent to screenwriters, and screenwriting teachers, textual analysis of 32 screenwriting manuals and supplementary historical and labour market data analysis (see Conor, 2014). Within this study, a number of ideal subject positions for the screenwriter were identified in screenwriting manuals, in screenwriting courses and in accounts of writing work from writers themselves; in particular, the 'egotist', the 'masochist' and the 'supplicant'. What is implicit although not acknowledged is that these subjects are also masculine in orientation although rarely acknowledged as such. And in a canonical portrait of screenwriting work such as *Adaptation* and the many characters embodied by Charlie Kaufman himself, screenwriting work is a deeply conflicted and tortured profession and is a masculine profession. These on- and off-screen constructions are also part of the larger discursive processes that shape screenwriters' experiences and the characterization of their profession. Screenwriting is characterized across a range of discursive and representative platforms as a profession that requires masculine mastery and egotism, a tortured and masochistic obsession with the work. It is simultaneously framed as a profession that is, by its nature, secondary and supplicative; someone else is always in charge which simply fuels the creative torture of the work. The conflicted but wholly masculine positionings within screenwriting work worlds are thus partially reflected and constituted via on-screen portrayals of the work. Using Kaufman and representations of screenwriting in *Adaptation* (2002), this article analyses the figure of the gendered screenwriter in the context of the contemporary socio-economy of the screenwriting labour force. This is a socio-economy in which inequalities are rife and in which very few people are able to make and sustain a living as a screenwriter.

'Egotist', 'masochist', 'supplicant'

Screenplay extract 1

Kaufman (V.O.)[7]

I am pathetic. I am a loser. I am fat.

McKee

So … what is the substance of writing?

Nothing as trivial as words is at the

heart of this great art, my friends.

McKee continues to talk but his voice goes under.

Kaufman (V.O.)

> *I have failed. I am panicked. I am fat.*
>
> *I have sold out. I am worthless. I . . .*

McKee

> *Literary talent is not enough. First,*
>
> *last, and always, the imperative is to*
>
> *tell a story.*

Kaufman watches with disdain as people take notes.

(Extract from *Adaptation*, 2002)

Inequalities determine who is in and who is out; who is able to experience, learn or undertake screenwriting work and who is not; who is able to take up a subject position within particular creative professions and what kinds of subject positions are possible. This first section identifies and further examines some of them: 'egotist', 'masochist' and 'supplicant',[8] all illuminated in the above exchange from *Adaptation* (2002). These are masculine positions and they are something slightly different to the very 'strident and assertive' masculinity that Allen (2013: 235) argues is often linked to the 'ideal' creative in discourses of cultural work. Rather than the masculine screenwriter as rational, hard-skinned and determined, these subject positions and those embodied in the character of Charlie Kaufman in the film, are conflicted, anxious and self-doubting. They are also performative. Butler's (1990, 1993) theory of gender performativity is particularly helpful here because, as Butler argues, gender performativity is constituted and regulated via repetitive discursive practices or 'repeated acts' (1990: 192). These practices are, as Butler writes, *'fabrications* manufactured and sustained through corporeal signs and other discursive means' (1990: 185, emphasis in original). Gender performativity is also vital and dynamic. It is a 'happening activity' as McRobbie (2005: 85) calls it, but it is never absolute. Thus, repeated and unquestioned framings of the screenwriter as male (and as white, well-educated, heterosexual, geek and 'egotist') that thread through the histories, contemporary accounts of screenwriting work, and *representations* of that work, serve to constitute a hegemonic understanding of the screenwriting labour force. They certainly are not stable or absolute but they are particularly potent in consecrated portrayals of screenwriting work such as that in *Adaptation* (2002). And crucially, this text is *also* vital and dynamic. The film itself is iterative, repeated across other sites (screenwriting manuals, screenwriting courses, interviews with screenwriters) as an influential and constitutive portrait of *the* screenwriter and the creative process of screenwriting.

The egotistic and masochistic screenwriter as ideal type is given full expression in the main characters of the film, the twin brothers Charlie and Donald

The Sociological Review, 63:S1, pp. 113–127 (2015), DOI: 10.1111/1467-954X.12244

Kaufman in *Adaptation* (2002), both played by Nicholas Cage. Charlie is the embodiment of the tortured creative, suffering for his art and suffering in life. He is struggling to adapt a book, 'The Orchid Thief' by Susan Orlean, into a screenplay and the film becomes a convoluted meta-narrative about these creative struggles and his own self-doubt. His twin brother Donald is the more successful, rational creative figure – he decides to become a screenwriter almost overnight and he gains mastery of the screenwriting profession by using exactly the tools that Charlie, the 'true' creative, abhors: screenwriting manuals, seminars, rules and conventions. Donald begins to write a serial-killer script ('*Silence of the Lambs* meets *Psycho*', Kaufman describes it, in the standard style of a script pitch) using Robert McKee's storytelling principles, whilst Charlie struggles to adapt Orlean's non-fiction book 'about flowers' for the screen, and becomes more unhinged and self-flagellating as the film progresses. Charlie's opening voiceover gives a flavour of this, a voiceover that continues throughout the film:

Screenplay extract 2

Kaufman (V.O.)

I'm old. I'm fat. I'm bald.

(reaches for notebook, catches sight of bare feet)

My toenails have turned strange. I am old. I am...

(Extract from *Adaptation*, 2002)

Caldwell (2008: 11) highlights a variant of 'worker masochism' as it is promoted in Hollywood trade publications and advertising for 'masculinised tools', just as Mahar (2001) identifies early advertising for film-making equipment as a masculine preserve, as the following section will discuss. In *Adaptation* (2002), creative masochism is necessary and torturous at the same time as it is rigorously masculine and self-oriented. Taylor helpfully contextualizes egotism and masochism as gendered subject positions (and for more on the gendered figure of the creative artist, see also Taylor's article in this collection):

> I referred earlier to the masculine image of the creative maker (the artist in the garret). It is notable that, as part of this characterization, responsibilities to others, including families, are famously cast aside.... both female and male participants referred to the 'selfishness' of their creative working ... The prioritizing of the commitment to the individual maker's own work conflicts with an other-directed-ness that operates not only in conventional caring roles, such as mothering, but also more generally as part of a feminine identity. (2011: 366–367)

The selfish and egotistical screenwriter as geek or nerd is a gendered image frequently evoked in portrayals of the screenwriter in film: Charlie Kaufman and his more successful twin Donald Kaufman in *Adaptation* (2002) or the New York playwright Barton Fink hired to write Hollywood studio films 'for hire' in the Coen Brothers' film of the same name (1991). In fact, *Adaptation* is constructed in such a way as to attract and promote fetishism and obsession with the form and structure of screenwriting itself. The film is about screenwriting work and the difficulties of that work and of any form of creative production. So, the convoluted chronology of the screenplay begins 'three billion years ago' as single-celled life develops on planet Earth. The film meshes various narrative strands together including the lives of the twin Kaufman screenwriters and the separate yet connected story of Susan Orlean (the role performed by Meryl Streep) as she researches her book and the orchid thief John Laroche (performed by Chris Cooper). And the script is peppered with 'in jokes' for its audience, especially for other screenwriters. The inclusion of the twins Charlie and Donald is itself a joke: they represent two very different trajectories of the profession. Donald is the successful blockbuster writer and also the sell-out. Charlie is the purist, the innovator but is, therefore, the tortured and less successful writer. And their dialogue is full of references to tropes of screen storytelling that then feature in the narrative itself: voiceover narration (used extensively but also ridiculed within the story by the guru Robert McKee, played in the film by Brian Cox); multiple personalities materialized via the twin brothers; and a *deus ex machina*[9] (again, McKee warns Charlie Kaufman against this: 'Don't you dare bring in a deus ex machina', and one is then used at the end of the film). All of this encourages a fetishization for screenwriting work and screenwriting lore and, as Proctor-Thompson (2013) notes in her discussion of the 'geek' subject in new media work, it privileges particular masculine creative subjects, and downplays others. Neither of the Kaufman brothers are physically strong or particularly strident (Charlie makes many references to himself as 'fat' and 'weak'), but they are self-oriented and obsessed with the work. And the screenwriter Charlie Kaufman's own success with this film and others, also reasserts his authorial power in the face of weakness or anxiety.

Screenwriting work in *Adaptation* (2002) is presented as self-oriented, torturous and conflicted. The professional characterization is also heteronormative. Donald Kaufman is framed as a 'successful' screenwriter in relation to not only his professional success (as a result of his application of storytelling formulae and screenwriting seminars) but also his self-confidence and his sexual prowess. In contrast, the character of Charlie Kaufman, tortured and masochistic, is also represented as a failure with women. When he is not writing he is depicted as routinely masturbating (as well as admonishing himself via voiceover for being 'bald', 'pathetic' and 'a loser'). There are numerous masturbation scenes in which he fantasizes about the women in his life: Valerie his agent (performed by Tilda Swinton), Susan Orlean herself and his love interests Amelia (Cara Seymour) and Alice (Judy Greer). This is in contrast to Donald's successful relationship with Caroline (Maggie Gyllenhaal), a make-up artist (and a nicely sex-typed production role) who is supportive and adoring of Donald and his career. Thus to be a screenwriter in Kaufman's world is to be virile and sexually obsessed, homophilic and heterosexual (for more on heteronormativity and the sexualization of screenwriting language see Conor, 2014).

The Sociological Review, 63:S1, pp. 113–127 (2015), DOI: 10.1111/1467-954X.12244

The repeated construction of screenwriters as secondary, as fundamentally supplicative, is another challenge to the understanding of masculine creative genius as one of pure mastery and control. Macdonald's important work on screenwriting highlights the supplicant status of screenwriting work and the ways in which industry norms, embodied in the character of Donald Kaufman in *Adaptation*, repeat and reiterate this: 'a writer's general status in the workplace is as a supplicant, offering material and a level of skill to a market that is operated by others' (2004: 200). Supplication as a fundamental subject position for screenwriters is reflected in a 'know your place' discourse across a range of sites: screenwriting manuals, in published interviews with screenwriters, and in the director-as-auteur model in film theory. This is a key 'deficit identity' for the gendered screenwriter as Taylor and Reynolds term it; that is, an identity 'defined in terms of lack or what a person is not' (2005: 199, fn 1).[10] For Macdonald: 'A writer learns and adopts normative practices in order to work within the industry and has no means of engaging critically with these practices unless they have sufficient status to do so' (2004: 150). And deficit identities accrue to the character of Charlie Kaufman in *Adaptation* (2002), the [overweight, sweaty, 'pathetic', 'repulsive', 'I am nothing'] screenwriter for comic and dramatic effect. The creative and subjective anxieties given full-flight in *Adaptation* (2002) perhaps serve as a form of comic catharsis, both for the screenwriter Charlie Kaufman, and for the audience more generally, especially those with creative aspirations of their own. These are anxieties often tied directly to the nature of screenwriting as a 'secondary' and 'invisible' form of writing. However, in its narrative construction and its characterization, the film also shores up a particular and limited set of masculine screenwriting subjects: self-oriented creative, tortured genius, geeky fetishist. They are wholly masculine subjects, tightly regulated and situated forcefully within a spectrum of masculinities. And the comedic and knowing sensibility of the film and its 'complex' narrative also ensures the film can elide any serious critique. In fact, Kaufman's own position as a successful, visible and well-remunerated screenwriter has only been strengthened by the continued success of the film – *Adaptation* (2002) displays his control of his individual creative drive, his mastery of the screenwriting profession.

The socio-economy of screenwriting work[11]

Films such as *Adaptation* (2002) and characters such as Charlie and Donald Kaufman construct and consecrate representations of screenwriting work as masculine. In doing so, such representations effectively mask the fact that opportunities to participate in and perform this work are not evenly distributed, nor are the representative possibilities of the work. In fact, in the field of screenwriting work as in other cultural production industries discourses of egalitarianism are implicit; in statements from screenwriting gurus and manuals, for example, such as 'everyone is a writer' (Field, 1994). But contemporary data from a range of industries and places indicates levels of inequality and the very slow rates of change within this data.[12] In the UK industry, women represented 16 per cent of writers and 11.4 per cent of directors for UK independent British films in 2010–12 (British Film Institute, 2013). An earlier study titled 'Who writes British films' and surveying a sample of 60 films released in the UK in 2004 and 2005 found that the vast majority of the writers on those films were 'white (98%), male (82.5%), over the age of 46 (66%) and earned relatively high incomes' (UK Film Council, 2007: 7). And one of the only studies of its kind in the UK specifically focused on the lack of women screenwriters in the UK and found that women screenwriters were 'credited on less than 15 per cent of UK films made between 1999 and 2003' (UK Film Council, 2006: 1).

These stark inequalities are reflected in the most recent full Writer's Guild of America West (hereafter WGAW) Writers Reports (2011, 2013) that emphasize the lack of change in the diversity of Hollywood-based screenwriters in the years 2007–2009. 'Women writers remain stuck at 28 percent of television employment while their share of film employment actually declined a percentage point to 17 percent' (WGAW, 2011: 1). In 2009, ethnic minorities were under-represented by a factor of about 7 to 1 among employed film writers which is the 'smallest minority share of film employment in ten years (2011: 5). More recent statistics from the WGAW focused on television writing signal a very slow increase in the proportion of women television writers, indicating that between 1999–2000 and 2011–2012, women's share of this writing work increased by 5 percentage points, from 25 per cent to 30.5 per cent (2013: 2). In this time period, minority writers doubled their share (from 7.5 per cent to 15.6 per cent). However, this is still severe under-representation when considering the overall minority share of the US population (reported by the WGAW as 36.3 per cent in 2010). Lauzen's 'Celluloid Ceiling' report also reflects these trends:

> Women comprised 18% of all directors, executive producers, producers, writers, cinematographers, and editors working on the top 250 domestic grossing films of 2012. This percentage represents no change from 2011 and an increase of 1 percentage point from 1998. (2012a: 1)

These kinds of statistical patterns are also consistent (with small deviations) in other Anglophone screen markets (see Coutanche and Davis, 2013, for the Canadian picture, Screen Australia, 2013, and Davis, 2012 for a New Zealand perspective) and have been shown to be very slow to change and at times of economic crisis, worsening (see Skillset, 2009 and 2012 for UK statistics). A recent British Film Institute (2013) report, however, saw cause for optimism by noting that between 2010 and 2012 there was a 'breakthrough', with female screenwriters associated with 37 per cent of the top 20 UK independent films and 30 per cent of the most profitable UK independent films. And in early 2014, Sharma and Sender (2014) wrote a widely reported post with the heading: 'Hollywood movies with strong female leads make more money', after analysing the top 50 highest grossing Hollywood produced films and the numbers of those that passed the Bechdel Test; the Bechdel Test (or Bechdel-Wallace Test) being 'a diagnostic about the state of representations of women in pop culture in aggregate' and often used to refer to the representative numbers of women in film and television

The Sociological Review, 63:S1, pp. 113–127 (2015), DOI: 10.1111/1467-954X.12244

(Evans, 2013).[13] There is at least some indication then, that this socio-economy is not a static one. The mention of the Bechdel Test is particularly important here, as it indicates that to study inequalities in screen production industries requires an attention to inequalities *on*-screen as well as to inequalities within the labour force.

As the example(s) of Charlie (and Donald) Kaufman so aptly signal, screen-writers are directly involved in representational processes, in producing views on and of the world, images and narratives for others to consume and at times, and especially in the case of *Adaptation* (2002), images *about* creativity and the cre-ative process. Considering the statistical data presented so far, it is no surprise that many data sets also indicate consistent patterns of on-screen inequality. For example, Lauzen also tracks on-screen gender representations and in her 2012 report, 'It's a man's (celluloid) world', she writes:

> In 2011, females remained dramatically under-represented as characters in film when compared with their representation in the U.S. population. Last year, females ac-counted for 33% of all characters in the top 100 domestic grossing films. This represents an increase of 5 percentage points since 2002 when females comprised 28% of char-acters. While the percentage of female characters has increased over the last decade, the percentage of female protagonists has declined. In 2002, female characters ac-counted for 16% of protagonists. In 2011, females comprised only 11% of protagonists. (2012b: 1)

The Geena Davis Institute for Gender and Media commissioned research into representations of gender roles and occupations with similar results, including that females are not as prevalent as males in both film and television and across genres, that women continue to be stereotyped in domestic and heterosexual roles, for example, and that women are disproportionately sexualized in popu-lar and family entertainment (Smith *et al.*, 2013b). This research also found that women are much less likely than men to be shown working on-screen (only 20.3 per cent in family films and 34.4 per cent in prime-time television) and in inverse proportion to their representation in the US labour force as a whole (reported as 47 per cent, see Smith *et al.*, 2013b).

The researchers commissioned by the Geena Davis Institute write that males outnumber females 3 to 1 in family films and go on to highlight the fact that this ratio '...is the same as it was in 1946' (Smith *et al.*, 2013b: n.p.), another indica-tion of the entrenchment of inequalities both on- and off-screen. 'The Black List 3.0', an online forum for scriptwriting, script sharing and script-analysis, aggre-gated data on US 'spec' script sales[14] and found that the proportion of female 'spec' script sales is also decreasing. It was 14 per cent between 1991 and 2000, 13 per cent between 2001 and 2010 and only 9 per cent in 2011 and 2012 (see Orozco, 2013).

Plenty of tacit industrial knowledge circulates that justifies these contin-ued inequalities, making explicit links between professional practices on-screen and off. For example, the repetition of the 'what audiences want' argument, in which those audiences are regularly assumed to be adolescent boys; or routine

references to the perceived differences between the way men and women tell stories; or via the assumption that films written by men are simply more polished
and perform better at the box office. The analysis of box office data from the
British Film Institute (2013) and from Sharma and Sender (2014) clearly refute
this last assumption but these kinds of industrial theorizing, assumed to be 'natural law' as Caldwell puts it (2008: 18), are powerful and they are obfuscatory –
they mask another set of industrial truths, about the unstable and exclusionary
nature of the industry.[15]

Conclusion: creativity, screenwriting and gender

Screenwriting is a form of gendered creative labour. The screen production industries have, from their earliest days, been deeply unequal. Mahar's analysis of
early Hollywood links increased industrial specialization and efficiency to sex-
typing and increased discrimination against women filmmakers (2001: 103). Mahar writes: 'Seemingly gender neutral, the "new" American film industry was,
in fact, born masculine' (2001: 79), and in advertising and early film technology
development, men were depicted as camera operators, owners and exhibitors.
Whilst initially quite illustrative of the utopian vision of a creative industry as
'cool, creative and egalitarian' (see Gill, 2002), the screen production industries quickly became masculine, fraternalist and homophilic in orientation.[16] The
structural organization of screenwriting labour markets and the old and new
kinds of labouring practices within them, have then served to entrench, even
deepen these inequalities. Today, the organization of the Hollywood industry and
its film and television labour markets *builds* gender stereotyping and discrimination into everyday working practices and then sustains them via the reliance on
personal networks, reputation-based hiring and firing and mainstream marketing
strategies (for more on the gendered outcomes of networking and other informal
recruitment practices for screenwriters, see Wreyford in this volume and see also
Bielby, 2009). These inequalities are structural and historical in nature, although
they may also be hidden or unacknowledged. This is reflected not only in portrayals of screenwriting work like that of *Adaptation* (2002) but also in the un-
questioning use of masculine pronouns in screenwriting manuals, for example, or
blanket references to the 'Hero's Journey' in these texts, even alongside the voices
of both female and male screenwriters. This all effectively circumscribes screenwriting as a masculine profession, requiring masculine creative traits.[17] Importantly for an analysis of screenwriting as a form of creative labour, these accounts
of screen production as masculine and fraternalist echo findings from contemporary studies of gendered relations in other creative professions, from advertising to new media work (for example, Banks and Milestone, 2011; Gill, 2002;
Henderson, 2001; Nixon, 2003 and Nixon and Crewe, 2004).

More broadly, the neoliberal 'new cultural economy' in which screenwriters
now function, in modes that are often highly individualized and precarious, is
gendered and unequal. In a discussion of post-feminism and the ways in which
this can be linked to neo-liberal media and economic organization, Gill and

Scharff (2011: 7) ask: 'Could it be that neoliberalism *is always already gendered*, and that women are constructed as its ideal subjects?' (original emphasis). As many theorists have argued in recent and important feminist interventions,[18] it is now women who are primarily called upon to 'work' on themselves, to be 'top girls' as McRobbie (2009) puts it. It is often via the representative strategies of media texts of many kinds, including film and television that women are 'hailed' as ideal, neoliberal subjects. Yet women continue to have much less access to those representational strategies, to the conception and production of media, of narratives and characters, of images of creative work.

In neoliberal creative markets that require entrepreneurialism, fierce individualism and self-responsibility, the traditional language of equity is 'narrow and anodyne', as Allen puts it (2013: 237), and structural inequalities are 'individual, private problems, to be overcome by hard work, choice and self determination' (2013: 327). Not only is neoliberalism always/already gendered, but realms of creative production and cultural work are also always/already gendered and this affects which voices, narratives and subjects are visible and which are canonized. As Ball and Bell (2013: 551) note in their recent and important discussion of women's production histories in the UK, traditional film and auteur theory that privilege creative individuals such as Charlie Kaufman and other practices of film history are deeply gendered practices, meaning that women's labour is often invisible within them.

The gendered subjects that appear in discourse and representations of screenwriting work are self-oriented and self-responsible subjects: the 'egotist', 'masochist' or 'supplicant'. They must work on themselves and 'stay on top of it' or they suffer the effects (economic, psychological, physical etc.), of what Caldwell aptly terms 'trade pain' (2008). These ideal subjects illuminate the neo-Foucauldian 'enterprising self' as Du Gay (1996) calls it, those individualized selves who must be proactive, must seek out good working relationships that afford a measure of professional autonomy. As so many screenwriting manuals also command, they must watch consecrated films like *Adaptation* (2002) for professional development purposes, in order to constantly hone and develop their craft. From this angle, industrial insecurity, self-blame and 'trade pain' are 'common sense' and are just the ways things are, to be dealt with via further introspective examination and fetishization of the profession. The deeper concern here, is that self-blame and individualization are *not* distributed evenly and that 'ideal', performative screenwriting subjects work repeatedly to gender screenwriting work and *also* to deny inequalities and exclusions in this field, to make these inequalities 'unspeakable' as Gill (2011) argues.

If screenwriting work itself is often prone to invisibility, then the gendered dimensions of that work are even more deeply obfuscated (as Ball and Bell, 2013, also make very clear). Consecrated and repeated representations of screenwriting work as masculine, heteronormative and self-oriented are central to the imaginary of the screenwriting profession and although representations of screenwriting on film are relatively rare, they may be periodically refreshed and reanimated.[19] Those that are visible and durable, such as *Adaptation* (2002), are crucial sites of analysis when combined with an understanding of the past and present socio-economy of screenwriting work. This film is repeatedly evoked as canonical, an important and enduring embodiment of the particular difficulties of the screenwriting profession. In *Adaptation*, and in the texts that surround it (whether screenwriting manuals such as Robert McKee's, or screenwriting course syllabi, or interviews with Kaufman himself), particular subject positions are routinely framed as routine and necessary for screenwriters. These positions may be contradictory, requiring both a Charlie and a Donald Kaufman to give them expression: egotism and self-doubt, dominance and masochism, mastery and supplication. But they are powerfully and repeatedly evoked in work-worlds in which very few people are able to make or sustain a living. What needs much more visibility and attention is that these work-worlds, and representations of them, are deeply exclusionary. They are largely white and male. They are heteronormative. They are not other-oriented. And they are not open to alternative voices, subjects or representations.

Notes

1 The twin brother character is fictional but is listed as the official co-writer of the film.
2 See also McKee (1998) for the original manual upon which this seminar is based.
3 See: http://www.boxofficemojo.com/movies/?id=adaptation.htm.
4 See: http://old.bfi.org.uk/sightandsound/feature/49593 for an excerpt of Bean's 2003 review.
5 See *Rotten Tomatoes*: http://www.rottentomatoes.com/m/1118700-adaptation/ and *Metacritic*: http://www.metacritic.com/movie/adaptation.
6 The importance of this text is something that theorists also acknowledge. The cover of Maras's (2009) important book on screenwriting theory and history features an image of the character of Charlie Kaufman from the film, hunched over his typewriter.
7 V.O. is the standard screenplay abbreviation for 'voiceover'.
8 Note in this wider empirical study, I analysed these subject positions within the discourse of interviews with contemporary screenwriters and within screenwriting manuals. See Conor (2014).
9 Deus ex machina translates from the Latin as 'god in the machine'. It is often used in literature and drama to connote the sudden introduction of a person or thing used to resolve a seemingly irresolvable problem. In the case of *Adaptation (1999)*, an alligator serves as the deus ex machina at the end of the film.
10 Taylor and Littleton (2012) also discuss deficit identities in their narrative-discursive analysis of creative biographies and identities.
11 Note that I use some of these data sets more fully in my book, *Screenwriting: Creative Labour and Professional Practice* (2014), and that this section is a summary of issues more fully addressed there, especially in article 5.
12 With a few exceptions (such as Bielby and Bielby, 1996; Bielby, 2009) screenwriting research has not been concerned with inequalities in screenwriting work. Wreyford's article in this collection and more broadly is a crucial corrective to this gap.
13 See Evans (2013) for a full summary and further indicative links, and see Waldman (2014) for a critique of the test in light of Sharma and Sender's 2014 analysis.
14 'Spec' is an abbreviation of 'speculative' and refers to the market for speculative scriptwriting and sales, as opposed to the commissioning of scripts by production companies or producers.
15 See Christopherson (2008) and Smith *et al.* (2013a) for very recent accounts from women filmmakers themselves.

The Sociological Review, 63:S1, pp. 113–127 (2015), DOI: 10.1111/1467-954X.12244

16 For more on homophilic and exclusionary production spaces in the UK such as the BBC in the 1970s, see, for example, Sutherland (2013).

17 Out of the 32 'how-to' screenwriting manuals analysed in the broader study, four were written by women.

18 I am drawing on Foucauldian approaches to neoliberalism especially the work of Rose (1989, 1992, 1998, 1999). For important examples of the application of this kind of framework to the analysis of postfeminist media culture and young women as self-responsible neo-liberal subjects, see Gill (2008), McRobbie (2009) and Scharff (2012).

19 In the recent film *The Rewrite* (2014), for example, Hugh Grant plays a once-famous and now washed-up screenwriter turned teacher whose problems with young women and alcohol are solved by heterosexual and age-appropriate love.

References

Adaptation, (2002), Screenplay, written by C. Kaufman and D. Kaufman, directed by S. Jonze, USA: Good Machine, Intermedia, Propaganda Films, Saturn Films.

Allen, K., (2013), '"What do you need to make it as a woman in this industry? Balls!" Work placements, gender and the cultural industries', in D. Ashton and C. Noonan (eds), *Cultural Work and Higher Education*, 232–253, London: Palgrave Macmillan.

Ball, V. and Bell, M., (2013), 'Working women, women's work: production, history, gender', *Journal of British Cinema and Television*, 10 (3): 547–562.

Banks, M. and Milestone, K., (2011), 'Individualization, gender and cultural work', *Gender, Work and Organisation*, 18 (1): 73–89.

Barton Fink, (1991), *Film*, written by J. Coen and E. Coen, directed by J. Coen, USA: Circle Films, Working Title Films.

Bean, R., (2003), 'Sight and Sound's films of the decade: Adaptation', *Sight and Sound*, available at: http://old.bfi.org.uk/sightandsound/feature/49593.

Being John Malkovich, (2000), Screenplay, written by C. Kaufman, directed by S. Jonze, USA: Astralwerks, Gramercy Pictures, Propaganda Films, Single Cell Pictures.

Bielby, D., (2009), 'Gender inequality in culture industries: women and men writers in film and television', *Sociologie du Travail*, 51 (2): 237–252.

Bielby, W. and Bielby, D., (1996), 'Women and men in film: gender inequality among writers in a culture industry', *Gender and Society*, 10 (3): 248–270.

British Film Institute, (2013), '*Succes de plume?* Female screenwriters and directors of UK films, 2010–12', available at: http://www.bfi.org.uk/sites/bfi.org.uk/files/downloads/bfi-report-on-female-writers-and-directors-of-uk-films-2013-11.pdf.

Butler, J., (1990), *Gender Trouble: Feminism and the Subversion of Identity*, New York: Routledge.

Butler, J., (1993), *Bodies that Matter: On the Discursive Limits of Sex*, New York: Routledge.

Caldwell, J. T., (2008), *Production Culture: Industrial Reflexivity and Critical Practice in Film and Television*, Durham, NC: Duke University Press.

Christopherson, S., (2008), 'Beyond the self-expressive creative worker: an industry perspective on entertainment media', *Theory, Culture & Society*, 25 (7–8): 73–95.

Conor, B., (2014), *Screenwriting: Creative Labour and Professional Practice*, London: Routledge.

Coutanche, M. and Davis, C., (2013), '2012 report on Canadian screenwriters', 15 May, available at: http://www.ryersonrta.com/wp-content/uploads/2013/05/2012-REPORT-ON-CANADIAN-SCREENWRITERS.pdf.

Davis, M., (2012), 'A New Zealand problem or two', Wellywood Woman blog, 6 November. Available at: http://wellywoodwoman.blogspot.co.nz/2012/11/a-problem-or-two.html.

Du Gay, P., (1996), *Consumption and Identity at Work*, Cambridge: Polity Press.

Evans, S., (2013), 'What the Bechdel Test is and isn't', The Black Board forum, 20 August, available at: http://theblackboard.blcklst.com/forums/topic/what-the-bechdel-test-is-and-isnt/.

Field, S., (1994), *Screenplay: The Foundations of Screenwriting*, New York: Dell Publishing Co.

Gill, R., (2002), 'Cool, creative and egalitarian? Exploring gender in project-based new media work in Europe', *Information, Communication and Society*, 5 (1): 70–89.

Gill, R., (2008), 'Culture and subjectivity in neoliberal and postfeminist times', *Subjectivity*, 25 (1): 432–445.

Gill, R., (2011), 'Sexism reloaded, or, it's time to get angry again!', *Feminist Media Studies*, 11 (1): 61–71.

Gill, R. and Scharff, C., (2011), 'Introduction', in R. Gill and C. Scharff (eds), *New Femininities: Postfeminism, Neoliberalism and Subjectivity*, 1–17, London: Palgrave Macmillan.

Henderson, F., (2001), 'The culture behind closed doors: issues of gender and race in the writer's room', *Cinema Journal*, 50 (2): 145–152.

Kaufman, C., (2000), *Being John Malkovich*, London: Faber and Faber.

Lauzen, M., (2012a), 'The celluloid ceiling: behind-the-scenes film employment of women in the top 250 films of 2012', available at: http://womenintvfilm.sdsu.edu/research.html.

Lauzen, M., (2012b), 'It's a man's (celluloid) world: on-screen representations of female characters in the top 100 films of 2011', available at: http://womenintvfilm.sdsu.edu/research.html.

MacDonald, I. W., (2004), 'The presentation of the screen idea in narrative film-making', unpublished dissertation, Leeds Metropolitan University.

Mahar, K., (2001), 'True womanhood in Hollywood: gendered business strategies and the rise and fall of the woman filmmaker, 1896–1928', *Enterprise & Society*, 2 (1): 72–110.

Maras, S., (2009), *Screenwriting: History, Theory and Practice*, London: Wallflower Press.

McKee, R., (1998), *Story: Substance, Structure, Style and the Principles of Screenwriting*, London: Methuen.

McRobbie, A., (2005), *The Uses of Cultural Studies*, London: Sage.

McRobbie, A., (2009), *The Aftermath of Feminism: Gender, Culture and Social Change*, London: Sage.

Nixon, S., (2003), *Advertising Cultures: Gender, Commerce, Creativity*, London: Sage.

Nixon, S. and Crewe, B., (2004), 'Pleasure at work? Gender, consumption and work-based identities in the creative industries', *Consumption, Markets and Culture*, 7 (2): 129–147.

Orozco, S., (2013), 'Gender as represented in spec script sales', *Go into the Story*, available at: http://gointothestory.blcklst.com/2013/06/gender-as-represented-in-spec-script-sales.html (accessed 21 August 2013).

Proctor-Thomson, S., (2013), 'Gender disruptions in the digital industries?' *Culture and Organization*, 19 (2): 85–104.

The Rewrite, (2014), Film, written by M. Lawrence, directed by M. Lawrence, Castle Rock Entertainment.

Rose, N., (1989), *Governing the Soul: The Shaping of the Private Self*, London: Routledge.

Rose, N., (1992), 'Governing the enterprising self', in P. Heelas and P. Morris (eds), *The Values of the Enterprise Culture: The Moral Debate*, 141–164, London: Routledge.

Rose, N., (1998), *Inventing our Selves: Psychology, Power and Personhood*, Cambridge: Cambridge University Press.

Rose, N., (1999), *Powers of Freedom: Reframing Political Thought*, Cambridge: Cambridge University Press.

Scharff, C., (2012), *Repudiating Feminism*, Farnham: Ashgate.

Screen Australia, (2013), 'Number and proportion of male and female producers, directors and writers of Australian feature films, 1970–2011', available at: http://www.screenaustralia.gov.au/research/statistics/employmentfeaturefilmmakers.aspx

Sharma, V. and Sender, H., (2014), 'Hollywood movies with strong female roles make more money', *Vocativ*, 2 January, available at: http://www.vocativ.com/01-2014/hollywood-movies-strong-female-roles-make-money/.

Skillset, (2009), 'Skillset employment census 2009', available at: http://www.skillset.org/research/activity/census/article_7569_1.asp

Skillset, (2012), 'Skillset employment census 2012', available at: http://www.creativeskillset.org/research/activity/census/article_9235_1.asp

The Sociological Review, 63:S1, pp. 113–127 (2015), DOI: 10.1111/1467-954X.12244

Smith, S., Choeiti, M. and Pieper, K., (2013a), 'Exploring the barriers and opportunities for women filmmakers', Sundance Institute and Women in Film Los Angeles, available at: http://www.sundance.org/pdf/press-releases/Exploring-The-Barriers.pdf .

Smith, S., Choeiti, M., Prescott, A., and Pieper, K., (2013b), 'Gender roles and occupations: a look at character attributes and job-related aspirations in film and television', Geena Davis Institute on Gender in Media, available at: http://www.seejane.org/downloads/key-findings-gender-roles-2013.pdf

Sutherland, H., (2013), '"Trousered" and "sexless" at the BBC: women light entertainment makers in the 1970s and 1980s', *Journal of British Film and Television*, 10 (3): 650–663.

Taylor, S., (2011), 'Negotiating oppositions and uncertainties: gendered conflicts in creative identity work', *Feminism and Psychology*, 21 (3): 354–371.

Taylor, S. and Littleton, K., (2012), *Contemporary Identities of Creativity and Creative Work*, Farnham: Ashgate.

Taylor, S. and Reynolds, J., (2005), 'Narrating singleness: life stories and deficit identities', *Narrative Inquiry*, 15 (2): 197–215.

UK Film Council, (2006), 'Scoping study into the lack of women screenwriters in the UK', report prepared by Institute for Employment Studies, University of Sussex, available at: http://www.ukfilmcouncil.org.uk/media/pdf/4/r/0415womenscreen_-_FINAL_09.06.06.pdf

UK Film Council, (2007), 'Writing British films: who writes British films and how they are recruited', available at: http://www.ukfilmcouncil.org.uk/media/pdf/5/r/RHUL_June_27_2007_-_Final_for_Cheltenham.pdf

Waldman, K., (2014), 'The Bechdel Test sets the bar too low: let's write a new one', *Slate*, available at: http://www.slate.com/blogs/xx_factor/2014/01/07/the_bechdel_test_needs_an_update_we_ve_set_the_bar_for_female_representation.html

Writers Guild of America West, (2011), 'Recession and regression: the 2011 Hollywood writers report', available at: http://www.wga.org/uploadedFiles/who_we_are/hwr11execsum.pdf

Writers Guild of America West, (2013), 'WGAW 2013 TV staffing brief', available at: http://www.wga.org/uploadedFiles/who_we_are/tvstaffingbrief2013.pdf

The Sociological Review, 63:S1, pp. 113–127 (2015), DOI: 10.1111/1467-954X.12244
© 2015 The Author. Editorial organisation © 2015 The Editorial Board of the Sociological Review

Genre anxiety: women travel writers' experience of work

Ana Alacovska

Abstract: This article explores how the concept of genre can enrich our understanding of gender inequality in media industries. All media work takes place within genre-specific production worlds, which seem to be gender-segregated. By examining the gendered and gendering ideology of genres, an outcome of genre-gender discursive, historical and cultural crossover, we obtain a holistic view of the complexities of the psycho-biographical gender dynamics of media work. To this end, I trace the ways in which the andocentric genre of travel writing (a genre based on a masculine ideology) causes professional anxiety and constrains female travel writers' biographical identity work. By treating genres as mediators of work experiences and practices, I elucidate how contemporary female travel writers experience and cope with genre-induced anxiety.

Keywords: genre, gender inequality, biography, travel writing, media industries

Introduction

In this article, I am interested in exploring what the concept of *genre* could offer our understanding of gender in media work. How, if at all, can the concept of genre enrich the discussion of gender inequality in media industries? I will here elucidate the importance of genre and how it might help theorize persistent inequalities.

Despite the celebration of work in media industries as empowering, liberating and self-realizing, it has been found to be profoundly risky, insecure and taxing (Ross, 2003; Ursell, 2000). Hesmondhalgh and Baker (2011) documented the effects of working conditions (including project-by-project work, irregular employment, dismal pay, unpaid overtime and the internship system) on media workers' emotional and subjective experiences of work. They conclude that precarious systemic conditions heighten anxiety and stress. Gill (2002) and McRobbie (1998) contend that these structural conditions have been particularly disadvantageous to women, who are normatively expected to juggle non-negotiable

The Sociological Review, 63:S1, pp. 128–143 (2015), DOI: 10.1111/1467-954X.12246

family obligations with onerous career demands for unpaid labour, long working hours, self-promotion and intense networking.

Yet, such occupational conditions and the ensuing experiences of work, although perhaps more pronounced in media industries, are by no means specific to them. Kunda and Barley (2004) studying engineering contractors' work experiences in the Silicon Valley, conclude that the sense of risk, alienation, casualization and gender disqualification, is 'universal' to all 'itinerant professionalism' – temporary or intermittent knowledge-based jobs which are the mainstay of the 'knowledge economy'. Similarly, Gill (2009) reveals the precariousness of academic work and points to gender imbalances stemming from systemic changes: the neo-liberal reorganization of universities, the introduction of performance measurement audit systems, and de-unionization.

What, then, is 'particular' to media work? What may be specific to gender inequality in media industries? Media work occurs within and through genres because media industries produce, distribute and promote textual products categorized in genres for easier and more efficient management and marketing (Jensen, 1984; Negus, 1999). For Jensen (1984: 111), the cultural producers' experiences, beliefs and values are 'evidenced and enshrined in the cultural material', most notably, the semiotic and textual nature of genres. Every media worker operates and acts 'appropriately' in 'genre-specific worlds' because every genre has 'its own characteristic goals and values, costs and budgets and type of audience appeal', to which producers make 'big emotional' and 'professional investments' (Tunstall, 1993: 201–202). Media work is thus genre-related work. Arguing for the specificity of media production, Born (2010: 192) called for an empirical focus on 'genre-specific professional cultures', and Hesmondhalgh and Baker (2011: 91) contended that creative work can only be observed by going '*within* particular genre cultures'.

In this chapter I seek to embed media work in the gendered and gendering ideology of genres. I examine how genres influence professional identities and delineate appropriate gender conduct by empirically exploring the ways in which female writers draw upon the gendered resources inherent in a masculine genre when accounting for their work experiences and biographical standing.

Genres have already been theorized as not only 'systems of expectations' (Neale, 1990: 46) but also ideologically laden 'social contracts' (Jameson, 2006: 92) that mediate and frame the relationship between industries, texts and audiences. However, the links between texts and audiences have been soundly explored at the expense of the relationship between genres and actual producers. Reception studies of 'gendered genres' such as romances (Radway, 1984) and television melodramas (Ang, 1985) show the gendering effect of such 'women's genres', or what Kuhn (1984: 18) calls 'gynocentric genres', over female emancipation, education or imagination.

Simultaneously, 'women's genres' have been critiqued by feminist scholars for their ideological, 'oppressive' and 'subjectifying' 'performative' power to construct and foster 'a normative femininity' (Ferguson, 1983; Gough-Yates, 2003; McRobbie, 1996). Intrigued by the effectiveness of the romance she detects in

The Sociological Review, 63:S1, pp. 128–143 (2015), DOI: 10.1111/1467-954X.12246

actual reading practices, Radway quips that romance writers must have understood 'that the goal and raison d'être of the genre is its actual, though perhaps temporary effect on readers' (1984: 70). But what about a genre's 'actual' effect on 'actual' producers who act with and upon such effectiveness to inspire and emancipate, or perhaps even, subdue their readers? There is a rarely challenged and entrenched blindspot here because genres are first and foremost categories of 'labour and production' and only then of reception (Ricoeur, 1981: 136), even if authors themselves are the first ideal recipients of the genre (Macherey, 1978: 69). Genres affect producers as much as recipients. Yet very few studies recognize the performative power of genres over producers to act appropriately, adopt 'fitting' subject positions, and forge meaningful rapport with their own work. By implication, sparse attention is paid to how genres are brought to bear on and are mobilized in producer daily practice, as well as the ways in which genres constitute creative biographical selves and experiences of work (Bruun, 2010; Dornfeld, 1998).

This chapter therefore situates media workers' biographical selves and work experiences within genre-specific worlds. This seems all the more important when discussing gender imbalances because genres are ideologically gendered and exercise a gendering influence by providing culturally sanctioned codes for normatively appropriate femininity/masculinity (Derrida, 1980). Indeed, 'genres are built on premises about gender': genres both embody and fuel ideologically constructed gender identities (Gerhart, 1992: 189–190). By going 'inside' the 'andocentric' genre of travel writing (Wolff, 1993), I argue that a female worker's experience of gender inequality in media work, in addition to being 'an effect' of industrial working conditions, is a direct function of the discursively, culturally, historically and ideologically gendered and gendering logic of the genre in which she is professionally immersed and with which she identifies. I thus emphasize the salience of attending to *the effectiveness of genres* in relation to workers' sense of professionalism and career progress, as well as experiences of gender bias.

Gender-segregated genre worlds: gender, genre and media work

The junction between gender and genre in creative occupations has been well established, as I show below. The strength of this correlation is strong enough to warrant the talk of gender-segregated 'genre-specific worlds' (Tunstall, 1993). Gender segregation appears to parallel genre stratification. Typically, such parallelism is explained away with Bourdieusian-type 'homologies', a structural correspondence between consumption and production (Bourdieu, 1996). Genres with predominantly female audience are populated with women producers, and vice versa – genres popular with men are male-dominated. Thus, gender affiliation implies gendered occupational and genre association. Beyond such 'mirroring' homologies, which ultimately posit an essentializing, natural and commercially profitable homogeneity of female and male producing/consuming cultures, *how* and *why* such a gender-genre junction occurs or what types of occupational gendered subject positions genres could plausibly be expected to afford is largely left unexamined.

Tunstall finds that the experience of the female workers he studied at the BBC 'differed quite sharply between different genres' (1993: 178) with women encountering more derision, disrespect and entry barriers in the male genres of light entertainment, sports, news and current affairs than in children's programming, drama and documentary. Clawson (1999: 99) established that women musicians are both a 'numerical minority and 'symbolic anomaly' in the traditionally 'masculine genre' of rock (see also Schippers, 2002). In a large-scale study of contemporary Nigerian novel publishing, Griswold (2000) finds a statistical gender bias in favour of male authors for the entire genre of the novel, but especially in the sub-genres popular with male readership such as 'intellectual' and 'war' novels. Although Cantor (1971/1988: xviii) notices an increase in women TV producers in Hollywood in the mid-1980s, compared to the late 1960s, she finds that women are predominantly concentrated in genres with a female audience appeal such as domestic and situation comedies starring female actors. Lauzen (2013) finds that in the US top-grossing 250 films in 2012, women were disproportionally under-represented in creative and decision-making roles, faring worst in the male genres of action, horror and sci-fi. Gough-Yates (2003) and Ferguson (1983) describe a female occupational concentration in 'women's genres' such as 'women's magazines' in which editors, journalists and producers self-promote via claims to 'personify' and 'embody' the lifestyle and taste of young female readers.

The most significant work to argue that the occupational worlds surrounding specific genres are gendered, involving gender struggles for occupational genre predominance, is Tuchman's (1989) study of 19th-century English novel publishing. Through archival data, Tuchman meticulously documents that novel-writing was 'a female-dominated white-collar occupation' (1989: 5) centred on the sub-genre of romance that has been 'invaded' and 'redefined' by men predominantly because of masculine managerial and ownership control over major literary and publishing institutions. Other factors were also involved, including compulsory education, cheaper printing technologies, and international copyright protection. Yet, besides such structural explanations for the masculinization of the profession, Tuchman emphasizes another 'ideological' factor, that is, 'An ideology about how the work of the novelist was to be done' (1989: 9). Genre ideology enshrines professional norms that guide the gendering of the occupation of novel writing. For example, a newly expounded genre ideology of realism (a serious depiction of dignified male action) discursively 'edged out' the prevailing romance ideology (an entertaining portrayal of female sentiments) and so made 'writing [realist] novels seem an important enough activity to engage the best, the brightest, and the most talented men' (1989: 10). Tuchman is loyal to the production-of-culture 'desanctification' of creative work 'as just another white-collar job', so fails to elaborate further on the genre's (ideological) influence on the professional standing and self-understanding of 'edged out' female writers. Genres are not merely shaped by social and institutional determinisms, they

The Sociological Review, 63:S1, pp. 128–143 (2015), DOI: 10.1111/1467-954X.12246   131

'carry with them particular implications for social life' (Alexander and Smith, 2006: 146).

For Jameson (2006) and Macherey (1978), genres are not only reflective of so-cietal and historical conditions, but they produce and shape historical and subjec-tive consciousness and 'literary productions'. Genres 'interpellate' the producing subject into action, and thus it is pertinent to talk about 'genre ideology' (Bee-bee, 1994). This is manifested as practice, in 'use-value'. Producers understand themselves and act with the ideological resources, scripts, repertoires and pro-scriptions inherent in genres (Beebee, 1994). Thus, the (ideologically pragmatic) research emphasis should be on a genre's effectiveness, that is 'what genres do' first for their writers and only afterwards for their readers and society (Devitt, 2000: 704).

Gendered genres are doubly *effective* because they furnish socio-culturally sanctioned normative models for a producer's professional as well as gender-appropriate behaviour and experience. Both genre and gender are 'performative' – sustained through and sustaining performance as cultural producers mobilize and deploy genre norms and gender codes (Butler, 1986: 525; Derrida, 1980: 74).

In emphasizing the effectiveness of (gendered) genres, my approach builds on DeNora's (2002: 20) productive sociological proposal to follow how cultural ma-terials and resources (in her case Beethoven's music, its sonic structures, rhythm or pace), 'get into action' (to drive the gendering of piano playing in eighteenth-century Vienna). I also follow Nixon (2003) who argued that certain discursive scripts and semiotic repertoires accrued around the 'masculine' figure of the artist and the romantic notion of creativity generate gender tensions within advertis-ing departments. These scripts impose male-centered criteria for the evaluation of professional success and work quality, and hence propel male advertising prac-titioners' careers.

It is too simplistic to blame gender inequalities and anxieties solely on insti-tutional structures, once we realize that creative occupations represent gendered 'genre-specific worlds'. A focus on the gendering capacity of genre allows for a nuanced reappraisal of work experiences. This appraisal becomes even more salient if one remembers the inherently ambiguous nature of genres within media industries. Genres ensure that creative work and expression are 'structurally' and 'autonomously' possible (Grindstaff, 2002). Yet managers also transform genres into 'necessity in the workplace' (Ryan, 1991: 172), as a means by which they legitimize pressure and justify a castigation system. By examining the formative and structuring ideology of genres, we can hope to understand the complexities of the psycho-biographical gender dynamics of media work.

Some scholars (Adkins, 2013; Gill, 2011; Taylor and Littleton, 2006) recently proposed a focus on 'biographies' in the study of creative labour. To them, media workers' biographies are far more complex and richer than the notion of 'career' permits, owing to its accent on progression. This proposal is especially propi-tious because media workers' biographies doubly evoke genre, as constituents of individual identity, and of professional identity. The proponents of narrative (biographical) identity had argued that human lives are discursively constructed

The Sociological Review, 63:S1, pp. 128–143 (2015), DOI: 10.1111/1467-954X.12246

via genres because they provide the socio-cultural margin for the thinkable and the appropriate by furnishing the resources upon which people draw in identity work. Individual lives are *embedded* in genres (MacIntyre, 2011: 212). Such insights are all the more pertinent when applied to media workers who professionally identify with and are existentially beholden to the economic vitality of specific (sub-)genres.

A gendered genre: the masculine ideology of travel writing

Travel writing is a profoundly unequal and exclusive genre, as it embodies the Western 'ideology of travel'. Historically, travel writing has been the preserve of the well-heeled, muscular and educated man. Most of 'officially written' Western history is the result of an 'itinerant masculinity' (Smith, 2001: 2) in which women were relegated to 'home', and men were entitled to venture further afield in search of food, territories, capital, or epiphany, dispatching 'home' initiatory tales of survival, conquests and encounters with the erotic and the marvellous (Pratt, 1992). Travel is 'genderised' and becomes 'a gendering activity' (Leed, 1991: 113). To Clifford travel exercises gender-based discrimination, as '"good travel" (heroic, educational, scientific, adventurous, and ennobling is something men (should) do' while women travel only 'as companions' or 'as exceptions' (1997: 31). The genre of travel writing imbibes the gender imbalances of travel and becomes a gendered and a gendering genre.

Women were excluded from travel and thus impeded from travel writing by their required, imposed and stabilized femininity. Men were the *spiritus movens* of the public sphere and were destined to 'mobility' – to act, to progress and to move (Leed, 1991). By contrast, owing to their avowed biological nature – the need for mating stability and safety – women were socially and culturally attached to the domestic sphere, or as Leed argues, were doomed to 'sessility' – passivity, inaction and immobility (1991: 171). As Janet Wolff observes, such an ideologically constructed 'woman's place' renders 'invisible, problematic, and in some cases impossible, women "out of place"' (1993: 234). Travel is hence constitutive of masculinity, and it is the very antithesis of femininity. By implication, the genre of travel writing becomes 'an andocentric' genre – a genre of male identification that disqualifies women from participation and even pathologizes femininity (Wolff, 1993: 227). Men have 'culturally granted masculine authority' to work in certain genres which erects 'implicit barriers' and causes 'anxieties' to female professional authorship in those genres (Friedman, 1986: 205). The genre of travel writing, the genre of action, adventure and virility, is germane to the masculine prerogatives of mobility, but it is improper to women's 'obligatory' sessility. It embodies the 'masculine' pretensions to rigour, 'objectivity' and 'truth' (Fussell, 1980: 203), but it is unfitting with the female 'unstructured', 'sensual' and 'fluid' nature (Gledhill, 1997).

I do not wish to imply that women do not travel and write, but that female writers had to cope with the gendering genre ideology and self-consciously reassert their right to the genre. Historical biographical studies of 'wayward women' abound – that is, women who travelled and wrote in spite of all 'the ideological gendering of travel (as male)' (Wolff, 1993: 235; see also Robinson, 1990). However, it is this gendering of the genre that 'both impedes female travel and renders problematic the self-definition of (and response to) women who *do* travel' (Wolff, 1993: 235). As the andocentric genre enshrines normative male experiences and conventions, women in those genres are forced to 'conform, masquerade or rebel discreetly' (Clifford, 1997: 32). As 'the idea of man as risk-taking traveller' underpins the genre, women writers are compelled to fight against the marginalization of their authorship as less audacious and unremarkable (Bassnett, 2002: 225). Hence, travel writing as a masculine genre influenced historically the ways female travel writers made sense of themselves and negotiated their 'proper' professional and gender identities.

Such genre-gender crossover is even further complicated when brought into the publishing context. The ideology of the gendered genre afforded publishers 'legitimate' managerial (gendering) strategies for excluding female writers and imposing conditions on authorship. Some of these strategies involved enforcement of 1) pseudonyms, as publishers compelled women writers to use male-resembling noms-de-plume to meet readers' expectations of a male genre (Catling, 2000: 100); 2) disclaimers, as publishers required female authors to renounce publicly their 'normalness' as women, wives or daughters, to signal aberrant authorship so as to prevent competition with men on the book market (Siegel, 2004); and 3) 'proper' topics, as publishers approved female travel authorship only on gender-appropriate themes such as foreign customs, manners, food and dress (Pratt, 1992: 103–105).

The major advantage of historical-biographical studies of travel writing (Fussell, 1980; Smith, 2001) is that they always relate authorial experience of work to the relatively autonomous patterns of ideologically laden meaning inherent in the genre of travel writing. Yet, the major drawback is that they are *post hoc* and *post mortem* studies. These are studies that focus on singular, unitary, extraordinary after-the-fact, retrospective careers of dead writers rather than on a work-in-progress, ambiguous and heterogeneous, prospective biographical trajectory of a cohort of living writers. Hence, 'the writers' in biographical studies are 'implied authors' – inferred from the writing itself and from written personal documents: diaries, letters, notebooks. By contrast, in creative labour studies, the biographies are inductively inferred from 'biographical talk', which involves a systematic collection of interview data, such as life stories/life histories of flesh-and-blood professional creative workers within specific institutional contexts (Taylor and Littleton, 2006). Because biographical (identity) work is genre-bound work – writers draw on genre resources in constructing their professional identities – I re-examine below the 'biographical talk' of contemporary female travel writers in reference to the gendering/gendered ideology of travel writing.

However, first it has to be mentioned that the genre of travel writing is not only ideologically gendered but it is also racialized and ethnicized. Genre and race, similarly to genre and gender, are inextricably connected, effectuating genre-specific racial exclusion and marginalization within corporate cultures (see

Negus, 1999 on rap). Genre classification echoes racial segregation (Downing and Husband, 2005; Miller, 2010), with racialized genres carrying implications for producers' professional standing. Post-colonial scholars have indeed long criticized the genre of travel writing for its white Western middle-class ideology that renders racial and ethnic authorship unbefitting (Pratt, 1992). Regrettably, in this chapter, I could not tackle racial and ethnic inequality in media work, due to considerations of space. Nevertheless, I believe that the analysis of the effectiveness of genres will prove as productive for the future investigation of the particularities of ethnic and racial inequalities in media work, as it was for gender inequalities.

Data collection: gathering 'biographical talk'

Of 65 qualitative interviews with travel guidebook writers and producers that I conducted from 2008 to 2011, only 21 were with female writers, aged 22–55. Being freelancers, loosely affiliated with a plethora of transnational publication outlets, but unattached to any particular organization, and being literally 'itinerant professionals', unattached to any particular geographical location, travel writers were scattered around the globe. This created the problem of 'dispersed producers' for the empirical study of cultural production (analogous to the problem of 'dispersed audiences' for the empirical study of media audiences; see Radway, 1988) – imposing financial and logistical constrains upon the research. I thus conducted face-to-face, semi-structured interviews in Scandinavia, the Balkans and California (where I resided for extended periods). The remaining interviews were conducted via Skype and telephone, as these technologies proved expedient for reaching out to 'dispersed producers'. In this chapter, I focus exclusively on interviews with women writers. Ten women volunteered for a conversation upon seeing my solicitation messages on a number of occupational listservs, and the rest were accrued by snowballing at a considerable effort. The interviews lasted from one to two hours. My informants self-defined as professional freelance travel writers on the basis of their earning or striving to earn the bulk of their livelihood from travel writing, predominantly in the (sub-)genres of guidebooks and their offshoots – newspaper, magazine and web-based travel articles. I elicited biographical life-stories, inquiring particularly about experiences of work and attitudes towards professionalism and production practice. I was not explicitly probing about gender inequality and, unprompted, my informants spontaneously broached gender-related issues, especially when being asked about the tribulations of professional travel writing. This indeed testifies to the salience of both genre and gender to the ways female writers themselves understood their professional standing.

Plus ça change: 'not for girls' genre

The biographical studies of historical female travel writers concur that all female authors display an intense feeling for genre. Owing to this feeling, the female biographical consciousness was permeated and inflected with 'the protocols of gender out of which, through which, and against which they negotiate their movement from sessility to mobility' (Smith, 2001: 11). The gendered ideology of travel inflicted a distressing feeling of inadequacy. My interviews confirm that even contemporary female travel writers felt obliged to justify their 'ungirly' choice of genre and thus their professional career. Female authors were torn between justifying a professionally sound yet socially 'unnatural' behaviour such as disavowing children, marriage or settlement. Ten women I interviewed were in an established couple relationship. Four were mothers, three of only one child. The rest disclosed information neither about relationships nor motherhood.

To earn a living wage through travel writing, which would warrant professional engagement with the genre, my informants reported the need to travel at least three to four cumulative months a year. Women voluntarily questioned their 'gender normalcy' amidst the requirements for frequent travel, which appeared to call into question their 'proper' role as mothers or daughters:

> Now, every time I come back home after a period abroad I fear meeting that elderly lady with trillions of grandchildren from next door scornfully mumbling 'Oh, coming again back from travel work'. A single late-thirties women with no kids that travels for work is certainly not seen as cool anymore. Now I am seen as something of an anomaly. [laughs]. A spinster!

> Travel writing is not for girls, no esteem, too many personal sacrifices and debt, my father an accomplished writer used to say to me. Even though or should I say maybe because of having a regular stream of gigs, I cannot keep a boyfriend for more than a year. And, when I do find a boyfriend then I dread becoming a mother and everything goes to hell again.

The interviews revealed an inverse relationship between a female writer's perception of professional success and satisfaction with personal and family life, almost as if professional success excluded the possibility of intimate happiness and settled life.

'A male bastion': a feeling of trespassing

There are more subtle ways in which the masculine genre exacerbated the female authors' feeling of inadequacy or, as one informant said, 'an anxious feeling of trespassing onto a male bastion'. Female writers confessed to a burdensome injunction of abiding by genre norms that were thoroughly at odds with what they as women 'can' or 'cannot do' while travelling. Critically avowed 'good' travel writing entailed production practices that were incommensurate with the sociocultural expectations of 'female propriety' (a moral injunction) and which demoralized the reasonable expectation of non-hostile work environments (safety). The slippage between moral propriety, safety and success in the genre was the source of severe angst.

According to literary critics, good travel writing of all sub-genres builds on an author's curiosity and openness for adventure and foreign cultures, *his* navigation of the unknown, the dangerous and the prohibited, and *his* intrepid preparedness to enter into doubtful relationships and conflicts (Fussell, 1980; Bassnett, 2002). Such appreciatively normative criticism of 'good travel writing' solidified further the gendered genre ideology and in turn threatened the professional integrity of female travel writers. Within the genre world, respect for etiquette, good manners, vigilance or caution were commonly regarded as *not* conducive to good travel writing yet they were thought indispensable for unescorted travel by women. Thus, female writers were caught in a double bind; if they were deferent to genre norms, they risked their safety; if they were observant of gender norms, they would fail professionally:

> What I find most troubling in travel writing is its cocky prerogatives: embracing danger and almost kissing strangers. Look at Bill Bryson, Chatwin or the regular contributors to National Geographic, they go in a dark basement and brew slivovitz, drink with random hosts, go in a pub, strike a conversation with a stranger who happens to be a farmer and shows them all the back of Australia in a jeep. These are adventures by all counts. Can I jump headlong into such adventures? Once I was on assignment in Italy and went on an important archaeological site. A young male archaeologist approached me and we had a pleasant conversation, and he inferred I would be curious about going some 40 meters underneath behind closed bars in a cave that used to be Nero's golden home and for decades closed for visitors. That would have been a perfect travel story. I wandered away letting a good story fly away. 'Do not earn yourself a rape, woman', my inner voice panicked. The more palpable danger of having the ceiling fall over my head because of the heavy traffic above the cave hardly did cross my mind [laughs].

As the above excerpt shows, gendered genre norms complied with the commonsensical 'rhetoric of peril' (Siegel, 2004: 55) through which women's travelling bodies are socially and culturally constructed as 'innately weak' (Siegel, 2004: 61). Yet they also clashed with the realities of travel that present actual perils to women writers and require urgent safety precautions. For female writers, the anxiety arose from the need to stay vigilantly alert to travel hazards, while simultaneously eschewing and embracing, if only through self-irony, the professionally crippling 'rhetoric of peril' that precludes 'perilous' story-worthy experiences to happen ('a good story' slips by). Female travel writer's historical biographies are infused with impending risks of rape, mugging, and sequestration (Holland and Huggan, 2000: 111–116).

All the women writers I interviewed displayed awareness that the genre norms and production practices of travel writing were in direct conflict with the cultural prescriptions of femininity, which thus incurred a troublesome necessity to manage the discrepancy between gender and professional identity that seems to downgrade female performance and undermine women's professional confidence. The author of the previous excerpt, after having let 'the real story' rush past, settled for a 'gender-appropriate', yet less prestigious, 'write up of ancient Italian cuisine'. Another confessed:

> They say a good travel writer talks with everyone about anything. As a women writer I cannot simply smile at strangers and be friendly so as to elicit interesting (please

do hear sellable) stories. How easy is it to mistake a genuine work practice for an open sexual come-on? The apocryphal 'getting under the skin of the place' is one thing, while getting under my skirt is quite another. I cannot be rowdy or conspicuous. I would call in trouble. I stay as unassuming and as self-effacing as possible. I listen and observe, and get along well with elderly people and women pushing strollers. But this is nowhere near a travel adventure that sells on the market.

Some informants reported being repeatedly harassed by 'venomous' male colleagues for not being able to uphold the genre's 'male' prerogatives and norms. Condescending peer-criticism and accusations of professional dilettantism levelled at female writers undermined their self-confidence and pushed them to reconsider their 'fitness' for the genre.

I was commissioned by a respectable guidebook publisher to overhaul the content of an old edition. Once the guidebook was out, the old writer started pestering me with harassing emails. He accused me of being a 'travel dilettante' who's afraid to engage with the place 'after dark', who doesn't know as well as him to indulge in 'jolly banter' with locals, who stays away from skirmishes, who thus writes 'womanly' prose as 'stale and boring as a bad toast'. After the fourth email I started really to question my fit for this genre.

Biographical deliberations of 'fitting' or not into this genre were all too common within the genre world. Specific topics, styles and sub-genres were considered a better 'fit for women' – fashion, spa, well-being or gastronomy travel – whereas adventure or discovery travel were associated with men and generally commanded higher prestige. The traditional, binaristic gendering of sub-genres is not difficult to infer here. The evaluative genre categorization is gendered: low-prestige genres are associated with women writers (and readers) and possess 'inherently feminizing' qualities – emotions, pleasures, customs; whereas the high-prestige (sub-)genres are the preserve of men and exude 'masculine values' – seriousness, bravery and thought (Gledhill, 1997: 349).

Such gender-genre crossover had distinct implications for commissioning and editorial practices, and consequently fuelled the sense of individual anxiety and inadequacy. Female writers felt continually ousted by 'masculinist editors' who feared that 'serious' assignments on 'physically' and 'mentally' more demanding destinations or adventures would be damaged in an aesthetic and economic sense if entrusted to women. Apocryphal stories about female writers' travel tribulations that brought publishing schedules to a halt gained currency within the genre world and constituted onerous 'industry lore' (Havens, 2007), legitimizing women's exclusion, as in the following example:

As a women writer specialising in adventure and Asia, I am constantly anxious. Neither adventure travel nor Asia is taken to be a fit for female writers. When I pitch editors they expect me to whine about a broken nail and untidy lipstick rather than write about white water kayaking or north face ice-climbing. When I bid for guidebook gigs on Asia editors talk me off as unsuitable for such a manly task ... There is this story about a poor woman working on a guidebook who barely escaped a rape, frightened she called the publisher back home and requested they send in a companion so she can

The Sociological Review, 63:S1, pp. 128–143 (2015), DOI: 10.1111/1467-954X.12246

finish the job unhindered and sane. The publisher hardly broke even on that edition as the incident drained money... Instead they will offer I write about food-foraging or fashion in taigas or pickled food. Sometimes I feel these choices are made on my behalf not by myself.

Being constantly penalized for their genre-specific inadequacy, female writers succumb to a sort of self-perpetuating angst with which they reinforce the gender stereotypes. For economic reasons, some writers were forced to cede to the gendering power of genres and grudgingly accept predetermined genre choices such as writing about fashion, cuisine or spa travel. Three interviewees contemplated or attempted exit from travel writing towards 'female' genres, most notably cookbooks and gardening books, which would eliminate the exasperating need to always reassert one's eligibility and promised a balance between a family life and a creative job.

Others devised elaborate strategies for playing with gender stereotypes to resist genre choices 'being made on their behalf' and thus challenge the essentialisms inherent in gender-genre crossover. These strategies included 'cross-dressing' (dressing like a man) or hiring a local male companion. More significantly, three writers confided making an occasional use of cross-gender pseudonyms, and two of gender-predicting algorithms, to conceal their gender identity and increase the chances of being commissioned. One writer specialising in alpinism and mountain travel intimated her use of gender algorithms:

> Travel writing is virile and muscular. My readers are usually men. In the write-up of my articles I regularly use Gender Genie, an online tool that identifies an author's sex based on her writing. I mainly run my articles through to strengthen the robustness of my prose and gauge the use of language and approximate a manly tone.

Notwithstanding the scientific accuracy or reliability of gender-predicting algorithms or the frequency of cross-dressing and pseudonyms (more research is needed), the sheer 'occasional' use of them to attain or masquerade a genre-proper gender voice and production practice testifies to the obligation put on women to 'unsex' their expression and accept the genre on men's terms in order to sustain a professional career.

Conclusion

In this chapter, I pointed out that women travel writers are entrapped in a double bind: should they admit to the dangers of travel, harassment or insecurity, they would face charges of professional impropriety for work in a genre critically acclaimed for its masculine values of adventure, peril and skirmishes. Conflicts between gender norms and genre characteristics, deemed expedient for professional success, resulted in female workers' anxiety and feelings of inadequacy, which predictably devalued their work and crippled their personal advancement. Following Taylor and Littleton (2006: 33), one may say that the biographical identities of professionally successful female travel writers were 'troubled' because the genre ('the available narrative resources') and dominant gender norms ('safety' and 'closure') were difficult to harmonize in practice. As a consequence, women writers felt a constant need to reassert and restate their 'proper' professional and gender identity.

In the biographical accounts by male travel writers (which I did not discuss here), gender and consequently genre anxiety, did not surface. This is not to claim that the gendered/gendering ideology of travel writing has a zero impact on the ways men experience genre-specific professional success, but that men's experience of 'genre anxiety' are different in intensity, degree and shape from that of women. As I was not explicitly probing about gender, 'genre anxiety' remained concealed in men's biographical accounts.

The limited sample of interviewees in my study does not allow for generalization. However, I do believe that the in-depth interviewing, coupled with the analysis of genre ideology, complexifies the inquiry into gender inequality in creative labour. In emphasizing the genre-induced anxiety of travel writers, I suggest that travel writing is not merely reflective of gender inequalities, but it constitutes them. Genres possess the capacity to influence the ways female writers think, act and struggle for their own professional standing and career. It is impoverishing to seek occupational homologies between genres and genders as a function of audience appeal or institutional impositions without an explanation of *why* and *how* crossover happens. It is potentially more nuanced to see genres as ideological formations that affect the biographical selves and sense of success of actors who professionally inhabit genre-specific worlds. The alertness to a genre's effectiveness allows for familiar gender tribulations (negotiating motherhood or marriage and balancing household duties with professional work) to be seen in their genre-related specificity. Common gender tribulations acquire a particular shape and dynamism as they refract through the genres, which female producers are dependent on. These challenges take the form of anxiety of authorship, angst of gender-appropriate topics, styles and expression, and a sense of distress in relation to morality, safety and professional accomplishments. My argument is that the gender inequality in creative work cannot be comprehensively understood without a consideration of the role of genre in co-constituting gender tensions and anxieties. An overwhelming emphasis on genres obscures macro processes and institutional structures, but it allows the gendered genre-specificity of creative/media work to become obvious, especially as the publishing institutions themselves are not immune to the genre's effectiveness. The privileging of genres renders visible some less-researched coping strategies against institutionally endorsed genre-specific gender discrimination, such as gender-masquerading practices – the use of pseudonyms (see also Tuchman, 1989) and the use of gender-predicting algorithms – to simulate gender-proper expression or tone, and thus enhance employability and saleability. These practices require further investigation.

The privileging of the active (pragmatic-ideological) role of genres in the making of professional biographical selves evinces a more ambitious attempt at a rapprochement between the humanities – untestable and idiosyncratic genre interpretation – and the social sciences – replicable and generalizable

The Sociological Review, 63:S1, pp. 128–143 (2015), DOI: 10.1111/1467-954X.12246

insights into institutional structures, professions and work. In the name of this rapprochement, I hope that future studies will empirically test and validate the structuring power of the crossover between genre and gender within other genre-specific production worlds, of both andocentric and gynocentric kinds. For a holistic and a nuanced understanding of inequality in media work, greater attention should be paid to genres as mediators of working experiences and practices.

References

Adkins, L., (2013), 'Creativity, biography and the time of individualization', in M. Banks, R. Gill and S. Taylor (eds), *Theorizing Cultural Work: Labour, Continuity and Change in the Cultural and Creative Industries*, 149–160, London: Routledge.

Alexander, J. and Smith, P., (2006), 'The strong program in cultural sociology: elements of a structural hermeneutics', in H. Turner (ed.), *Handbook of Sociological Theory*, 135–150, London: Springer.

Ang, I., (1985), *Watching Dallas: Soap Opera and the Melodramatic Imagination*, London: Methuen.

Bassnett, S., (2002), 'Travel writing and gender', in P. Hulme and T. Youngs (eds), *Travel Writing*, 225–241, Cambridge: Cambridge University Press.

Beebee, T., (1994), *The Ideology of Genre*, University Park, PA: Pennsylvania State University Press.

Born, G., (2010), 'The social and the aesthetic: for a post-Bourdieuian theory of cultural production', *Cultural Sociology*, 4 (2): 171–208.

Bourdieu, P., (1996), *The Rules of Art*, Palo Alto, CA: Stanford University Press.

Bruun, H., (2010), 'Genre and interpretation in production: a theoretical approach', *Media, Culture and Society*, 32 (5): 723–737.

Butler, J., (1986), 'Performative arts and gender constitution: an essay in phenomenology and feminist theory', *Theatre Journal*, 40 (4): 519–531.

Cantor, M., (1971/1988), *The Hollywood TV Producer: His Work and his Audience*, New Brunswick: Basic Books.

Catling, J., (2000), *A History of Women's Writing in Germany, Austria and Switzerland*, Cambridge: Cambridge University Press.

Clawson, M. A., (1999), 'Masculinity and skill acquisition in the adolescent rock band', *Popular Music*, 18 (1): 99–114.

Clifford, J., (1997), *Routes: Travel and Translation in the Late Twentieth Century*, Boston, MA: Harvard University Press.

DeNora, T., (2002), 'Music into action: performing gender on the Viennese concert stage, 1790–1810', *Poetics*, 30: 19–33.

Derrida, J., (1980), 'The law of genre', *Critical Inquiry*, 7 (1): 55–81.

Devitt, A., (2000), 'Integrating rhetorical and literary genre theory', *College English*, 62 (6): 696–717.

Dornfeld, B., (1998), *Producing Public Television, Producing Public Culture*, Princeton, NJ: Princeton University Press.

Downing, J. and Husband, C., (2005), *Representing Race*, London: Sage.

Ferguson, M., (1983), *Forever Feminine: Women's Magazines and the Cult of Femininity*, London: Heinemann.

Friedman, S., (1986), 'Gender and genre anxiety: Elizabeth Barrett Browning and H.D. as epic poets', *Tulsa Studies in Women's Literature*, 5 (2): 203–228.

Fussell, P., (1980), *Abroad: British Literary Travelling between the Wars*, Oxford: Oxford University Press.

Gerhart, M., (1992), *Genre Choices, Gender Questions*, Oklahoma: University of Oklahoma Press.

Gill, R., (2002), 'Cool, creative and egalitarian: Exploring gender in project-based new media work in Europe', *Information, Communication & Society*, 5 (1): 70–89.

Gill, R., (2009), 'Breaking the silence: the hidden injuries of neo-liberal academia', in R. Flood and R. Gill (eds), *Secrecy and Silence in the Research Process: Feminist Reflections*, 228–244, London: Routledge.

Gill, R., (2011), 'Creative biographies in new media: social innovation in web work', in P. Jeffcutt and A. Pratt (eds), *Creativity and innovation and the cultural economy*, 1–20, London: Routledge.

Gledhill, C., (1997), 'Genre and gender: the case of soap opera', in S. Hall (ed.), *Representation: Cultural Representation and Signifying Practices*, 339–386, London: Sage.

Gough-Yates, A., (2003), *Understanding Women's Magazines: Publishing, Markets and Readership*, London: Routledge.

Grindstaff, L., (2002), *The Money Shot: Trash, Class and the Making of TV Talk Shows*, Chicago: University of Chicago Press.

Griswold, W., (2000), *Bearing Witness: Readers, Writers and the Novel in Nigeria*, Princeton, NJ: Princeton University Press.

Havens, T., (2007), 'Universal childhood: the global trade in children's television and changing ideals of childhood', *Global Media Journal* 6 (10), available at: http://lass.purduecal.edu/cca/gmj/sp07/gmj-sp07-havens.htm

Hesmondhalgh, D. and Baker, S., (2011), *Creative Labour: Media Work in Three Cultural Industries*, London: Routledge.

Holland, P. and Huggan, G., (2000), *Tourists with Typewriters: Critical Reflections on Contemporary Travel Writing*, Ann Arbor, MI: University of Michigan Press.

Jameson, F., (2006), 'Magical narratives: on the dialectical use of genre criticism', in *The Political Unconscious*, 103–150, New York: Routledge.

Jensen, J., (1984), 'An interpretive approach to culture production', in D. R. Willard and B. Watkins (eds), *Interpreting Television: Current Research Perspectives*, 98–118, Beverly Hills, CA: Sage Publications.

Kuhn, A., (1984), 'Women's genres', *Screen*, 25 (1): 18–29.

Kunda, G. and Barley, S., (2004), *Gurus, Hired Guns, and Warm Bodies: Itinerant Experts in a Knowledge Economy*, Princeton, NJ: Princeton University Press.

Lauzen, M., (2013), *The Celluloid Ceiling: Behind-the-scenes Employment of Women on the Top 250 Films of 2012*, San Diego: Diego State University, available at: http://womenintvfilm.sdsu.edu/files/2012_Celluloid_Ceiling_Exec_Summ.pdf

Leed, E., (1991), *The Mind of the Traveller: From Gilgamesh to Global Tourism*, New York: Basic Books.

Macherey, P., (1978), *A Theory of Literary Production*, London: Routledge.

MacIntyre, A., (2011), *After Virtue*, London: Bloomsbury.

McRobbie, A., (1996), '"More"! New sexualities in girl's and women's magazines', in J. Curran, D. Morley and V. Walkerdine (eds), *Cultural Studies and Communications*, 172–194, London: Arnold.

McRobbie, A., (1998), *British Fashion Design: Rag Trade or Image Industry?*, London: Routledge.

Miller, H. K., (2010), *Segregating Sound: Inventing Pop and Folk Music in the Age of Jim Crow*, Durham, NC: Duke University Press.

Neale, S., (1990), 'Questions of genre', *Screen*, 31 (1): 45–66.

Negus, K., (1999), 'The music business and rap', *Cultural Studies*, 13 (3): 488–508.

Nixon, S., (2003), *Advertising Cultures: Gender, Commerce, Creativity*, London: Sage.

Pratt, M. L., (1992), *Imperial Eyes: Travel Writing and Transculturation*, London: Routledge.

Radway, J., (1984), *Reading the Romance: Women, Patriarchy and Popular Literature*, Chapel Hill, NC: University of North Carolina Press.

Radway, J., (1988), 'Reception study: ethnography and the problems of dispersed audiences and nomadic subjects', *Cultural Studies*, 2 (3): 358–376.

Ricoeur, P., (1981), 'The hermeneutical function of distanciation', in B. J. Thompson (ed.), *Hermeneutics and Social Sciences: Essays on Language, Action and Interpretation*, 131–144, Cambridge: Cambridge University Press.

Robinson, J. (1990), *Wayward Women: A Guide to Women Travellers*, Oxford: Oxford University Press.

Ross, A., (2003), *No-collar: The Human Workplace and its Hidden Costs*, Philadelphia: Temple University Press.

The Sociological Review, 63:S1, pp. 128–143 (2015), DOI: 10.1111/1467-954X.12246

Ryan, B., (1991), *Making Capital from Culture: The Corporate Form of Capitalist Cultural Production*. Berlin: Walter de Gruyter.

Schippers, M., (2002), *Rocking Out of the Box: Gender Maneuvering in Alternative Hard Rock*, New Brunswick, NJ: Rutgers University Press.

Siegel, K., (2004), 'Women's travel and the rhetoric of peril', in K. Siegel (ed.), *Gender, Genre and Identity in Women's Travel Writing*, 55–72, London: Peter Lang.

Smith, S., (2001), *Moving Lives: Twentieth-century Women's Travel Writing*, Minneapolis: Minnesota University Press.

Taylor, S. and Littleton, K., (2006), 'Biographies in talk: a narrative-discursive research approach', *Qualitative Sociology Review*, 2 (1): 22–38.

Tuchman, G., (1989), *Edging Women Out: Victorian Novelists, Publishers, and Social Change*, New York: Routledge.

Tunstall, J., (1993), *Television Producers*, London: Routledge.

Ursell, G., (2000), 'Television production: issues of exploitation, commodification and subjectivity in UK television labour market', *Media, Culture and Society*, 22 (6): 805–825.

Wolff, J., (1993), 'On the road again: metaphors of travel in cultural criticism', *Cultural Studies*, 7 (2): 225–241.

The Sociological Review, 63:S1, pp. 128–143 (2015), DOI: 10.1111/1467-954X.12246
© 2015 The Author. Editorial organisation © 2015 The Editorial Board of the Sociological Review

The heroic body: toughness, femininity and the stunt double

Miranda J. Banks and Lauren Steimer

Abstract: This article explores the role of stunt women in film and television production, and considers their contribution to the construction of on-screen action heroines. Combining feminist theory with interviews with professional stunt women, the article illuminates stunt women's strategically hidden professional labour: on the set, on the screen, and in the popular press.

Keywords: stunting, film, television, bodies, screen heroines

Introduction

Nancy Thurston: These people have nobody to trust, and if they can't trust their stunt person, then we can't get them to do anything. They tell us their fears.

Maria Kelly: Yes, because a woman needs to know that another woman out there is going to be covering her ass for her (4 April 2004).

In 1996, Lucy Lawless, television's Xena, fell off a horse while rehearsing a skit for *The Tonight Show* and fractured her pelvis. News reports months later reassured readers that Lawless had returned to the set, but 'for a while doubles would handle her stunts' (Anonymous, 1996; Graham, 1997). The reports implied that Lawless performed her own stunt work, and it was only because she was injured that stunt doubles would take over. Yet stunt workers perform the vast majority of the action sequences on television and in film, including those in *Xena: Warrior Princess* (1995–2001), which concerned the exploits of a female warrior set on a path of redemption. While rarely discussed in the press, at *Xena* conventions the crew would explain how seven different women were needed to play the heroine: Lawless, one primary stunt double (Zoë Bell),[1] and five others who specialized in everything from horse riding, to flying stunts, to weapon skills, to a 'polite nudity' double. Each was hired to create the illusion that one character, played by the main actor, performs every action within the series. Thus, while the star plays the primary character, she does not commonly contribute to the most

The Sociological Review, 63:S1, pp. 144–157 (2015), DOI: 10.1111/1467-954X.12245
© 2015 The Authors. Editorial organisation © 2015 The Editorial Board of the Sociological Review. Published by John Wiley & Sons Ltd, 9600 Garsington Road, Oxford OX4 2DQ, UK and 350 Main Street, Malden, MA 02148, USA

physically demanding elements of body-spectacle that cement that character's status as an 'action' heroine. The corporeal contributions of the stunt double greatly inform the reception of the character, and the star, as dynamic and empowered. The production process seams actor to stuntwoman and the success of the final product depends on viewers seeing actor and stuntwoman as one: namely, the character. Editing creates this seamless transition from actor to stuntwoman to actor. The pro-filmic act of doubling, or 'covering', translates into a comparable erasure off-screen. The stuntwoman's body is diegetic (present in the narrative world) but her identity hides in plain sight between two cuts.

While the actor might be adored for her looks or her dramatic abilities, it is the stunt double's body, a body that seemingly jumps over fences, kicks a man across a room, and fights to the death with multiple opponents, that is integral to the visual pleasures derived from these visceral spectacles. But in the media's coverage of action-adventure programmes, it is the star, not the double who is celebrated as the vigorous, heroic performer. The subtle erasure of the stunt person, or the downplaying of her role in the creation of the heroine, is not unique to women. We believe stuntmen equally experience this same erasure. However, the processes of, and the logic behind, this erasure in both behind-the-scenes interactions as well as after-the-fact interpretations, call for a sex-specific analysis.

This article addresses gender disparity in the Hollywood stunt industry and the discursive erasure of stuntwomen's labour. This erasure is a process that is deeply rooted in the marketing of 'authentic' action stardom and perpetuated by female stars for whom stuntwomen-as-doubles risk their bodies and their lives. We provide a living history of women in the contemporary stunt industry. What little scholarly work there is on stuntwomen has not focused on issues of gender. Here, we seek to identify the processes and effects of the production and reception of the action heroine in relation to her stuntwomen.[2] We elaborate upon our research methodologies for this project, which include first-person interviews with stuntwomen as well as historical and contemporary periodical research on the star interviews and marketing campaigns that erase the stuntwoman from production. The history of the stunt industry is described in brief and the place of women in that history is addressed specifically, as we consider the work-life and career limitations of the modern stuntwoman. Lastly, this essay considers the erasure of the stuntwoman and her labour via media coverage of the female action star in film and television.

Methodology

While there is a substantial corpus of scholarship on stars and gendered structures of performance, studies of gender and creative labour have been few and far between until the publication of this anthology. Banks (2009) explores the gendered labour structures that inform creative labour in Hollywood. Her earlier study stressed the importance of collecting first-hand accounts from women working in the industry as a means to offset the misleading statistics on the status of female below-the-line labourers (2009: 87–90). Though this project was concerned with the 'women's work' of costume design, together we share this larger focus on the methodologies that scholars should employ when undertaking feminist production studies, namely harvesting information from practitioners and the pressing need for feminist approaches to 'explore and uncover' gender bias that affects below-the-line labourers (2009: 95–97).

Today there are over 200 professional stuntwomen working in Hollywood, yet the long history of their contributions to the film and television industry is barely acknowledged, let alone understood.[3] What we offer here is a study of the history of this simultaneous fascination with, and erasure of, the female stunt double in films and television programmes starring action heroines, as seen through articles in the popular press about the films or series, the star, or even the stuntwoman. The work for this article also involved personal interviews with women working as stunt performers in the film and television industries. Between 2003 and 2009 we spoke with members of the Stuntwomen's Association of Motion Pictures at an association meeting, and conducted individual interviews with stuntwomen Jeannine Epper, Shauna Duggins, Nancy Thurston, Maria Kelly and Zoë Bell. This research on women working in the contemporary stunt industry greatly informed our analysis of a type of hidden labour within the entertainment industry that is integral to the magic of the moving image.

This article is the product of shared interest in the living conditions of working women in film and television industries and a surplus of research on action stars and their doubles. As well as the interviews with stuntwomen both of us have conducted trade union policy and magazine research on stuntwomen and female action stars in the course of other writing projects and we conceive of this article as a locus of that scholarship on stunting, gender, industry, and labour. Banks' groundwork on stuntwomen in the popular press originated in interviews and archival research conducted at the Margaret Herrick Library and is historiographic in nature. Steimer's research focuses on contemporary stuntwomen and action actresses and requires regular reviewing of entertainment, fitness, 'women's' and fan magazines as publicity vehicles for action genre films and television shows with a female lead. We envision our periodical research as a necessary supplement to the knowledge acquired via our interviews. This essay integrates two distinct approaches as we study stunt women's labor: first, a direct study of their professional experiences through interviews, on-set observations, and reading of professional policies and contracts; and second, through close analysis of their representation in popular newspapers and magazines. It is by looking among, between, and across these primary and secondary materials that we find answers to some of these important questions. While crossing over these academic divides as we explore these media forms is theoretically and methodologically complicated, the challenges that it presents are worth the struggle. Because in answering these questions about how these disciplines converge through the study of gender and labour, we better understand the different voices

The Sociological Review, 63:S1, pp. 144–157 (2015), DOI: 10.1111/1467-954X.12245

that converge in the processes of production, distribution, and consumption of the particular texts.

A brief history of Hollywood stunting

The technical erasure of the double has been a part of motion picture history since its inception. In early American cinema (1895–1929), film directors discovered that creating exciting action sequences necessitated the use of stunt doubles, as actors' skills at stunt work were not always up to the needs of a sequence. Bean (2002: 407) provides a detailed analysis of the early actresses of adventure films who regularly, and often ignorantly, threw themselves in harm's way for the camera and for their film fans. Stunting grew as a more common profession in Hollywood during the studio era. But with the breakdown of the studio system in the 1960s, most stunt people began to 'work both cards', finding work both through the Screen Actors Guild (SAG) and the Screen Extras Guild (SEG) to make ends meet. As stuntman Loren Janes explained, by the 1960s, 'the new heads of the studios didn't know a stuntman from a grip' (Setlowe, 1996). It was at this point that the Stuntman's Association of Motion Pictures (SAMP) was formed.

By the end of the 1960s, stunt work was still considered men's work even though films and television series starred women in action-oriented roles. Men outnumbered women in the profession at a ratio of five-to-one, and many stuntmen were hired to double for women. SAMP's first meeting was held in a SAG boardroom and was attended by forty of the top stuntmen in Hollywood. No women were invited (Setlowe, 1996). The founders of SAMP established their group as a fraternal organization not open to women. The group looked after the interests of its members by providing a legitimate organization for directors and casting agents to contact when hiring for films or television programmes, and SAMP soon emerged as a huge force within the industry. As one casting director admitted without giving his name, '[stuntmen] run their own empire. It's the most incredible fraternity I've ever seen' (Robb, 1983).

During this time, women were also denied access to on-set leadership roles in their industry like that of stunt coordinator. The role of the stunt coordinator was established when film-makers needed to hire someone to organize sequences that necessitated the use of multiple stunt people. Stunt performers who find consistent work in the industry have historically moved up in the hierarchy of the stunt labour force from individual stunts, to 'utility' stunts,[4] to stunt doubling, to work as a stunt coordinator, and finally (for the rare few) to work as a second unit director. Often the stunt coordinator was chosen for the position because he doubled for the main actor – and was therefore centrally involved in most of the stunts within the film or television programme. Soon it became clear that stunt coordinators would hire their teams from within their own organization.[5] This practice was not just exclusive, it was discriminatory: stunt coordinators were almost all white men, and therefore hiring from within their organizations meant the exclusion of women and minority stunt people. Accounts from stuntwomen in our interviews do discuss cross-gender and cross-race stunting, although exact numbers are difficult to procure. While often if the central character was a woman or a minority – or both – the stunt double for that particular actor would be matched well (for example, African-American stuntwomen Peaches Jones and Jadie David doubled for Theresa Graves on ABC's 1974 policewoman series *Get Christie Love*). But the most common discrimination occurs with all of the secondary or utility stunt work – not in doubling for the star, but rather in action sequences with long shots or second unit stunt work, where multiple stunt people perform or drive cars in the background. These kinds of stunts, where the camera is at a great distance from the stunt person, are not sex, race, or age specific, and yet, these jobs have historically gone to young white men. Even in films and television programmes starring mostly women or minorities, the stunt coordinator was generally a white male.

In the mid-1970s, stuntwomen began organizing on their own. In 1976, the Stuntwomen's Association of Motion Pictures (SWAMP) was established – the same year that the now coed Stunts Unlimited elected two women to its membership, Kitty O'Neil and Janet Brady. SWAMP organized with the intention of attaining better working conditions and higher wages for their members. As one of their first acts as an association, they created a directory, listing member's professional skills and physical attributes, highlighting the strength and diversity of talents available to stunt coordinators, directors, and casting agents (Anonymous, 1977). In one of its first actions, SWAMP fought for the hiring of more stuntwomen and female stunt coordinators. As SWAMP Secretary Sunny Woods explained in a 1977 article in *Variety*: 'There is no clear studio policy. Lacking that, a male coordinator with jobs to fill naturally turns to the people in his own organization, or to his friends, and they are men' (Mayer, 1977). At the time, men were still more inclined to hire men – even as doubles for women. One possible option to transform the industry was to invite women into the male stunt organizations, thereby facilitating the hiring of stuntwomen. But the stuntmen in power clearly stated their disinterest, even disgust, at the notion of opening their associations to women. Bill Lane, SAMP president and the head of SAG's stunt and safety investigation team, was one such stunt coordinator who even in 1983 refused to conceive of such a change:

> It says 'stuntmen,' it doesn't say 'stuntwomen' … it doesn't say stunt-persons either…. [SAMP is] a fraternal organization… It was set up that way (to be for men only) 22 years ago. At that time, they didn't have the ERA (Equal Rights Amendment) or any of the other **** like that… We have enough of our own problems – we don't need the women's. (Robb, 1983)

Considering the level of discrimination, it was clear why some women felt, and still feel, that 'getting the job is harder than doing the job' (A.P.T., 2000).

Some stuntwomen saw that the best method for bettering their situation was to become stunt coordinators themselves. In 1976, Julie Anne Johnson was the first female to hold such a position on a major TV show, earning approximately $1,500 a week as the stunt coordinator for *Charlie's Angels* (1976–81). It is not surprising that it was a female-dominated action programme that broke the long-standing tradition and gave a woman the job of stunt coordinator. Soon after, Donna Garrett, a twenty-year veteran, was tapped as stunt coordinator for *Cagney & Lacey* (1981–88) (Platt Jacoby, 1988). At this time, SWAMP worked to gain the 'right of first refusal', which meant that any job doubling for a woman must first be offered to a stuntwoman, and only if she refuses could it then be offered to a stuntman (Mayer, 1977).

Transformation within the industry has been slow, and stunting is still a male-dominated industry. Yet the small but growing number of stuntwomen-turned-stunt coordinators are slowing transforming the profession, and are hiring from within their own organizations.[6] Three key reasons for the increase in female stunt coordinators in the United States are: the creation of a SAG policy of Non-Discrimination and Diversity that requires stuntwomen to be employed to double for female actors; the creation of multiple female trade collectives in the tradition of SWAMP that operate to market their members to coordinators; and the increase in lead stunt doubling roles for women after the success of *Xena: Warrior Princess* heralded a new wave of programmes featuring fighting female figures on television (*Buffy the Vampire Slayer* 1997–2003; *Dark Angel* 2000–2002; *Alias* 2001–2006 etc.) and altered the expectations and requirements for television action sequences.

The nature of stunt work

While early stunt work was often based around horse tricks and fight scenes, over time the stunts have only become more technically and physically challenging. In the 1960s and 1970s stuntwomen found work in the industry because of specialized skillsets in acrobatics, motorcycle driving, and via the nepotistic structures common to guild work. Jeannie Epper, the stunt double for Lynda Carter in *Wonder Woman* (1975–79), worked her way into the industry with help from her father, stunt legend John Epper. John taught his children horse stunts at an early age and Jeannie's first on-camera stunt was riding bareback down a cliff (Epper, 2004). Debbie Evans, the motorcycle double for Wonder Woman in the 1970s and, more recently, for Carrie Anne Moss in the intense freeway chase sequence from *The Matrix Reloaded* (2003), found work in the stunt industry in the mid-1970s because she was the women's world motorcycle trial champion. While Evans and Epper have had very long careers in the stunt industry compared to contemporary stuntwoman (many of whom retire after having a child), neither of these grand dames of American stunting are commonly recruited as a stunt coordinator for big budget feature films. Stuntwomen find that they are offered far less work as they grow older.

The impact of ageism in Hollywood is felt across the industry. There is very little longevity for women in the field; if pregnancy and child-rearing does not slow them down, it does usually make them less available. In response to this ageism, many stuntwomen undergo plastic surgery, an attempt to make their faces match the youthfulness of their bodies and to stay in the running for stunting opportunities. (The documentary *Double Dare* [Micheli, 2004], covers this issue thoughtfully.) One of the key issues that affects the longevity of a stuntwoman's career is the glass ceiling between doubling and coordinating. Stuntmen with long and storied careers can extend their working life with work as coordinators and second unit directors, while this is not so for most stuntwomen of Evans and Epper's generation.

Many of the younger stuntwomen working in the industry today rely on their diversified training in multiple martial art forms, wire-work, precision driving and gymnastics, as well as a host of additional skillsets. It is now common for many stuntwomen who have the combination of talent and good fortune to land doubling work for lead heroines to supplement their previous martial arts skills or gymnastics training by attending stunt driving classes, high diving classes, or diversifying their fighting portfolio by studying an ever-increasing array of martial art forms. While the stuntwomen of the 1970s learned many new stunts on the job, it is becoming increasingly common for stuntwomen entering the industry today to go to 'stunt school' in order to increase their opportunities for employment by adding new skills to their résumés. Stuntwomen in their 20s and 30s that have made their careers doubling for actresses cast as action heroines express how they hope to find work as coordinators later in life. With their diversified portfolios, a small but increasing number of stuntwoman have chipped away at the glass ceiling as coordinators like Zoë Bell for low budget action films like *Bitch Slap* (2009), Jill Brown for *30 Rock* (2006–2013), and Jo McLaren for most recent iteration of the BBC science-fiction series *Doctor Who* (1963–89; 2005–present).[7]

The working day of any stuntperson, male or female, involves the ever-present risk of career-ending injury and stunt people must devote hours away from the set to the maintenance of their physique. As Stevie Meyers, former President of SWAMP explains, stunt people are professionals, and therefore are exceptionally careful. Their bodies are their livelihood: 'The work may be potentially dangerous, but if one of us is doing something that isn't safe, then it's not a stunt…. A stunt is planned with precision and executed with care' (Lamb, 1971). Stuntmen and women are paid the same amount as per SAG policy: currently a US$859 minimum day rate and a US$3200 minimum weekly rate (The National Stunt and Safety Department of the Screen Actors Guild, 2011). They can increase their pay by agreeing to do more treacherous stunts, but the risks entailed in doing these more complex stunts make their work exponentially more dangerous. Even an average day of stunt work may leave a stunt person's body traumatized, and if a stunt person is seriously injured she or he is quickly and easily replaced. Stuntwomen Nancy Thurston and Maria Kelly (2004) explain the difference between a stuntwoman and the actress she doubles for:

Kelly: We're dispensable; they're not. We get hurt, just bring in a replacement. They get hurt, production is closed down.

Thurston: Or if an actor suddenly doesn't like you or somebody else new comes along and they like them better – unless you're in someone's contract, you're not guaranteed to stick with someone.[8]

Dana Hee was Jennifer Garner's stunt double on *Alias* until part way through the first season when she hurt her hand. She was replaced by Shauna Duggins who was contracted for a number of years to be Garner's double on all of her film and television projects. There are no guarantees in Hollywood, and the stunt industry is no exception.

Other than the limited room for career advancement, the primary gendered differences in the lived relationship to work for male and female stunt performers in the US are the degree to which stuntwomen must maintain slim yet discretely muscular physiques and the less forgiving costume requirements for women, which leave little room for protective devices and increase the risk of injury. While the actors strive to stay thin, stuntwomen must be both slim (to match the stars) and muscular (in order to perform the feats required for the stunt) – a body type that is extremely difficult to maintain. Jeannie Epper contends that stuntwomen are put under much more pressure to maintain their figures than stuntmen. 'The men don't have to wear skimpy clothes like we do. So I think that as a young person choosing to be a stuntwoman, I had no idea what it was going to do to myself. The diets you go on, the strenuous getting up at five in the morning to go to the gym' (Epper, 2004). Stuntwomen are also expected to be just as thin, if not thinner, than the actors they work with so that there is space in their costumes to wear protective gear. The nature of female costumes makes this a challenge stunt-men face far less. When describing her work on television's *Charlie's Angels*, Julie Ann Johnson explained, 'They dress us in shorts or negligees, not to mention high heels, and then tell us to fall down a flight of stairs … When the scene calls for long pants, they are often too tight to allow for padding. So we are more suscepti-ble to bruises, rug burns, and splinters than the boys are' (Chase, 1980). Even the wigs they are asked to wear can prove to be occupational hazards.[9] The lack of protective equipment makes difficult stunt work exponentially more dangerous. While doubling for Lynda Carter on *Wonder Woman* in the 1970s, Epper had no space for padding in her red, white, and blue corseted costume. Essentially, she performed countless high falls, horse stunts, and fistfights practically naked. Twenty years later, Zoë Bell donned a similarly revealing costume as Xena that also left very little room for padding. Even Belinda McGinley had only a tank top and shorts to protect her from a cinematic tsunami as she doubled for Naomi Watts in *The Impossible* (2012).

A distinction must be made here between the strong body and the muscular body. While stuntwomen must be strong, these women cannot become too mus-cular – otherwise they look too masculine, and therefore 'unattractive'. In 'Pump-ing irony: the muscular and the feminine', Mansfield and McGinn explain that a woman with a hard body is still considered shocking and transgressive (1993: 54). The bodies of the main actors are deemed feminine and attractive, but the type of musculature that it takes to perform these types of stunts is sometimes seen as too hard for the average viewer, and so the stuntwoman cannot look as if she is muscular enough to perform the stunts she does. To maintain the illusion, some stuntwomen have gone so far as to re-femininize their bodies by masking their muscles through plastic surgery, and in particular, breast augmentation. A stuntwoman's body must also match the bodies of the actors in order to help maintain the illusion of seamlessness that confirms the actor's standing as both heroic and physically adept.

'Stand aside, stunt double!': the actor as heroine

Many popular press articles about action stars tend to focus on a given star's unique physical prowess, which depends on an erasure – or dismissal – of the stuntwoman. We have found that there is also a common trend in these profiles to comment on how the stars are fully capable of performing most of their own stunt work. Many articles even include a guide for readers on how they, like these stars, can become superhero-tough. The authors of these articles clearly imply that the actors are the ones doing the stunts, and that the stars' figures are not only achievable, but once achieved, will be capable of great heroism and toughness.[10] In most of these articles, if the star's stunt double is mentioned, the author will work to reassure readers that the star performs most of her own stunts, dismissing the labour of her on-screen double.[11]

In these articles about female stars of action films and series comments are routinely made about how the stars, because of their years playing sports or tackling an extraordinary career or life experience, can perform their own stunts. In a discussion of Lynda Carter as television's new Wonder Woman in an October 1976 *Time* cover story, the author pointed to Carter's athletic skills as well as her previous achievements as being key to the skills she brings to her new role:

> Carter, 24,... is a former swimming champion and ballet student with the physical skills to do most of her own stunts. She is convinced the show has value because it 'shows that women don't have to be unattractive to be independent'. (Anonymous, 1972)

The goal here was to promote the notion that Carter is herself a 'wonder woman' – tough and beautiful, athletic and feminine, in a way that is not only deemed a positive portrayal of womanhood, but clearly attainable for the average woman. The representations of stars in these articles, just like their characters, pick and choose from traditional discourses of feminism and femininity with blithe dismissals of gender politics.

More recently, the representation of the uncomplicated dualities of feminism is designed to imply that any woman can be, or ideally should be, every woman – careerist, crime-fighter, responsible family member and super-citizen. The mainstream media's prevailing vision of today's American woman is one of a veritable super-heroine – able to single-handedly find success in her career and at home, juggle work and familial responsibilities, stay fit and be a capable domestic goddess, comfortable in her womanhood, both as a feminist and as feminine. An excellent contemporary example of this can be found in a *People* magazine article tellingly titled 'Kate Winslet did her own *Divergent* stunts – while pregnant' in which the author quotes the film's director Neil Burger on Winslet's commitment to life and work:

... there is a scene where she fights Shailene and she was like, you know, taking the falls and I'm like, 'Stop, you're pregnant.' But she was still wanting to do it with as much action ... [Winslet's] a committed actress and she's a committed mother, too. But she is just completely there, and you kind of just have to stop her. (Billups, 2014)

The article does not mention Winslet's stunt double for *Divergent* (2014), Karin Silvestri, and equates falling onto a padded mat with doing all of her own stunts and engaging in fights. In these articles, it is often equally necessary to conceal that taking on a role of action star necessitates depending on others – whether on the set, for example, directors, writers, producers, the camera department, make-up artists, costume designers, and stuntwomen – or off – including agents, managers, friends and family, nannies, assistants, and personal trainers. This having-it-all mantra clearly plays into what Gill (2007) has called the rhetoric of a post-feminist sensibility.

Contemporary articles find it not enough simply to praise the physical prowess of the star, but surprisingly argue that the stuntwoman is *unessential* to the production of the programme. In its featured article entitled 'Stand aside, stunt double!', *SELF* magazine placed the fresh-faced Jennifer Garner on their cover alongside the tag line, '*Alias* star Jennifer Garner on turning 30 and taking fitness to a whole new level (stunt doubles, step aside)' (Cohen, 2002). By repeating this comment twice as prefaces to the article itself, it sets the reader up to believe that Garner the actor is as tough and capable as the character she plays. Garner reinforces this apparent contradiction by describing how she acts out all of her own stunts – whether or not it is used in the programme: 'I do 95% of my own stunts', Garner proudly tells the magazine. Garner, like other stars, must work out to stay slim, but the actual need for the star to be tough or physically fit seems to be played up for the press (Cohen, 2002). An extremely similar quotation from Lynda Carter appeared in 1976 in *Variety*: 'I have a stunt double who is an aerial acrobat. She jumps from a teeterboard and is propelled in the air. It's very dangerous work. But I do 90% of my stunts. It's very exhausting' (Kaufman, 1976).

In June 2000, *In Style* featured the stars of five syndicated action-adventure programmes. Each profile offers two pictures, one with the star in costume, and another with her body in motion, exercising. Each profile offers details on the eating habits, exercise regimens, personal struggles with maintaining their 'fighting weight', and often some personal thoughts on toughness and femininity. Lucy Lawless is praised for her fitness schedule on the set:

Getting back into fighting shape after having her baby was a battle Lawless faced with her usual gusto ... Lawless does a lot of her own stunts, even learning kung fu and sword fighting for her role ... Above all, Lawless says, Xena keeps her inspired. 'I like playing a character who's strong and courageous. I have no visible male support. Just because a woman is strong doesn't mean she's not feminine'. (Corcoran, 2000: 301)

Tia Carrere, star of the *Tomb Raider*-inspired television series that ran from 1999–2002, *Relic Hunter*, comments on how strong she has to be for her role: 'You can hurt yourself in the kinds of fight scenes I do ... You really have to have stamina'

(Corcoran, 2000: 304). Carrere gives the impression here that her character's battles are all her own (the 'scenes I do'), and that the average woman (the implied 'you') could do them (Corcoran, 2000: 304). Each of these profiles offer readers the information, and seemingly, the inspiration to become like these women, who are described in these pages as accomplished kick boxers, sword fighters and rock climbers.

A stuntwoman's job is to take calculated risks. They are compensated for their work but also for their willingness to go unseen, even to let someone else take the credit. Talking together, stuntwomen Nancy Thurston and Dana Reed discussed the propensity for actors to say they do their own stunts. Thurston shrugged her shoulders and said, 'If they want to say that they do their stunts, fine [laughing]. As long as I get my paycheck, I don't care.' Dana Reed added, 'We'll be laughing – all the way to the bank' (Thurston and Reed, 2004). As for their erasure within the press, stuntwomen realize that part of their jobs entails staying on the sidelines – or even out of sight. One singular example of a prominent stuntwomen speaking the truth to power occurred as a response to the publicity materials for the television programme *Buffy The Vampire Slayer* that detailed Sarah Michelle Gellar's childhood training in *taekwondo* and her workout regimen for the stunts on *Buffy*. Gellar's stunt double Sophia Crawford decried this in an interview, claiming that the suggestion that Gellar performed her own stunts was 'a lie':

> I've gone through lots of pain to make Buffy appear to be able to fight. I'm the only performer on screen who has been working on the show from the start that most people don't even know they are watching. [Interviewers should] ask [Gellar] to step out onto the stage and perform some of those spinning kicks of 'hers' and flipping onto her back on the concrete. See if you think it looks the same. (Crawford, 1999)

It is rare for stuntwomen to speak so candidly about the erasure of her contributions to a character that occur when stunt labour is conflated with actor's labour. Crawford made these comments that tear apart the seams between her stunting body and Gellar's body and the following season she was replaced as Gellar's double and Crawford's husband, *Buffy* stunt coordinator Jeff Pruitt, was replaced as well. Pruitt later posted a 'behind the scenes' video archive of the stunt coordination process on *Buffy* that aptly demonstrates and clearly delineates between Gellar's and Crawford's physical contributions to the character (Pruitt, 2013).

Conclusion: giving credit where credit is due

Although stunting is applauded by the crew and celebrated by audiences, stunt workers themselves rarely receive screen credit for their work. Films now sometimes include in their end titles a specific stunt person as an actor's double, but that is a new phenomenon. Not one of the television series in this study lists a specific stunt double in the credits, and only a small number of more recent programmes have begun to credit the stunt coordinator with an individual title card at the end of each episode. The reason for this erasure of stunting is critical. As Setlowe (1992) explains in *Variety*, for the illusion of the narrative to hold together, the stunt person's work must not only be invisible, but unacknowledged. 'To acclaim what stuntmen and women, stunt coordinators, and special second-unit directors do is to publicly acknowledge that the star did not do it. It is to destroy the very illusion everyone is working so hard to create' (1992: 53). This erasure through illusion not only occurs within films and television series, but also in the minds of most viewers.

The function of this article has been threefold: charting the history of women in the stunt industry; identifying the working conditions and gendered limitations inherent in stunting in the American film and television industries; and shedding light upon the process by which stuntwomen's labour is consistently expunged from the historical record via popular media accounts of the production process. The primary purpose of these accounts is to reinforce the daredevil nature of the action star at the expense of making the stunt person invisible. Our goal in writing this article has been to give credit to the labouring bodies of stuntwomen, to give voice to their concerns, and to write them back into media histories.

What is clear is that film and television producers, actors, stunt professionals, journalists, and viewers find pleasure seeing, and critically deconstructing, women in action. But there is more than one woman responsible for the representation of this character – not just the creator of the programme, the writers, or the star who plays her, but also the stunt coordinator and in particular, the stuntwoman. The labour of multiple bodies – real and fictionalized, celebrated and hidden – is necessary to create and maintain the illusion. If we ignore this labour, then we are only seeing part of the picture.

Notes

1 Bell became the primary stunt double for Lawless in 1998 when Geraldine Jacobsen retired from the role (Bell, 2009).
2 Though we realize that such projects are not mutually exclusive, both would be animated by feminist/structuralist concerns, and both are equally important.
3 For contributions by industry professionals see Baxter (1974) and Sullivan and Sullivan (1983). And for scholarly discussions of stunting see Bean (2002), Smith (2004), Smith *et al.* (2006) and Steimer (2009).
4 When a single stunt person performs multiple different stunts for one production while not working as a stunt double for a primary actor, the stunt person is credited with 'utility' stunts.
5 At various points in time, concerns about nepotism by stunt coordinators have made the Screen Actors Guild (SAG) take action. None of the stunt organizations are officially sanctioned by SAG. SAG issued warnings that were designed to prevent stunt coordinators from taking 'illegal' kickbacks or agent percentages as commission. See Anonymous (1970, 1992), General subject files (n.d.) and Robb (1983).
6 It is hard to estimate precisely how many women are getting regular stunt coordinating work.
7 Bell was trained as a gymnast and supplemented her portfolio with techniques learned during a 'trial-and-error' process on *Xena* and her Hong Kong-style wirework training on *Kill Bill* (Bell, 2009). Jo McLaren is a British stuntwoman trained in martial arts and was the uncredited stunt double for Angelina Jolie as the eponymous *Lara Croft: Tomb Raider* (2001). The UK system for stunt work is far more regimented in regard to certification in a wide variety of skillsets and has allowed for slightly more upward career movement for stuntwomen than in the US.

8 Usually, a stuntwoman is contracted for a scene, a series, or for a film. It is rare that a stuntwoman signs a contract with a particular actor rather than for a series or film (Stuntwomen's Association of Motion Pictures, 2004).

9 Stuntwoman Diane Peterson complained about the hazards of wearing a wig while stunting. In response to a question by an interviewer about the worst thing about her job, Peterson replied, 'Wearing those damn wigs. The bobby pins they use are like daggers' (Anonymous, 1991).

10 The tag line for the article reads, 'The gods may have blessed them with athletic prowess, but TV's superwomen still have to do their share of crunches. Check out how these tough, beautiful babes stay ready to rumble' (Corcoran, 2000).

11 There are numerous examples of this for various actors including Anne Francis and Diana Rigg (Anonymous, 1970; Lewis, 1965). Lynda Carter only conceded that she did not do her own aerial work – although discussions with Epper (2004) seem to prove otherwise.

References

Anonymous, (1970), 'Stuntmen warned by SAG on agency', *Variety*: 1, 5.

Anonymous, (1972), 'TV's super women', *Time*: 70.

Anonymous, (1977), 'Stuntwomen publish listings with photos', *Variety*, available from LexisNexis.

Anonymous, (1990), 'Emma Peel appeal: designers raid the closet of our favorite sixties heroine', *San Francisco Focus*, available from LexisNexis.

Anonymous, (1991), 'Diane Peterson: standing in Jessica Lange's shoes, she thrives on double trouble', *People*: 69.

Anonymous, (1992), 'Chairman of old boy's club', *Variety*: 58.

Anonymous, (1996), 'Xena falls short of TV image: actress fractures pelvis on shoot', *The Times-Picayune*: A43.

A.P.T., (2000), 'Guilds: stuntwomen's association', available from LexisNexis.

Banks, M., (2009), 'Gender below-the-line: defining feminist production studies', in V. Mayer, M. Banks and J. Caldwell (eds), *Production Studies: Cultural Studies of Media Industries*, 87–98, New York: Routledge.

Baxter, J., (1974), *Stunt: The Story of the Great Movie Stunt Men*, Garden City, NY: Doubleday.

Bean, J., (2002), 'Technologies of early stardom and the extraordinary body', in J. Bean and D. Negra (eds), *A Feminist Reader in Early Cinema*, 404–443, Durham, NC: Duke University Press.

Bell, Z., (2009), *Personal interview by Lauren Steimer*.

Billups, A., (2014), 'Kate Winslet did her own *Divergent* stunts – while pregnant', *People*, available at: http://www.people.com/people/article/0,20798259,00.html

Chase, J., (1980), 'Women daredevils', *Cosmopolitan*, 233–237.

Cohen, B., (2002), 'Stand aside, stunt double!', *SELF*: 38–39.

Corcoran, M., (2000), 'Action figures', *In Style*: 300–301.

Crawford, S., (1999), 'Buffy stunts: interview', *Femme Fatales*, 8 (3): 23.

Epper, J., (2004), *Personal interview by Miranda J. Banks*.

General subject files, (n.d.), *Fairbanks Center for Motion Picture Study at the Academy of Motion Picture Arts & Sciences, Margaret Herrick Library*. Beverly Hills, CA.

Gill, R., (2007). `Postfeminist media culture: elements of a sensibility', *European Journal of Cultural Studies*, 10 (2): 147–166.

Graham, J., (1997), 'The fall and rise of Xena: horse spill behind her, Lucy Lawless charges ahead', *USA Today*: 3D.

Kaufman, D., (1976), 'TV's Wonder Woman, Lynda Carter, takes series (and life) seriously', *Variety*, available from LexisNexis.

Lamb, D., (1971), 'Stuntwomen stand on feats', *Los Angeles Times*: E1.

Lewis, R., (1965), 'Honey West's earrings explode: so does Anne Francis', *TV Guide*: 24.

Mansfield, A. and McGinn, B., (1993), 'Pumping irony: the muscular and the feminine', in S. Scott and D. Morgan (eds), *Body Matters: Essays of the Sociology of the Body*, 50–69, London: Falmer Press.

The Sociological Review, 63:S1, pp. 144–157 (2015), DOI: 10.1111/1467-954X.12245

Mayer, B., (1977), 'Stuntwomen jump on studios for favoring men in hiring, even as femme star doubles', *Variety*, available from LexisNexis.

Micheli, A., (2004), *Double Dare*. Runaway Films.

National Stunt and Safety Department of the Screen Actors Guild, The, (2011), '*Stunt & Safety Digest 2011–2014: Theatrical Motion Pictures and Television*, Los Angeles, CA: 6.

Platt Jacoby, N., (1988), 'Thrills and spills', *Elle*: 151.

Pruitt, J., (2013), '*Buffy-Doppelgangland-Earshot-stunt home movies* [video], available at: https://www.youtube.com/watch?v = ex9_pANdH4I.

Robb, D., (1983), 'Okay on the job, but no room for women in two of three stuntmen's orgs', *Variety*: 14.

Setlowe, R., (1992), 'Hollywood's Hitmen: Stunt work is as old as film itself and as new as tomorrow's final cut.', *Daily Variety*, 53–54.

Setlowe, R., (1996), 'Shows of derring-do', *Variety*: 25.

Smith, J., (2004), 'Seeing double: stunt performance and masculinity', *Journal of Film and Video*, 56 (3): 35–53.

Smith, J., Solomon, M., Banks, M. and Rehak, B., (2006), 'Stunt/work: performers, technology, and new media', *Society for Cinema and Media Studies Conference*, Vancouver, Canada.

Steimer, L., (2009), 'From *wuxia* to *Xena*: translation and the body spectacle of Zoë Bell', *Discourse*, 31 (3): 359–390.

Stuntwomen's Association of Motion Pictures, (2004), *Personal interview by Miranda J. Banks*.

Sullivan, G. and Sullivan, T., (1983), *Stunt People*, New York: Beaufort Books.

Thurston, N. and Kelly, M., (2004), *Personal interview by Miranda J. Banks*.

Thurston, N. and Reed, D., (2004), *Personal interview by Miranda J. Banks*.

The Sociological Review, 63:S1, pp. 144–157 (2015), DOI: 10.1111/1467-954X.12245
© 2015 The Authors. Editorial organisation © 2015 The Editorial Board of the Sociological Review

Part 5: Boundary-crossing

When Adam blogs: cultural work and the gender division of labour in Utopia

Ursula Huws

Abstract: Taking as its starting point the current resurgence of interest in Utopian alternatives to capitalist forms of production, including those based on cultural co-production, this chapter takes a critical look at Utopias, from Thomas More to the present day, which propose idealized future societies in which people are emancipated from exploitative labour relations. It examines the ways in which these Utopias have envisaged cultural labour – whether as specialist artistic occupations or as a general creative dimension of all labour – and relates this to the gender divisions of labour envisaged for these idealized societies. It concludes that most Utopias fail to imagine future changes in the social division between paid and unpaid work. Where these have gone beyond a model of small self-sufficient agrarian communities, even if they have envisaged changes in the technical division of labour, they have reproduced existing gender divisions of labour, excluding unpaid reproductive work from their visions of emancipation and work-sharing. In so doing, they have constructed cultural labour as something which is supported invisibly by the reproductive labour of others.

Keywords: utopia, division of labour, history, capitalism, reproductive labour

When Adam delved and Eve span, who was then the gentleman?

(John Ball, speaking at Blackheath, after his liberation from imprisonment in the Archbishop's Palace in Maidstone by the Kentish rebels in the Peasants' Revolt of 1381)

Introduction

'Why study cultural work?' asked Mark Banks, opening his presentation at a workshop in London in summer 2012, on 'Cultural Work, Subjectivity and Technology'. Why indeed? And why now? The train of thought sparked by these questions led me to the starting point for this chapter, which is the proposition that 'cultural' or 'creative' work represents a kind of ideal type of unalienated labour and, as such, plays a central role in any vision of an alternative future.

The Sociological Review, 63:S1, pp. 158–173 (2015), DOI: 10.1111/1467-954X.12247
© 2015 The Author. Editorial organisation © 2015 The Editorial Board of the Sociological Review. Published by John Wiley & Sons Ltd, 9600 Garsington Road, Oxford OX4 2DQ, UK and 350 Main Street, Malden, MA 02148, USA

An examination of the ways in which cultural labour is portrayed in Utopian representations of the future of the work can, I surmise, tell us a great deal about how work is understood by the authors of these Utopian visions, including the ways that these understandings are gendered. This seems to be a timely question to address in the context of the current wave of imaginings of a post-capitalist future economy based on a free exchange of goods organized online between autonomous creative workers (see for instance, Barbrook, 2007; Dyer-Witheford, 1999, 2013) using 'peer-to-peer' modes of production (eg Bauwens, 2006; Rigi, 2012; Siefkes, 2012) and this chapter represents an attempt to sketch out a feminist response to such proposals. How have Utopian visionaries imagined the division of labour in future societies? Do their visions really open up the possibility for all labour to be satisfying and unalienated? Or might the freedom of some workers to be creative be underpinned by the less satisfying – even coerced – labour of others?

It is, of course, dangerous to project the contemporary concepts of 'cultural' or 'creative' labour backwards into historical contexts where the term would have had little meaning, if any. I have developed functional definitions of these terms in the context of the political economy of contemporary capitalism elsewhere (Huws, 2007, 2010). Here I use the terms more loosely to refer to artistic and intellectual labour as conceived by the authors in question. Depending on the author, the category might include the labour of priests and scholars as well as visual artists and musicians, whether carried out as specialist tasks (and incorporated into occupational identities) or integrated into the daily activities of the general population. Sketching the history of Utopias over the last 500 years also involves tracing the emergence of separately visible forms of cultural labour from their antecedents in other activities in which they were formally embedded, for example in pedagogy, art or craft production

A renaissance utopia

A good place to start any discussion of idealized imaginary futures is with Thomas More's 16th-century classic *Utopia*, which gave us the term. His vision is surprisingly feminist to modern eyes. Although in his Utopia women are assigned tasks (working with wool and flax) which he regards as less physically taxing than those assigned to men (which are named as masonry, smith's work and carpenter's work) they are expected to work on similar terms:

> Every family makes their own clothes; but all among them, women as well as men, learn one or other of the trades formerly mentioned. Women, for the most part, deal in wool and flax, which suit best with their weakness, leaving the ruder trades to the men. (More, 1901: n.p.)

However, working hours are short – six hours a day, three before and three after dinner. The remaining time is devoted to scholarship.

The Sociological Review, 63:S1, pp. 158–173 (2015), DOI: 10.1111/1467-954X.12247

The rest of their time besides that taken up in work, eating and sleeping, is left to every man's discretion; yet they are not to abuse that interval to luxury and idleness, but must employ it in some proper exercise according to their various inclinations, which is for the most part reading. It is ordinary to have public lectures every morning before daybreak; at which none are obliged to appear but those who are marked out for literature; yet a great many, both men and women of all ranks, go to hear lectures of one sort of other, according to their inclinations. (1901: n.p.)

Scholarship, one form of cultural labour, is therefore an activity in which everyone participates and is distinguished from entertainment, which is another: 'After supper, they spend an hour in some diversion, in summer in their gardens, and in winter in the halls where they eat; where they entertain each other, either with music or discourse' (1901: n.p.).

Nevertheless, whilst everyone participates in culture, it is assumed to be produced by specialists, with 'study' contrasted with and counterposed to 'labour'. There is an intellectual elite, but this is not hereditary, with social mobility in and out of it, its membership subject to social approval. Cultural products (other than books) do not figure strongly in this analysis. And, whilst it is clear that craft is involved in most labour, creativity does not feature in More's account as such. On the contrary, there is an emphasis on avoiding luxury, finery, products that are 'vain and superfluous' and those that 'can tempt a man to desire more' (1901: n.p.).

The emergence of class analysis

More's early 16th-century world is one without employment relations in which production is organized within family units and the only hierarchical relations are between priests and scholars and those who do manual work – a relationship that does not involve direct expropriation although it may involve some subsidy from the latter to the former. Over the next 200 years, as capitalism developed, such a simple organization of labour became harder to imagine. Quesnay's (1758) *Tableau Économique* portrayed an economy based on three distinct economic classes: landowners, farmers and 'sterile classes' (so called because he thought they consumed everything they produced and, unlike the agricultural sector, were unable to produce an economic surplus and contribute to growth). We can presume that artists, scholars and priests were all included in this 'sterile' class (insofar as they were not also agricultural workers or landowners). Two decades later, Smith (1776) was able to present the world with a developed model of a division of labour whose rationale was to increase workers' productivity in the interests of their employers:

The division of labour, however, so far as it can be introduced, occasions, in every art, a proportionable increase of the productive powers of labour. The separation of different trades and employments from one another seems to have taken place in consequence of this advantage. (1776: n.p.)

The Sociological Review, 63:S1, pp. 158–173 (2015), DOI: 10.1111/1467-954X.12247

Whilst Quesnay (1758) and Smith (1776) attempted to analyse the economy as it actually was, other 18th-century writers were more prescriptive, sketching out how it might be. Rousseau, who helped prepare the ground for the French Revolution, makes an interesting contrast with More. Whilst in agreement with him on the evils of idleness and luxury – indeed going further than More in blaming the arts and sciences for contributing to the corruption of man (in his *Discourse on the Sciences and Arts,* 1750), Rousseau was emphatically less egalitarian in his attitude to women. In his idealized world, portrayed in *Emile* (1762), boys are to be encouraged to learn manual skills requiring creativity and thought, but girls should only be educated to be helpmeets for the boys. The equality he advocated so eloquently (in his *Discourse on Inequality*, 1754) is an equality between men that explicitly excludes women, as Wollestonecraft (1792) pointed out. Cultural labour, here, is emphatically masculine.

Utopian socialism

The French revolution (which can be regarded in this context as a Utopian project in its attempt to bring a new social order into being) and its failure, provoked a new wave of Utopian thinking, some leading to actual experiments in setting up model communities, and some existing primarily as unrealized blueprints. One of the most influential of these 'Utopian Socialists', as they were later designated by Engels (1880a), was Claude Henri de Rouvroy, Count of Saint-Simon, whose ideal industrial society was divided into three classes: 'gentlemen' (also referred to as 'proprietors'), 'men of genius' and 'the rest of the people'. He envisaged that the two former groups would be elected by the latter and that the 'men of genius' would be representative of both the arts and the sciences, with a panel of eighteen being elected, comprised of: three mathematicians, three physicists, three chemists, three physiologists, three authors, three painters and three musicians. These 'men of genius' take the place of religious leaders and ensure a kind of technocratic rational economic progress bringing continuous social improvement (anticipating some of the ideas of Saint-Simon's pupil, Auguste Comte). What we might now think of as professional cultural workers therefore played a prominent role in social management.

> I think that all classes of society would be happy in the following situation: spiritual power in the hands of the scientists; temporal power in those of the proprietors; power to nominate those called upon to carry out the functions of the great leaders of mankind in the hands of everyone; the reward for those who govern to be – esteem. (Saint-Simon, 1803: n.p.)

Saint-Simon's Utopian society (contrasted by him with the industrial society of the early 19th century which he regarded as exploitative, divided immorally between 'working people' and 'idlers' or 'thieves') is a co-operative one in which there is full employment. Artistic labour is included as a separate category of labour, contributing to the general good and deserving to be paid for so doing.

After working hard for six days a week, everyone enjoys a cultured leisure on the seventh,

> On Sundays, you find delight in eloquence, you take pleasure in reading a well-written book, in looking at beautiful pictures or statues or in listening to music which holds you entranced. Hard work is necessary before a man can speak or write in a way which will amuse you, or can paint a picture or carve a statue which pleases you or can compose music which affects you. Is it not fair, my friends, that you should reward the artists who fill the pauses in your work with pleasures which enlarge your minds by playing on the most delicate nuances of your feelings? (Saint-Simon, 1803: n.p.)

Although Saint-Simon himself had rather little to say about gender, the reader can assume that his 'men of genius' and artists were male. However, his followers, beginning with Enfantin (1796–1864) proselytized the gradual emancipation of women, which had become a central concern among Saint-Simonians by 1831 (Moses, 1984: 42).

Meanwhile, on the other side of the Channel, Robert Owen was setting up a model community, in the cotton mills of New Lanark in Scotland in which a kind of enlightened paternalistic capitalism was established which in some ways anticipated the social democratic welfare states of the 20th century. New Lanark, managed by Owen from 1800 to 1825, had free medical care, a crèche for working mothers, pensions for the elderly and infirm, free education – starting 'almost as soon as they can walk' (1816) and continuing into adulthood in the form of evening classes. There were concerts and museums as well as gardens to enjoy during leisure hours. Owen was an advocate of the 8-hour working day, though in practice, at a time when it was normal to work 16 hours a day in the cotton industry, the working day in the New Lanark was 10 hours.

His views on gender were outspoken. He was against marriage, and approvingly quoted contemporary feminists 'Mrs Jamieson, Miss Martineau and Mrs Grimstone' in support of his denunciation of a woman's condition in contemporary marriage:

> Her only duty is obedience, rendered to her legal Lord and Master. The law has arranged that she should have no control even over her own earnings; that she should yield a devoted submission to her master's will; and, no matter what his iniquities, remain bound to him, his inalienable property, his legal slave. (Owen, 1839: 877)

His 'new social mechanism' was designed to produce equality between men and women, and the provision of childcare services at least partly to enable women to participate fully in paid labour (it was also intended to ensure the children's education, including their moral education). But he thought that the working classes in their present state ('the most oppressed and degraded class in society') were incapable of grasping the mechanisms by which they were oppressed or comprehending the 'new scientific arrangements' required for the betterment of society (Owen, 1839: 596). They would need to be educated, and educated moreover by the 'directing class', before they could be trusted to collaborate in the building of 'communities ... of superior knowledge, manners, wealth and

The Sociological Review, 63:S1, pp. 158–173 (2015), DOI: 10.1111/1467-954X.12247

happiness' (Owen, 1839: 597), envisaged, not as a classless society but as a collaboration between workers and capitalists. Cultural workers are enlisted in the service of the capitalists as part of this educational project.

It is perhaps in the work of Fourier, the third Utopian Socialist identified by Engels (1880a) that we find the most detailed, if bizarre, prescription for a Utopian organization of economic activity, as well as the most trenchant critique of industrial capitalism, a critique which anticipates Marx's concept of alienation in several respects. Fourier pinpoints the potential attraction of work as a pleasurable activity and contrasts it with the reality of coerced labour.

In contrast with the rather dour work ethic promulgated by Owen, Fourier insists that work should be engaging and voluntary. He repeatedly asserts that different people are attracted to different kinds of activity and that any activity becomes boring very quickly. Indeed he stipulates that 'the industrial sessions be varied about eight times a day, it being impossible to sustain enthusiasm longer than an hour and a half or two hours in the exercise of agricultural or manufacturing labour'. He also writes approvingly of the pleasures of voluptuousness, eating and drinking and political intrigue ('cabalism') and finally of the passion of 'harmonism' or 'unityism' which motivates one to 'reconcile his own happiness with that of all surrounding him and of all human kind'. In his 'associative' Utopia the pursuit of such passions will lead to the situation where 'a general perfection in industry will be attained by the universal demands and refinement of the consumers, regarding food and clothing, furniture and amusements' (Fourier, 1822: n.p.).

Fourier was in favour of free love and tolerant of homosexuality and his ideal world can at first glance seem to resemble a 1960s hippy Utopia. However, any investigation of how he proposed to reach this relaxed and emancipated state reveals him to have been someone who might have been characterized in the 1960s as 'a control freak', with an obsession with micro-managing labour processes comparable to that of his near-contemporary Charles Babbage (1791–1871) or, a century later, Frederick Winslow Taylor.

Fourier provides a particularly vivid example of the contradiction that is central to so many libertarian Utopias: the more individual freedom is desired in the idealized future, the more coercive the means to achieve it. To take another example, whilst he advocates sexual freedom, he also stipulates that men, women and children should eat separately. There is strict segregation by age in the living arrangements in his Utopia.

Like Owen, he envisages his ideal communities being set up in a collaboration between enlightened capitalists and workers. Society is organized in 'phalanxes', each made up of 1,600 people preselected by class and occupation: 'At least seveneighths of the members ought to be cultivators and manufacturers; the remainder will consist of capitalists, scholars, and artists.' Profits are to be distributed unequally: '5/12 to manual labour, 4/12 to invested capital, 3/12 to theoretical and practical knowledge'. Cultural workers (the 'scholars and artists') are thus conceived as a separate class, deserving of additional reward, along with capitalists. The principle here is that 'every one, man, woman, or child, be remunerated in proportion to the three faculties, capital, labour, and talent' (Fourier, 1822: n.p.). He envisages that differences between these groups will erode over time, through the joint education and upbringing of children of all classes, helped by the way, in his view, that rich people are attracted to manual labour.

After Marx

The three Utopian Socialists identified by Engels (1880b) all have in common an idea that Utopias can be brought into being through an alliance between enlightened capitalists and workers. Most also picture a future that includes many features of an idealized pre-industrial economy, with people living in small communities and an emphasis on agriculture and craft manufacture. For future Utopians, Marx's ideas introduced a fundamental change in this regard. Once an idea of capitalism as an antagonistic relationship between labour and capital had been established, it was impossible to imagine a future of unalienated labour without also imagining, as its precondition, the abolition of capitalism as a system. And this was not a process that could take place voluntarily. Morris, the Marx-influenced Utopian of the later 19th century (in his 1890 *News from Nowhere*) presupposes that a revolution has taken place, described in politically sophisticated detail in a chapter called 'How the change came'. Morris (1890), who was also strongly influenced by Ruskin, is eloquent on the topic of the creativity of labour (something I discussed in Huws, 2007) but his Utopian solution to challenging the waste and alienation produced in the capitalist 'World Market' is to revert to a romanticized mediaeval rural economy in which production is craft-based. Morris was in favour of free love and, in his views on gender relations, followed Engels (1880b) who memorably conjectured that 'after the impending overthrow of capitalist production' there will emerge:

> a generation of men who never in their lives have known what it is to buy a woman's surrender with money or any other social instrument of power; a generation of women who have never known what it is to give themselves to a man from any other considerations than real love, or to refuse to give themselves to their lover from fear of the economic consequences. (Engels, 1880b: n.p.)

Nevertheless, like Ruskin (and, indeed, like Marx and Engels) Morris did not challenge either heterosexuality (indeed, despite his rejection of enforced monogamy, he seems to have been as homophobic as most of his contemporaries) or the gender division of labour. Whilst he took from Marx a strong sense of the destructiveness of capitalism, especially to individual creativity and to the natural world, he did not follow him in regarding the additional productivity released by capitalist machinery and a developed division of labour as creating the potential for a communist future with access to cheap goods for all. His Utopia was a place where Adam continued to delve, and Eve to spin, their gratification coming from an intrinsic pleasure in the work itself and the fact that the products of their labour were not wrested from them.

The Sociological Review, 63:S1, pp. 158–173 (2015), DOI: 10.1111/1467-954X.12247

The technophile, H.G. Wells, lampooned this position in his 1905 *A Modern Utopia,* calling it:

> a bold make-believe that all toil may be made a joy, and with that a levelling down of all society to an equal participation in labour … It needed the Olympian unworldliness of an irresponsible rich man of the shareholding type, a Ruskin or a Morris playing at life, to imagine as much. Road-making under Mr. Ruskin's auspices was a joy at Oxford no doubt, and a distinction, and it still remains a distinction; it proved the least contagious of practices. (1905: n.p.)

Wells' alternative Utopia reflects his position as a middle-class professional writer and Fabian fellow-traveller, who enjoyed an active and promiscuous sex life. It is a vision which purportedly (Smith, 1986) had a greater influence on Beveridge than any other text when he was designing the post-World War II British Welfare State. It is essentially the vision of a benevolent one-party dictatorship seeking to balance the freedom of the individual with the general social good. Individual freedom is important to Wells, and this is integrally linked with creative freedom: 'To have free play for one's individuality is, in the modern view, the subjective triumph of existence, as survival in creative work and offspring is its objective triumph' (1905: n.p.).

So too is (heterosexual) sexual freedom. In his new world, childless marriages expire after a few years and motherhood is subsidized by the state. In pursuit of such freedoms individuals are allowed to own personal property and accorded considerable privacy. However, all land and natural resources are owned by the state. Wells envisages machinery and energy playing an increasingly important role in production (thereby reducing the role of labour) and proposes that units of energy are used as the sole currency (thus encouraging the location of industry in regions where energy costs are lowest). He also anticipates the state's requirement to keep track of the population through technologies of identification and surveillance:

> The new [Utopia] must square itself to the needs of a migratory population, to an endless coming and going, to a people as fluid and tidal as the sea. It does not enter into the scheme of earthly statesmanship, but indeed all local establishments, all definitions of place, are even now melting under our eyes. Presently all the world will be awash with anonymous stranger men.

> Now the simple laws of custom, the homely methods of identification that served in the little communities of the past when everyone knew everyone, fail in the face of this liquefaction. If the modern Utopia is indeed to be a world of responsible citizens, it must have devised some scheme by which every person in the world can be promptly and certainly recognised, and by which anyone missing can be traced and found. (1905: n.p.)

Perhaps his most important message, though, is that there is a clear distinction to be made between satisfying creative work on the one hand and routine and degraded work on the other, and the notion that technology can liberate humankind from the latter, enabling time to be devoted to the former and thereby prefiguring many more recent Utopias.

> The plain message physical science has for the world at large is this, that were our political and social and moral devices only as well contrived to their ends as a linotype machine, an antiseptic operating plant, or an electric tram-car, there need now at the present moment be no appreciable toil in the world, and only the smallest fraction of the pain, the fear, and the anxiety that now makes human life so doubtful in its value. There is more than enough for everyone alive. (1905: n.p.)

This idea that drudgery will be eliminated sits rather uncomfortably alongside a strong work ethic ('The permanent idleness of a human being is not only burthensome to the world, but his own secure misery', Chapter the Fifth, Section 3). Here, the state plays a role in guaranteeing some sort of employment to all. Domestic labour is not discussed. Wells seems to think that housework can be automated out of existence. His minutely detailed description of a Utopian bedroom tells us – inadvertently – a lot about the labour of an Edwardian housemaid:

> The room is, of course, very clear and clean and simple … There is no fireplace, and I am perplexed by that until I find a thermometer beside six switches on the wall. Above this switch-board is a brief instruction: one switch warms the floor, which is not carpeted, but covered by a substance like soft oilcloth; one warms the mattress (which is of metal with resistance coils threaded to and fro in it); and the others warm the wall in various degrees, each directing current through a separate system of resistances. The casement does not open, but above, flush with the ceiling, a noiseless rapid fan pumps air out of the room. The air enters by a Tobin shaft. There is a recess dressing-room, equipped with a bath and all that is necessary to one's toilette, and the water, one remarks, is warmed, if one desires it warm, by passing it through an electrically heated spiral of tubing. A cake of soap drops out of a store machine on the turn of a handle, and when you have done with it, you drop that and your soiled towels and so forth, which also are given you by machines, into a little box, through the bottom of which they drop at once, and sail down a smooth shaft … Beside the bed, and to be lit at night by a handy switch over the pillow, is a little clock, its face flush with the wall. The room has no corners to gather dirt, wall meets floor with a gentle curve, and the apartment could be swept out effectually by a few strokes of a mechanical sweeper … You are politely requested to turn a handle at the foot of your bed before leaving the room, and forthwith the frame turns up into a vertical position, and the bedclothes hang airing. You stand at the doorway and realise that there remains not a minute's work for anyone to do. (1905: n.p.)

From our 21st-century viewpoint we can appreciate the prescience which foresaw central heating, air conditioning, en-suite bathrooms, laundry chutes and minimalist decor. But the idea that all these things would maintain and dust themselves seems naive, to say the least. And what happens to that dirty laundry when it reaches the bottom of the chute?

As the 20th century unfolded, with all its horrors, Dystopias (such as Aldous Huxley's 1931 *Brave New World* and George Orwell's *1984*) were more easily envisaged than Utopias. One exception, Charlotte Perkins Gilman's 1915 *Herland,* presents a feminist vision of a world run entirely by women who have learned to reproduce by means of parthenogenesis. Its main descriptive focus is on the quality of relationships and how children are educated. Little attention is paid to industrial organization and we are left to assume that this is essentially a pre-capitalist world, with the sort of updated medievalism characteristic of Morris's (1890) *Nowhere*, albeit without a gender division of labour. Later 20th-century feminist Utopias, such as Ursula Le Guin's 1969 *Left Hand of Darkness* and Marge Piercy's 1976 *Woman on the Edge of Time,* retained the strong emphasis on equality but replaced Perkins Gilman's (1915) segregated woman-only world with androgynous ones, in some ways resembling hippy communes, in which creativity is more a taken-for-granted dimension of everyday life than the basis for a distinctive career as a cultural worker. Although both Le Guin (1969) and Piercy (1976) contrast these Utopian worlds with oppressive, hierarchical Dystopian ones, with rigid sex-roles, clearly based on critiques of the here-and-now of contemporary capitalist societies (albeit transferred to a fictional planet in Le Guin's science fiction account) neither grapples with the problem of how the capitalist mode of production, and the division of labour that underpins it, can be transformed to bring such a Utopia into being.

Modern utopias

It was later in the 20th century that attention turned once again to such questions. The context was the end of the period of relative post-war prosperity and low unemployment in Western economies that began to unravel around the time of the 1973 oil crisis. A generation of Marxist-influenced intellectuals who had been formed in this optimistic earlier period was now faced with the reality of rising unemployment, the decline of traditional industries, and with them the occupations that had formed the basis of workplace-based trade union organizations, as well as the introduction of new technologies that seemed to bring the promise of hugely increased productivity in the future whilst, in the here-and-now, directly contributing to the degradation of labour and the destruction of jobs. Prominent among this generation of Utopians were André Gorz (1982, 1985) and Ivan Illich (1982), each of whom produced a significant corpus of work. They were followed by others, writing in English, such as Jeremy Rifkind (1995) and Stanley Aronowitz and William DiFazio (1994).

I have discussed the Utopian visions of Gorz and Illich elsewhere (Huws, 1991), my main criticisms being their failure to recognize the ways in which paid labour in the 'productive' economy was underpinned by unpaid reproductive work and the ways in which the relationship between 'productive' and 'reproductive' labour has shifted historically as a result of commodification (see Huws, 2003, 2014a for a fuller discussion of this shift). Contemplating the enormous destructiveness and waste of capitalism's inexorable drive to the creation of endless new products, each with its in-built obsolescence, and attempting to find a more equitable division of labour, both Illich (1982) and Gorz (1982, 1985), in their different ways, proposed a future model of work sharply differentiated into two spheres. The first of these, the sphere of necessity, is characterized by highly automated, centrally planned heteronomous activity, and is concerned purely with supplying the goods required to meet basic human needs. Work in this sphere is routinized and fragmented and alienating, but, because it is so highly automated and efficiently managed, it requires only a very small total number of person-hours, so, with everyone doing their share, it takes up only a minimal fraction of the working day, week or year. The other sphere is characterized by autonomous activity. Here, work is creative, individualistic and unalienated. The implication is that the goods and services produced in this way are luxuries, rather than necessities, but neither Illich nor Gorz advocates the socialization of any of the activities currently carried out unpaid by women as housework (and typically taking up considerably more time per week than the 40-odd hours of most paid full-time employment). Despite some pious nods in the direction of men doing a larger share of this domestic labour (but no indication of what mechanism will be used to oblige them to do so), the implication is that domestic labour will remain as exploitative, repetitive and resource-intensive (because of the lack of economies of scale) as it is at present (Huws, 1991).

Illich (1982) addressed the gender question quite explicitly, arguing in *Gender* that the contemporary subjugation of women is a side-effect of capitalism, and specific to Western cultures, advocating a return to a romanticized 'natural' pre-capitalist division of labour. Gorz (1985) simply takes the existing state of technological development (and its associated division of labour) as a given, recognizes that it is unpleasant and alienated, and seeks to minimize the amount of it that any given person has to do. The as-yet-uncommodified unpaid labour that sits beyond this field of vision is simply ignored. He shows no concern about how the cooking will be done, the house kept clean or the children cared for whilst his protagonist Utopians are writing their poetry or composing their symphonies.

The work of this generation of Utopians remains influential and, along with the ideas of Hardt and Negri (2000, 2004, 2009) and their many Autonomist followers, seems to have been the strongest influence on the current wave of Utopian thinking.

In the intervening period, technological development has progressed and new aspects of life brought within the scope of capitalist commodity production, including art and culture, public services and sociality itself (see Huws, 2014b). The Internet and 3D printers have joined the automated factories envisaged by Gorz (1985) and Rifkind (1995), blurring the boundaries between production and consumption and between paid and unpaid work and generating new kinds of intangible commodities.[1] Whilst the welfare states foreshadowed by Wells have morphed into new opportunities for capital accumulation (see Huws, 2012) the mass surveillance of the population which he saw as an inevitable feature of rational state planning (but which Orwell, 1949, and Huxley, 1998, viewed in a more sinister light) has become an everyday reality.

Because many of the new commodities are immaterial, with content comprised of digitized information, cultural labour has moved from the periphery to the centre of attention of the intellectuals studying these developments. No longer the preserve of an elite caste (as envisaged by More and the 19th-century

Utopian Socialists), or a taken-for-granted aspect of all production processes (as seen by Ruskin and Morris) or even an activity to be carried out by all in their leisure time (as in the Utopias imagined by feminists and the late 20th-century advocates of 'the end of work'), cultural production is now regarded as a central site of struggle. Whether this is seen as a simple contest between labour and capital or a more complex reconfiguration of antagonisms, in which individuals are reconstituted both as producers and as consumers of culture, varies considerably from author to author. There is now a copious literature on the phenomena conceived, *inter alia,* as 'playbour' (Kücklich, 2005), 'prosumption' (Comor, 2010; Toffler, 1980), and 'co-creation' (Banks and Humphreys, 2008; Prahalad and Ramaswamy, 2000) but the debate remains open. A detailed discussion of this literature is beyond the scope of this paper.

Even while following many of the same principles as their late 20th-century predecessors, the new Utopias, with their close attention to informational and cultural commodities, are distinctively different in their imagined details and in many of their central preoccupations. Of these new Utopians, Nick Dyer-Witheford (1999, 2013) provides what seems to be both the most comprehensively researched and elegantly argued account, so I will focus mainly on his work here.

Two key ingredients of his new world are some form of universal basic income for all and a radically reduced working day, achieved through the increased productivity brought about by technology. It is perhaps unfair to expect a detailed discussion of how, politically, such changes can be introduced. Both these demands do, however, raise major questions about the extent to which it is possible to bring about such changes at the level of a nation state (or indeed any other geographical or administrative unit) in the context of globally integrated markets, including labour markets.

To these two ingredients, Dyer-Witheford (2013) adds a third: the free exchange of information; and a fourth: the use of the potential of information technology to compute large amounts of data in real time both for the rational management of markets and to enable decentralized democratic decision making:

> . . . use of the most advanced super-computing to algorithmically calculate labour time and resource requirements, at global, regional and local levels, of multiple possible paths of human development; selection from these paths by layered democratic discussion conducted across assemblies that include socialized digital networks and swarms of software agents; light-speed updating and constant revision of the selected plans by streams of big data from production and consumption sources; the passage of increasing numbers of goods and services into the realm of the free or of direct production as use values once automation, copy-left, peer-to-peer commons and other forms of micro-replication take hold; the informing of the entire process by parameters set from the simulations, sensors and satellite systems measuring and monitoring the species metabolic interchange with the planetary environment. (Dyer-Witheford, 2013: 20)

In principle, this solution avoids the contradiction between security and democracy, exemplified by Wells, whereby the provision of a secure basic income and essential services for all requires a top-down paternalistic state. Dyer-Witheford (2013) puts centralized planning in the hands of decentralized decision-makers, in an approach that is similar in some ways to that of John Chris Jones (2000) in *The Internet and Everyone,* which draws on cybernetics to imagine a world in which the Internet can enable the development of new mutually shaped social forms.

In practice, however, in several of its features this approach replicates some of the problems raised by its predecessors. Although this vision is predicated on the further development of existing technologies, it does not take account of new technologies that might be developed in the future that fall outside the scope of this cybernetic market-like network. Indeed, this network seems to constitute something of a closed world, internally sensitive but impervious to external influences. For instance, it imagines sophisticated feedback mechanisms triggered by sensors monitoring the planetary environment but this presupposes knowledge of where to put the sensors. How might it cope with unforeseen biological or climatic phenomena? It also seems to be based in an essentialist notion of how social needs are constituted, not seeing them as socially and culturally shaped and changing over time. Who, for instance, could have foreseen thirty years ago that access to broadband might become seen as essential to the ability to function fully as a citizen? Nor does this model propose mechanisms by which such new technologies might be created and adopted. Like earlier Utopias, it seems to take for granted that the commodities that will be produced, distributed and consumed will be functionally similar to those that already exist, meeting needs that are already met through the market (at least for those who can afford them) under the present capitalist system.

Furthermore, it does not give any serious consideration to the activities currently carried out outside the market, by unpaid labour – the reproductive tasks that take up such a high proportion of most people's time. A conservative analysis of the available time use statistics (Ramey, 2008) estimated that in 2005 US women were spending 29.3 hours per week on average on 'home production' (compared with 46.8 in 1900) and men 16.8 hours (compared with 3.9 in 1900). Yet, despite considerable attention to the topic of 'free labour' (Terranova, 2000), in the general literature in this field, there is almost no discussion of how domestic reproductive work will be organized in these putative new Utopias. To be fair, Dyer-Witheford does discuss domestic labour in *Cyber-Marx,* referring to the 'wages for housework campaign' and the concept of 'zerowork' (1999: 435–436) but this is mentioned very much in passing in the context of a discussion about whether such labour is necessarily alienating. Housework appears in his Utopia only as a class of activity that, along with creative work, can be carried out in the leisure time that will be made available to all by the general reduction in paid working time, achieved through the application of labour-saving technologies in the workplace. There is no discussion of who will do this work or how its nature might be changed. In most of the other new Utopian literature it is barely mentioned. Whilst cultural labour and the production of information commodities are the focus of fascinated attention, reproductive labour appears to arouse little

The Sociological Review, 63:S1, pp. 158–173 (2015), DOI: 10.1111/1467-954X.12247

more than a yawn, and the dependence of the former on the latter is rendered invisible.

Conclusion

History tells us that unpaid reproductive activities can be seen as a sort of reservoir from which new commodities can be generated (see Huws, 2003 for a discussion of this). Indeed, I would contend that it is only possible to understand the capitalist system's extraordinary ability to extricate itself from its periodic crises, confounding the prophecies of those who assume that it will implode from its own contradictions, by this continuing ability to generate commodities for which new markets can be found. So long as there is unpleasant or repetitive unpaid work to be done, there will always be a market for new products that promise to make it easy, fun and apparently unlaborious. And new industries will arise to create and distribute them. A vision of the future that filters reproductive labour out of view thus runs the risk of failing to predict the next big wave of commodification. And a Utopia that focuses only on those activities that currently take place visibly within the market runs the risk of leaving the gender division of labour intact and disregarded. While Adam blogs, we must ask, who is cleaning the toilet?

Note

1 I have discussed this blurring of boundaries, elsewhere. See for instance, Huws, 2013.

References

Aronowitz, S. and DiFazio, W., (1994), *The Jobless Future*, Minneapolis: University of Minnesota Press.
Banks, J. and Humphreys, S., (2008), 'The labor of user co-creators', *Convergence*, 14 (4): 401–418.
Barbrook, R., (2007), *The Cyber-communist Manifesto*, available at: http://www.imaginaryfutures.net/2007/04/18/by-richard-barbrook/
Bauwens, M., (2006), 'The political economy of peer production', *Ctheory. Net*, available at: http://www.ctheory.net/articles.aspx?id=499.
Comor, E., (2010), 'Digital prosumption and alienation', *Ephemera*, 10 (3/4): 439–454.
Dyer-Witheford, N., (1999), *Cyber-Marx: Cycles and Circuits of Struggle in High-Technology Capitalism*, Urbana-Champaign, IL: University of Illinois Press.
Dyer-Witheford, N., (2013), 'Red plenty platforms', *Culture Machine*, 14: 1–27, available at: http://www.culturemachine.net/index.php/cm/article/download/511/526
Engels, F., (1880a [1970]), 'Socialism: Utopian and scientific', in *Marx/Engels Selected Works, Volume 3*, available at: http://www.marxists.org/archive/marx/works/1880/soc-utop/index.htm
Engels, F. (1880b), *The Origin of the Family, Private Property and the State*, available at: http://www.marxists.org/archive/marx/works/1884/origin-family/ch02d.htm
Fourier, C., (1822 [1972]), 'Attractive labour' from *Théorie de l'unité universelle: The Utopian Vision of Charles Fourier*. Selected Texts on Work, Love, and Passionate Attraction. Translated, edited and with an introduction by Jonathan Beecher and Richard Bienvenu. London: Jonathan Cape, available at: http://www.historyguide.org/intellect/fourier.html.
Gorz, A., (1982), *Farewell to the Working Class*, London: Pluto Press.

Gorz, A., (1985), *Paths to Paradise: On the Liberation from Work*, London: Pluto Press.

Hardt, M. and Negri, A., (2000), *Empire*, Cambridge, MA: Harvard University Press.

Hardt, M. and Negri, A., (2004), *Multitude: War and Democracy in the Age of Empire*, New York: Penguin.

Hardt, M. and Negri, A., (2009), *Commonwealth*, Cambridge, MA: Harvard University Press.

Huws, U. (1991), 'What is a green-red economics? The future of work', *Z magazine*, September.

Huws, U., (2003), *The Making of a Cybertariat: Virtual Work in a Real World*, New York: Monthly Review Press.

Huws U., (2007), 'The spark in the engine', *Work Organisation, Labour and Globalisation*, 1(1): 1–10.

Huws, U., (2010), 'Expression and expropriation: the dialectics of autonomy and control in creative labour', *Ephemera*, 10 (3/4): 504–521.

Huws, U., (2012), 'Crisis as capitalist opportunity: new accumulation through public service commodification', *Socialist Register*, 48.

Huws, U., (2013), 'Shifting boundaries: gender, labor and new information and communication technologies', in C. Carter, L. Steiner and L. McLaughlin (eds), *Routledge Companion to Media and Gender*, 147–156, London: Routledge.

Huws, U., (2014a), 'The underpinnings of class in the digital age: living, labour and value', *Socialist Register*, 50.

Huws, U., (2014b), *Labour in a Digital Global Economy: The Cybertariat Comes of Age*, New York: Monthly Review Press.

Huxley, A., (1931 [1998]), *Brave New World*, New York: HarperCollins.

Illich, I., (1982), *Gender*, New York: Pantheon Books.

Jones, J.C., (2000), *The Internet and Everyone*, London: Ellipsis.

Kücklich, J., (2005), 'Precarious playbour: modders and the digital games industry', *The Fibreculture Journal*, 5.

Le Guin, U., (1969), *Left Hand of Darkness*, New York: Ace Books.

More, T., (1901), *Ideal Commonwealths*, New York: P.F. Collier & Son. The Colonial Press, available at: http://oregonstate.edu/instruct/phl302/texts/more/Utopia-trade.html

Morris, W., (1890 [2003]), *News from Nowhere*, available at: http://www.marxists.org/archive/morris/works/1890/nowhere/nowhere.htm

Moses, C. G., (1984), *French Feminism in the 19th Century*, Albany, NY: State University of New York Press.

Orwell, G., (1949), *1984*, available at: http://wikilivres.ca/wiki/Nineteen_Eighty-Four

Owen, R., (1816), *Address to the Inhabitants of New Lanark*, available at: http://www.marxists.org/reference/subject/economics/owen/

Owen, R. (1839) *New Moral World, Volume 6*, available at: http://books.google.co.uk/books?id=RXtGAAAAMAAJ&printsec=frontcover&dq=new+moral+world+robert+owen+volume+6&hl=en&sa=X&ei=UpGIUoWsEeag7Aaa2oDYAQ&ved=0CDMQ6AEwAA#v=onepage&q=new%20moral%20world%20robert%20owen%20volume%206&f=false

Perkins Gilman, C., (1915 [1979]), *Herland*, New York: Pantheon Books, available at: http://www.gutenberg.org/files/32/32-h/32-h.htm

Piercy, M., (1976), *Woman on the Edge of Time*, New York: Fawcett Crest.

Prahalad, C. K. and Ramaswamy, V., (2000), 'Co-opting customer competence', *Harvard Business Review*, January/February.

Quesnay F., (1758), 'Tableau Économique. 'Third' edition', reprinted in M. Kuczynsi and R. L. Meek (eds), *Quesnay's Tableau Économique*, New York: A.M. Kelley, 1972, available at: http://www.marxists.org/reference/subject/economics/quesnay/1759/tableau.htm

Ramey, V., (2008), *Time Spent in Home Production in the 20th Century: New Estimates from Old Data*, Working Paper 13985, Cambridge, MA: National Bureau of Economic Research, available at: http://www.nber.org/papers/w13985.pdf?new_window=1

Rifkind, J., (1995), *The End of Work: The Decline of the Global Labor Force and the Dawn of the Post-Market Era*, New York: Putnam.

The Sociological Review, 63:S1, pp. 158–173 (2015), DOI: 10.1111/1467-954X.12247

Rigi, J., (2012), 'Peer-to-peer production as the alternative to capitalism: a new communist horizon', *Journal of Peer Production*, 1, available at: http://peerproduction.net/issues/issue-1/invited-comments/anew-communist-horizon/

Rousseau, J-J., (1750 [1997]), *'The Discourses' and Other Early Political Writings*, trans. V. Gourevitch, Cambridge: Cambridge University Press.

Rousseau, J-J., (1754), *'Discourse on Inequality'*, trans. G.D. H. Cole, available at: http://www.nutleyschools.org/userfiles/150/Classes/5377/DiscourseonInequality.pdf (accessed 12 February, 2015).

Rousseau, J-J., (1762[1979]), *Emile, or On Education*, trans. with an introd. by A. Bloom, New York: Basic Books.

Saint-Simon, C-H., (1803), *Letters from an Inhabitant of Geneva to his Contemporaries*, available at: http://www.marxists.org/reference/subject/philosophy/works/fr/st-simon.htm

Siefkes, C., (2012), 'Beyond digital plenty: building blocks for physical peer production', *Journal of Peer Production* 1, available at: http://peerproduction.net/issues/issue-1/invitedcomments/

Smith, A., (1776), *An Inquiry into the Nature and Causes of the Wealth of Nations*, available at: http://www.adamsmith.org/smith/won-b1-intro.htm.

Smith, D. C., (1986), *H.G. Wells: Desperately Mortal*, New Haven and London: Yale University Press.

Terranova, T., (2000), 'Free labor: producing culture for the digital economy', *Social Text*, 18: 33–58.

Toffler, A., (1980), *The Third Wave*, New York: Bantam Books.

Wells, H. G., (1905), *A Modern Utopia*, available at: http://www.gutenberg.org/dirs/etext04/mdntp10h.htm

Wollestonecraft, M., (1792), *A Vindication of the Rights of Woman with Strictures on Political and Moral Subjects*, available at: http://www.gutenberg.org/catalog/world/readfile?fk_files=3275304

The Sociological Review, 63:S1, pp. 158–173 (2015), DOI: 10.1111/1467-954X.12247
© 2015 The Author. Editorial organisation © 2015 The Editorial Board of the Sociological Review

A new mystique? Working for yourself in the neoliberal economy

Stephanie Taylor

Abstract: This article discusses the growing UK trend of people working for themselves. Beginning with the example of a media representation, it explores the wider implications of a discursive drift by which discourses of entrepreneurialism and contemporary creative work converge on the new figure of the worker who leaves paid employment for the supposed satisfactions of working from home. The article argues that, in contrast to the heroic masculine figures of the entrepreneur and artist, this is a feminized low-status worker. Its celebration is part of a 'new mystique' resembling the 'housewife trap' described by Friedan (1963) half a century ago, because for increasing numbers of people, both male and female, working for yourself amounts to exclusion to an almost subsistence level of economic activity on the margins of the neoliberal economy.

Keywords: entrepreneurialism, creative work, feminization, discursive drift

Introduction

Growing numbers of UK workers in a wide range of fields are now involved in some arrangement of working for themselves, including self-employment, freelancing or running their own small businesses. Research indicates that many of these workers suffer the uncertain incomes, fragile career trajectories and general precarity which have long been recognized as the experience of workers in the cultural and creative industries (eg Gill and Pratt, 2008). In addition, recent media representations exemplify a discursive drift by which working for yourself in any field is characterized using the now established discourses of contemporary creative work, including the associations with art which have functioned as an attraction for creative workers, a focus for their aspirations, and an inducement for them to tolerate difficulties and uncertainty (eg McRobbie, 1998; Taylor and Littleton, 2012). This article argues that central to this discursive drift is neither the 'fundamentally masculine' (Ahl and Marlow, 2012) figure of the successful entrepreneur nor the masculine artist but a novel, feminized (though not inevitably female) figure, who works on a small scale, mostly alone and from home, motivated by the hope of self-fulfilment and freedom as alternative rewards to a

The Sociological Review, 63:S1, pp. 174–187 (2015), DOI: 10.1111/1467-954X.12248
© 2015 The Author. Editorial organisation © 2015 The Editorial Board of the Sociological Review. Published by John Wiley & Sons Ltd, 9600 Garsington Road, Oxford OX4 2DQ, UK and 350 Main Street, Malden, MA 02148, USA

steady income and secure employment. The article proposes that this feminized figure is part of a 'new mystique', resembling the 'housewife trap' made famous by Betty Friedan (1963) which invited women to move back from the paid work-force to the home and domesticity. The new mystique attached to working for yourself is part of a process of exclusion by which increasing numbers of work-ers, both male and female, are encouraged to accept a marginalized position in the neoliberal economy.

The first section of the article describes the trend and situation of people work-ing for themselves, drawing on recent research. The next section discusses one ex-ample of a recent media representation of these workers to draw out some of the parallels with work in the contemporary cultural and creative industries (CCI) and outline the discursive drift by which discourses of entrepreneurialism and creative work converge. The following sections discuss two figures central to these discourses, the entrepreneur and the creative artist, to show their gendering and explore its wider implications, including in relation to home as the site in which people are working for themselves.

Working for themselves: the people and the problems

Statistics on employment in the UK indicate that an increasing number of peo-ple are working for themselves. Discussion is complicated by the variety of pos-sible arrangements and categories: these people include those described as self-employed, freelance or owning their own small businesses, with some differences of meaning in those terms. A recent UK report by Conor D'Arcy and Laura Gar-diner refers to the 'self-employed' and cites the following definition from EURO-STAT: 'Self-employed persons are the ones who work in their own business, farm or professional practice' (quoted in D'Arcy and Gardiner, 2014: 8). However, the authors note that other criteria may be used, sometimes for tax purposes. Their own definition includes individuals who run their own businesses, with the possi-bility of hiring other people; provide their own equipment and decide when, how and where to work; and have several customers at the same time. Like the EU-ROSTAT definition, this encompasses terms used by other sources on employ-ment research, including, to cite a few examples from different national contexts, 'homeworking' (Dex, 2009), 'home-based businesses' (Clark and Douglas, 2010; Loscocco and Smith-Hunter, 2004) and 'home-based work' (Tietze *et al.,* 2009). For the purposes of this article, my interest, paralleling D'Arcy and Gardiner's, is in people who are in an alternative situation to full-time paid employment by others, and work largely or entirely from home. Hereafter I adopt the language of particular sources when citing them and otherwise refer to these people as working for themselves.

D'Arcy and Gardiner (2014) report that self-employment has been increasing in the UK since the 1960s but has accelerated since 2008 to the point that in 2014 the self-employed amount to nearly 15 per cent of all employment, or one in seven. D'Arcy and Gardiner interpret the increase partly as a structural change, reflecting general changes in the way people work which include rises in portfolio careers and precarious working. (These have been widely discussed as features of work in the cultural and creative industries, or CCI: eg Gill and Pratt, 2008.) However, they suggest that the increase in self-employment is also partly cyclical and an effect of the recession, in that some people are becoming self-employed because paid employment is not available. There are also increasing numbers of people who are self-employed part-time, sometimes combining this work with paid employment.

Describing the UK self-employed, D'Arcy and Gardiner (2014) note that there has been an increase in the proportion who are women, although this is still less than half overall and smaller than the proportion in other OECD countries. (On various definitions, 2011 figures showed the proportion of UK women working for themselves was below the OECD average: OECD, 2013: 69.) There are also increasing numbers of older self-employed people, including those over 60. Mirroring trends in the workforce as a whole, self-employed and employed, there has been an increase in the proportion of self-employed people educated to degree level or higher and working in service sectors; 18 per cent more in information and communications, 10 per cent more in arts and leisure and 49 per cent in other service sectors. Some of these will include workers in the CCI which, as a sector, has been noted to have a very high proportion of 'micro-businesses' (Miles and Green, 2008).

Earlier research provides some general background on why working for yourself might appear an attractive option. In a review of survey-based research on work, Shirley Dex (2009) notes that in the late 20th and early 21st century the UK workforce has become both better qualified and more dissatisfied. There has been an increase in work strain, especially among women employees, and also a general decline in 'rates of organisational commitment, or commitment to the organisation's values'. Dex notes that these were 'very low among employees in Britain around the turn of the Millennium' (2009: 17). Workers are less deferential and expect more autonomy than in the past. Dex also reports that, despite predictions in the 1960s that people would become more instrumental, working primarily for money and losing 'the traditional work ethic', recent surveys indicate that UK workers are still committed to 'work as a central life interest' and they value 'intrinsic aspects of work and having interesting work' over 'a high income' (2009: 16). Although she acknowledges the difficulty of prediction, Dex proposes that 'The trend towards so-called *humanization* of work is likely to continue', for instance, through opportunities for 'increased autonomy', 'self-development' and 'greater employee involvement' (2009: 18). The dissatisfactions and expectations she describes suggest that people who are unhappy working for others, eager to do interesting and satisfying work which uses their skills, and willing to risk some earning disadvantage, might see working for themselves as a desirable alternative to paid employment which offers the 'humanization' they are seeking.

Research on people starting their own businesses has indicated that 'lifestyle issues' are more likely to motivate women than men (Walker and Webster, 2007: 125) and a particular group working for themselves are those who researchers

The Sociological Review, 63:S1, pp. 174–187 (2015), DOI: 10.1111/1467-954X.12248

have dubbed 'mumpreneurs', that is, women who 'set up a business in order to enable them to both work and care for young children' (Duberley and Carrigan, 2012: 629). Carol Ekinsmyth offers a more specific definition, that the mumpreneur has '*configured* her business around her caring role rather than simply juggling the two' (2013: 2, emphasis in original), facilitated by new ICTs. (Ekinsmyth notes that this definition could equally embrace a male parent.) She suggests that mumpreneurship is a 'spatial phenomenon' since it involves 'creatively building businesses around the sociospatial routines of daily childcare' (2013:2). The key space would seem to be home as the double site of living and earning.

An optimistic view of the phenomenon of mumpreneurship could be that it amounts to a reconstruing of business practice in order to take account of additional, non-economic values, thereby achieving some of the humanization referred to by Dex (2009). However, researchers have found that women who attempt to reconcile the demands of a business with domestic responsibilities are likely to experience long working hours, conflicts around space and time which result in 'tension and stress' (Thompson *et al.,* 2009: 229), and also reduced returns and survival prospects. Rather than being a magic solution, mumpreneurship is therefore potentially 'a "no win" situation' (Thompson *et al.,* 2009: 235). Other researchers suggest that mumpreneurs are additionally likely to be overburdened because they are attempting to reconcile a business career with contemporary requirements for a form of intensive mothering which is 'wholly child-centred, emotionally involving and time-consuming' (Duberley and Carrigan, 2012: 633) and even a 'fetishization of the maternal' (Littler, 2013).

The problems of mumpreneurs echo those found to be part of the more general experience of working for yourself. For anyone working at home, the boundaries between work and non-work time are likely to become blurred so that work overflows into other areas of life. (This kind of overflow is exacerbated by new technologies, in the phenomenon which Gregg, 2011, calls 'presence bleed'.) Another problem is the loss of the social contacts obtained in more conventional working situations. D'Arcy and Gardiner (2014: 19) report that 83 per cent of the self-employed do not employ anyone else and Dex (2009) has noted the isolation faced by people who work from home in any capacity, whether as casual workers, employees or 'entrepreneurs'. On the financial side, D'Arcy and Gardiner suggest that their research 'paints a worrying picture of the security and vulnerability of self-employed people' (2014: 5). The self-employed are a cause for concern since they earn less than the employed (typically, about 40 per cent less, though part of this may be due to reduced hours) and their earnings have fallen faster in the recession than the earnings of the employed. They are also less likely to be contributing to a pension. D'Arcy and Gardiner's (2014) evidence of the lower earnings of self-employed people is echoed by research on home-based businesses which has found that these 'are likely to be relatively small in scale, insecure and offer poor returns' (Thompson *et al.*, 2009: 228). A further finding is that such businesses have poor prospects for growth.

The new entrepreneurs?

The trend of working for yourself has received considerable media attention in UK 'quality' papers. Some recent articles refer to the problems ('Many 'self-employed' women earn less than £10,000 a year': Fisher, 2014) but many, perhaps unsurprisingly, tend to be upbeat. For example, one headline claims 'Generation of entrepreneurs grows up in the downturn' (Allen, 2014), although the sub-head warns 'More jobless youth are choosing self-employment but it's not an easy option'. A Technology feature 'The best of British startups' celebrates 'technology clusters' as part of an 'urban renaissance' and 'a broader economic story, with more new businesses started in the UK last year than at any time in our history' (Silva, 2014). Another article notes that 'More than 520,000 new businesses registered with Companies House during 2013, a rise of 8% on 2012 and a record high, according to website StartUp Britain' (Prosser, 2014: n.p.).

A further article which I will discuss in detail, by Emine Saner, was published on *The Guardian* website on 24 November 2013 with the more ambivalent headline 'Cottage industries: all homework and no play?' (Saner, 2013a), and then, in a slightly abridged version, with a different headline, 'Home alone', in the print edition of the same newspaper on Monday 25 November 13 (Saner, 2013b). Both versions are sub-headed with the claim that 'Cottage industries are booming in the UK – the number of people working from home has doubled in the past 10 years', firmly presenting the people discussed as examples of a trend. The article invites readers to meet six[1] 'entrepreneurs' who work from home, three women and three men 'whose longest commute is to their kitchen'. The reference to 'cottage industries' in the headline (Saner, 2013a) is yet another variation on the terminology for working for yourself. The word 'cottage' perhaps adds an implication of tradition and even cosiness but this term is not used by any of the interviewees, at least as they are quoted. Instead, three of the six refer to having 'a business' or 'a company' so correspond to the situation variously described by research sources as a 'home-based business' (eg Clark and Douglas, 2010; Loscocco and Smith-Hunter, 2004), small business or 'micro-business' (eg Miles and Green, 2008). The other three describe themselves differently. One refers to 'working from home', which he contrasts with two previous experiences, working for a company, and employing other people. Another has 'an office at home' and 'about 40 clients', and the last refers to himself as 'freelance' and 'self-employed'.

Saner's article follows a familiar journalistic format in which the six people featured are presented in turn, with accompanying photos. Two are in the fashion industry, one as a designer of ethically sourced clothes and the other, formerly a teacher of fashion design, running a children's clothing company. Two of the interviewees exemplify the novel occupations generated by social media: one is a social-media consultant and one a former designer who is now a design blogger. The fifth interviewee is a taxidermist who emphasizes that his work, whether on commission or for 'stock' pieces that he will sell, is motivated by his passion for wildlife. The sixth interviewee is a recruitment consultant for 'high-calibre staff ... managing directors or part-time financial directors'. Their supposedly

The Sociological Review, 63:S1, pp. 174–187 (2015), DOI: 10.1111/1467-954X.12248
© 2015 The Author. Editorial organisation © 2015 The Editorial Board of the Sociological Review

first person accounts appear to have been edited down from answers to questions (which are not included) about their respective employment histories, financial situations, motivations for working from home and day-to-day working experience. Because of the editing process, it could be argued that the article presents the author's rather than the interviewees' claims and positionings, since the latter are quoted selectively. Here, my interest is in the whole article as one among the related media representations.

A first point to note is that the article is extremely positive in both its overall narrative and in some of the interviewees' specific claims. The shift to working for yourself is presented as an improved situation for each of them, and a solution to previous problems or dissatisfaction. For example, one interviewee says: 'At one point, I was employing eight people but I didn't like the relentlessness of it'. He now works by himself, on a smaller scale and with a lower turnover, because 'It is more important to me to do good work'. Another comments 'I don't think I could go back to being an employee'. Two of the interviewees fit the category of mumpreneurs, discussed in the previous section. One of them gave up 'a really good job' to run a children's clothes company from home because she did not want to 'work long hours with a commute and three children in childcare'. She is 'happier to have a cut' in her income than return to her previous commuting situation because 'the bonus for me is that I can work around my children'. The second woman had taken a career break when she had her children and did not want to return to a job in the City with 'very limiting' hours and a long commute. She set herself up as a recruitment consultant and now organizes her work time 'so I can fit it around my children'. She received help from 'other mothers' to set up the business initially and now lists many women with children among the candidates for whom she finds work.

Although the overall implication of Saner's article is that the positives of working for yourself outweigh the negatives, it does acknowledge the kinds of difficulties discussed in the previous section, including in its headline 'Home alone'. Alongside a few mentions of the flexibility of working for yourself, such as 'sneaking away' if there's 'a lull', there are many references to hard work and long hours. Interviewees describe having no holidays, as already quoted, working in the evenings, having 'less time to spend with friends' and getting a dog as an incentive 'to get me out of the house'. The two mumpreneurs organize their work around their children: 'Once they're asleep at night I can carry on if there are still things to do'. Interviewees are also quoted as referring to loneliness: 'I do miss working with a group of people at times'; 'It can be a bit lonely'; 'It can be a bit of a downer being by yourself'. Most notably, all of the accounts contain some reference to precarious financial situations: 'Any profit I make I put back into the company. I don't have sickies'; 'it's not lucrative'; 'It was tough financially to begin with'; 'I'm currently having to spend vital cash flow on legal fees to protect my intellectual property'; 'It does get a bit scary when the money isn't coming in quite as regularly'; 'I'm making the most of it while it lasts because you never know what's going to happen'. The article also indicates that for at least an initial period, all of the interviewees depended on other financial support, provided, respectively, by a spouse, 'an investment portfolio', alternative forms of work, and the redundancy payment from a previous job.

The article is summarized here in some detail because of the apparent parallels with work in the contemporary cultural and creative industries. Echoing researchers' findings that cultural and creative workers claim to 'love' what they do (eg Gill, 2007; Taylor and Littleton, 2012), Saner's interviewees' accounts refer to 'passion': 'doing something that is your passion'; 'I'm passionate about wildlife'; 'It's a job I'm passionate about so it's quite easy to keep motivated'. Creative work is regarded by its practitioners as personal in the sense of being closely matched to their interests and experience (Taylor and Littleton, 2012) and the accounts in Saner's (2013a) article indicate a similar emphasis, for example, in the many references to what the various interviewees 'want' and what is 'important to me', as does the more general narrative of the article, that financial precariousness, long hours and loneliness are compensated by the satisfaction of pursuing a personal project or vocation. The accounts in Saner's (2013a) article also accord with Mark Banks' claim that many creative workers are motivated by 'a multitude of moral and political impulses' (2007: 187). For example, the first interviewee in the article is a fashion designer who had previously worked for companies in which 'their priorities were margins and profits'. She explains that she started her own business because she wanted instead 'to produce my own designs, but in a more responsible, thoughtful way. I wanted clothes that were still beautiful and well-cut … but were still ethically sourced', made from sustainable fabrics. Another interviewee claims as an additional benefit of running a business that 'I feel I'm helping indirectly to generate a manufacturing base in this country again, however small. I do feel proud of that'.

What then is the significance of these parallels and overlaps with creative work? The contemporary creative sector has always been broadly defined (eg Department of Culture, Media and Sport, 2001) and Fuller *et al.* (2013) suggest that recently the reference of creativity 'has expanded to include virtually all the performative labours producing the information economy, from computer coding to legal research' (2013: 144). It would therefore be possible to argue the specialisms of at least some of the six home-based interviewees in Saner's (2013a) article locate them *within* the sector, as creative workers. However, this is not how Saner categorizes them. Rather, the parallels which I have described are a further example of a discursive drift by which discourses of entrepreneurialism and creative work converge. The significance of the drift becomes clear through a closer examination of the gendering of two figures, the creative artist and the entrepreneur, which are central to these discourses and underlie discussions of people working for themselves, including in Saner's article.

Gendered figures

This section will consider the implications of the images of two figures associated with contemporary work. The first is the entrepreneur whose personal enterprise, such as a willingness to pursue opportunities and take risks, is of course central to

The Sociological Review, 63:S1, pp. 174–187 (2015), DOI: 10.1111/1467-954X.12248

the market-driven accounts of economic development associated with neoliberalism. The entrepreneur is also associated with working for yourself. D'Arcy and Gardiner note that: 'For those who see high rates of self-employment as positive, much is made of the entrepreneurialism and innovation associated with going it alone' (2014: 17). Also, since 2011, unemployed people in the UK who become self-employed have been able to claim the New Enterprise Allowance (NEA), apparently in an expectation that the imagined inactivity of the unemployed person will be transformed into the commendable activity of the entrepreneur. The second figure is the creative artist or auteur (McRobbie, 1998) whose image underlies many now-established understandings of careers and work practices in the CCI. The congruence between the agentic individual figures of the entrepreneur and the creative artist, pursuing their respective business and creative projects, was recognized in early discussions of the CCI. Kate Oakley notes that entrepreneurship has been a key notion in the policies which defined cultural and creative industries in the late 20th and early 21st centuries (2009: 291). Angela McRobbie, discussing young fashion designers in the 1990s, saw a 'fusion of entrepreneurial values with a belief in the creative self, with the latter providing a rationale for the former' (1998: 83).

A less commonly noted connection is that the entrepreneur and the creative artist are both masculine figures. Helene Ahl and Susan Marlow suggest that 'the defining characteristics of the entrepreneur are also those which define masculinity' (2012: 544). Ahl (2006) analysed research articles and 'foundational' economic texts about entrepreneurs, referring to an index of the characteristics associated with masculinity and femininity compiled by the psychologist Sandra Bem. Ahl's finding was that the attributes of the entrepreneur are both positive and masculine; the femininity characteristics identified by Bem were either the opposite of entrepreneurial, or not related to it at all. Ahl concludes that the image of the entrepreneur is that of 'a heroic self-made man' (2006: 599). In a strikingly similar summary, Alison Bain, discussing female artistic identity, writes: 'In contemporary Western mythology, the artist is understood to be male. The dominant cultural myth is of the "artist as male hero"' (2004: 172). This probably derives from the celebrated named figures of European art, especially in the 19th century, the vast majority of whom were men.

Subsequent to McRobbie's claim, quoted above, researchers have explored in more detail how contemporary creative workers are influenced by the image of the artist, including how the value attached to being creative can lead them to blur the boundaries between work and non-work, and to accept uncertain career trajectories and limited financial rewards for their work (at least in the short-term) (Taylor, 2011; Taylor and Littleton, 2012). However, the research indicates that the aspirations of contemporary creative workers are not wholly consistent with an elite masculine artist figure who pursues a creative vocation with ruthless selfishness, occupying an outsider position because he rejects the values and conditions of participation in the mainstream economy. Instead, many workers appeared to be influenced by a creative figure who occupies a different kind of marginalized economic position, turning away from participation in the competitive context of professional 'art worlds' (Becker, 1982) in order to carry out an almost therapeutic, personal creative project. In the terms of a 'hierarchical gendered ordering where femininity is associated with deficit' (Ahl and Marlow, 2012: 545), this is a feminized figure, consistent with the larger sociological thesis of the feminization of work as a general contemporary phenomenon which impacts on both women and men (eg Adkins and Jokinen, 2008). The feminization thesis is complex but two key arguments are that with the spread of short-term employment and portfolio working, the 'atypical and precarious working conditions that formerly fell to women are currently becoming common among men as well' (Veijola and Jokinen, 2008: 175), and that contemporary work increasingly requires forms of relating and communication skills which entail the emotional work and 'affective labour' conventionally done by women more than men. It is this second, feminized creative figure, I suggest, who is more relevant to the discursive drift described in the previous section, and to the situation and aspirations of the people working for themselves who are the focus of this article.

A new mystique

As Saner's headline 'Home alone' indicates, for many people working for themselves, the site of their work is also the place where they live. Home as a place of work has complex, and of course gendered, associations that are further complicated by the discursive drift between creative work and working for yourself. Conventionally, home is the site of the unpaid domestic work of women, and its supposed attractions (some of which are indicated in Saner's article) derive in part from the disconnect with paid employment. Home is a place of freedom in contrast to the restrictions of conventional workplaces, a place to be with children instead of apart from them, a place in which personal values can be prioritized and, from all of these expectations, a place in which the worker is able to be whole or complete, retaining some authenticity of self which is assumed to be lost or at least jeopardized in the conflicts of different, larger employment contexts. Such positive images are central to discussions of work-life balance which generally assume some process of encroachment or contamination whereby the larger worlds of work threaten the containment of the home (eg Gregory and Milner, 2009).

A different set of associations follow from the Romantic associations of the workshop and studio as spaces in which creative makers both live and work. The workshop is associated with the continuation of work outside the capitalist economy. It is implicitly contrasted with the separated work and living spaces of industrialized working life, the factory and the home, and therefore with the alienation of the industrial factory worker whose work is only for others. However, it is a masculine space because it is the site for non-domestic work, for the activities of the craftsman, in contrast to the conventional crafts of women (for instance, in textiles) most of which are directly linked to the home. The image of the studio is also masculine, heavily influenced by biographies of 19th-century European male artists which were publicized as selling points for their work (eg White and White, 1965). As part of the elite masculine image of the artist, the

The Sociological Review, 63:S1, pp. 174–187 (2015), DOI: 10.1111/1467-954X.12248

studio is a site for painting or other creative work, and also sleeping, eating, drinking and receiving visitors and prospective buyers who come to view work. It is a space of relative poverty, following from the rejection of participation in 'ordinary' work or routine employment in the capitalist economy, and of responsibility for earning to support other people financially. It is also, however, a space of privilege, in that a choice has been made to prioritize creative work over the claims of others. The 'selfishness' of this prioritizing, to use a term from contemporary creative workers' own accounts (Taylor and Littleton, 2012), conflicts with the other-directedness that operates not only in caring roles, such as parenting, but also more generally as part of a contemporary feminine identity (Taylor, 2011).

Alison Bain (2004), conducting research with Canadian women visual artists found that possession of a studio was a 'powerful identity marker for them' precisely because of the gendered associations. Having a studio functions as part of these women's claim to belong to a profession which is still largely male-dominated. But although it was the aspiration of Bain's participants to have their own studios, she found, in an example of the difficulties of resisting expectations of other-directedness, that many of the women also had to fight to *protect* their claims to the studio as their own space, for example, if it was in or near a family home, to close the door and resist the encroachment of other people and their belongings.

For people working for themselves, the reassurances of home as a safer place and the creative promises of the workshop and studio as living/working sites potentially merge in the feminized creative figure discussed earlier, to promote a withdrawal from the challenges of paid employment and a return to this more private and personalized site. This kind of '"turning away" from wider social issues and publics' (Littler, 2013: 235) has been described as a contemporary 'retreatist fantasy' (2013: 239). It also recalls the fantasy discussed by the US feminist writer Betty Friedan in the early 1960s. She argued that women's hard-won fights for the right to escape from home, become educated and work as professionals were being subverted through a revived 'mystique of feminine fulfilment' (1963:18) which was supposedly to be attained through women's return to the home and domesticity. The mystique was reinforced institutionally, for example, through college courses which educated women to be good wives and mothers. Friedan suggested that, as a consequence, a new generation of women were suffering 'by choosing femininity over the painful growth to full identity, by never achieving the hard core of self that comes not from fantasy but from mastering reality' (1963: 181). (This of course invokes again a deficit model of femininity.) The tone is harsh. Friedan criticizes a 'sick society' which ignores and wastes women's strength and abilities. Then she suggests:

> Perhaps it is only sick or immature men and women, unwilling to face the great challenges of society, who can retreat for long, without unbearable distress, into that thing-ridden house and make it the end of life itself. (1963: 232)

The Sociological Review, 63:S1, pp. 174–187 (2015), DOI: 10.1111/1467-954X.12248
© 2015 The Author. Editorial organisation © 2015 The Editorial Board of the Sociological Review

183

The contemporary self-employed, freelancers and owners of small businesses, female and male, who are the focus of this article, would probably distance themselves from such narrow ambitions, yet the celebrations of working for yourself which I have discussed can be seen as the latest variant of the phenomenon which Friedan (1963) describes and as part of a new mystique which again potentially excludes women, and others, by encouraging them to return home, in the guise of a different set of priorities.

Interestingly, Friedan herself referred to such variants. Her criticisms extended to women with 'small businesses that open and close with sad regularity' (1963: 347). She also noted, sarcastically, the attraction of creative work:

> The 'arts' seem, at first glance, to be the ideal answer for a woman. They can, after all, be practiced in the home. They do not necessarily imply that dreaded professionalism, they are suitably feminine, and seem to offer endless room for personal growth and identity, with no need to compete in society for pay. (1963: 348)

However, she went on to separate the situation of the 'amateur or dilettante' from professional women creatives (1963: 348). The distinguishing features of the latter, in her account, are that they enter the competition, seeking appropriate pay, peer recognition and social status. More generally, she is arguing for the fuller participation of women in contrast to their exclusion at home: a woman needs 'work in which she can grow *as part of society*' (1963: 345, emphasis added).

A premise of Friedan's argument is therefore that such work exists out there, in society, to be won through effort, even if there are barriers to break down. The different circumstance of many of the people working for themselves in the UK today is that the work may not be there, because of the recession and, in the longer term, because of the structural changes which have resulted in more and more precarious working. Other writers (eg Morgan and Nelligan, this volume) have noted that neoliberal economies require a new kind of worker. This is a person who is mobile and malleable, infinitely energetic and ambitious, living in the present and ready to adapt to the immediate demands of changing markets. The ultimate false promise of working for yourself may be that it offers a viable alternative for people who do not conform to this masculine ideal, for instance, because of their caring responsibilities, maturity or work history.

Conclusion

This article has discussed the current trend of people working for themselves, exploring one newspaper article as an example of media representations of such workers. Following the premises of a narrative-discursive approach (eg Taylor and Littleton, 2006, 2012), a newspaper article like that by Emine Saner (2013a, 2013b), however conscientiously sourced, can be analysed as a construction.

The Sociological Review, 63:S1, pp. 174–187 (2015), DOI: 10.1111/1467-954X.12248
© 2015 The Author. Editorial organisation © 2015 The Editorial Board of the Sociological Review

It invokes well-established notions and narratives, such as those linked to entrepreneurial and creative discourses. The recognizable and familiar character of these discursive and cultural resources is what makes the construction persuasive, because it apparently makes sense.

Saner's article presents a range of people who turn from paid employment to working for themselves, thereby achieving a better lifestyle and resolving conflicts, for example, between earning and caring for children. The article invites identification with this supposedly liberated new kind of worker. Littler (2013: 228) notes that the 'formulation' of a figure as a social type can be 'actively used' within a certain context to shape ideas about a role and way of living. In these terms, the presentation of working for yourself in Saner's article and others can be understood as 'part of the process whereby contemporary media negotiate a work world where, whether by accident or by design, "the individualism of self-realization … has … become an instrument of economic development"' (Couldry and Littler, 2011: 268, citing Honneth, 2004). However, in contrast, to the heroic and masculine figure of the conventional entrepreneur, the hypothetical new worker is a feminized figure, retreating from the pressures of the conventional working world and often accepting an almost subsistence level of earning on the margins of the neoliberal economy.

A conventional narrative of entrepreneurship, consistent with the market-driven focus of neoliberalism, is that the currently small-scale projects of the people now working for themselves will expand to drive future economic development; this is the narrative attached to the New Enterprise Allowance. However, an alternative view, more consistent with feminization, would be that people working for themselves are not the potential drivers of future prosperity but the marginal figures excluded from it. This interpretation is supported by D'Arcy and Gardiner's (2014) finding that the growth in the self-employed is partly accounted for by people over 60, many of whom work part-time, and that another significant group are people who are self-employed as a second job. These groups do not appear in the self-employed statistics at all but amount to about 1 per cent of all employees! (D'Arcy and Gardiner, 2014: 18). Taken together with the cyclical rise in self-employment, these statistics and the example of mumpreneurs suggest that the relevant narrative of working for yourself may be less about career beginnings, prospective expansion, ambition and entrepreneurial success than about sustaining yourself through difficult circumstances, like unemployment, and coping with inadequate pensions, insufficient earnings and the need to raise the next generation. The move from conventional employment to this new situation, presented positively in Saner's article, is of course a move to precariousness consistent with the general thesis of the feminization of work. The larger narrative of neoliberalism here is that of creeping privatization, exclusion and the personalization of responsibility for dealing with circumstances – retirement, caring responsibilities, unemployment and under-earning – which formerly warranted support from a welfare state.

The Sociological Review, 63:S1, pp. 174–187 (2015), DOI: 10.1111/1467-954X.12248
© 2015 The Author. Editorial organisation © 2015 The Editorial Board of the Sociological Review

Note

1 There are six in the online article and five in the shorter print version.

References

Adkins, L. and Jokinen, E., (2008), 'Introduction: gender, living and labour in the fourth shift', *NORA – Nordic Journal of Feminist and Gender Research*, 16 (3): 138–149.

Ahl, H., (2006), 'Why research on women entrepreneurs needs new directions', *Entrepreneurship Theory and Practice*, 30 (5): 595–621.

Ahl, H. and Marlow, S., (2012), 'Exploring the dynamics of gender, feminism and entrepreneurship: advancing debate to escape a dead end?', *Organization*, 19 (5): 543–562.

Allen, K., (2014), 'Generation of entrepreneurs grow up in the downturn', *The Guardian*, 13 May.

Bain, A., (2004), 'Female artistic identity in place: the studio', *Social & Cultural Geography*, 5 (2): 171–193.

Banks, M., (2007), *The Politics of Cultural Work*, Basingstoke and New York: Palgrave Macmillan.

Becker, H., (1982), *Art Worlds*, Berkeley, CA: University of California Press.

Clark, D. and Douglas, H., (2010), 'Micro business: characteristics of home-based business in New Zealand', *Small Enterprise Research*, 17: 112–123.

Couldry, N. and Littler, J., (2011), 'Work, power and performance. analysing the "reality" game of *The Apprentice*', *Cultural Sociology*, 5 (2): 263–279.

D'Arcy, C. and Gardiner, L., (2014), *Just the Job – or a Working Compromise? The Changing Nature of Self-employment in the UK*, Resolution Foundation.

Department for Culture, Media and Sport, (2001), *Creative Industries Mapping Document*, London: HMSO.

Dex, S., (2009), 'Review of future of paid and unpaid work, informal work, homeworking, the place of work in the family (women single parents, workless households), benefits, work attitudes motivation and obligation', *Beyond Current Horizons: Technology, Children, Schools and Families*, available at: www.beyondcurrenthorizons.org.uk

Duberley, J. and Carrigan, M., (2012), 'The career identities of "mumpreneurs": women's experiences of combining enterprise and motherhood', *International Small Business Journal*, 31 (6): 629–651.

Ekinsmyth, C., (2013), 'Mothers' business, work/life and the politics of "mumpreneurship"', *Gender, Place and Culture: A Journal of Feminist Geography* (published online 18 July): 1–19.

Fisher, L., (2014), 'Many "self-employed" women earn less than £10,000 a year', *The Observer*, 9 March: 17.

Friedan, B., (1963 [1971]), *The Feminine Mystique*, London: Victor Gollancz.

Fuller, G., Hamilton, C. and Seale, K., (2013), 'Working with amateur labour: between culture and economy', *Cultural Studies Review*, 19 (1): 143–154.

Gill, R., (2007), *Technobohemians or the New Cybertariat? New Media Workers in Amsterdam a Decade after the Web*, Amsterdam: The Institute of Network Cultures.

Gill, R. and Pratt, A., (2008), 'In the social factory? Immaterial labour, precariousness and cultural work', *Theory, Culture & Society*, 25 (7-8): 1–30.

Gregg, M., (2011), *Work's Intimacy*, Cambridge: Polity Press.

Gregory, A. and Milner, S., (2009), 'Editorial: work-life balance: a matter of choice?', *Gender, Work and Organization*, 16 (1): 1–13.

Honneth, A., (2004), 'Organized self-realization some paradoxes of individualization', *European Journal of Social Theory*, 7 (4): 463–478.

Littler, J., (2013), 'The rise of the "yummy mummy": popular conservatism and the neoliberal maternal in contemporary British culture', *Communication, Culture and Critique*, 6: 227–243.

Loscocco, K. and Smith-Hunter, A., (2004), 'Women home-based business owners: insights from comparative analyses', *Women in Management Review*, 19 (3): 164–173.

McRobbie, A., (1998), *British Fashion Design: Rag Trade or Image Industry?*, London: Routledge.

The Sociological Review, 63:S1, pp. 174–187 (2015), DOI: 10.1111/1467-954X.12248

Miles, I. and Green, L., (2008), *Hidden Innovation in the Creative Industries*, London: NESTA.

Oakley, K., (2009), 'From Bohemia to Britart: art students over 50 years', *Cultural Trends*, 18 (4): 281–294.

OECD, (2013), *Entrepreneurship at a Glance*, Paris: OECD Publishing, http://dx.doi.org/10.1787/entrepreneur_aag-2013-en (accessed 4 November 2014).

Prosser, D., (2014), 'Join the small business boom with a start-up supporter deal', *The Observer*, 1 January.

Saner, E., (2013a), 'Cottage industries: all homework and no play?', *The Guardian*, 24 November, available at: http://www.theguardian.com/money/2013/nov/24/cottage-industries-homework-working-from-home.

Saner, E., (2013b), 'Home alone', *The Guardian*, 25 November.

Silva, R., (2014), 'The best of British startups', *The Observer*, 12 January: 15.

Taylor, S.,(2011), 'Negotiating oppositions and uncertainties: gendered conflicts in creative identity work', *Feminism and Psychology*, 21 (3): 354–371.

Taylor, S. and Littleton, K., (2006), 'Biographies in talk: a narrative-discursive research approach', *Qualitative Sociology Review*, 2 (1): 22–38.

Taylor, S. and Littleton, K., (2012), *Contemporary Identities of Creativity and Creative Work*, Farnham: Ashgate.

Thompson, P., Jones-Evans, D. and Kwong, C., (2009), 'Women and home-based entrepreneurship: evidence from the United Kingdom', *International Small Business Journal*, 27 (2): 227–239.

Tietze, S., Musson, G. and Scurry, T., (2009), 'Homebased work: a review of research into themes, directions and implications', *Personnel Review*, 38 (6): 585–604.

Veijola, S. and Jokinen, E., (2008), 'Towards a hostessing society? Mobile arrangements of gender and labour', *NORA – Nordic Journal of Feminist and Gender Research*, 16 (3): 166–181.

Walker, E. and Webster, B., (2007), 'Gender, age and self-employment: some things change, some stay the same', *Women in Management Review*, 22 (2): 122–135.

White, H. and White, C., (1965 [1993]), *Canvases and Careers: Institutional Change in the French Painting World*, Chicago and London: University of Chicago Press.

Hungry for the job: gender, unpaid internships, and the creative industries

Leslie Regan Shade and Jenna Jacobson

Abstract: This paper examines the experiences of young Canadian women working in Toronto and New York who have undertaken unpaid internships in the creative sector. Interviews focused on their internship experiences, ability to secure paid employment, knowledge of the legal status of unpaid internships, and familiarity with emergent activism against unpaid internships. Findings reinforce the class-based privilege of unpaid internships in the creative sector. Despite the economic precarity of unpaid internships, the young women articulated strong desires to find meaningful, secure, and paid employment.

Keywords: internship, youth employment, class, labour law, women

Introduction

> When you intern, the first couple of days you have a lot of questions, and one of the worst questions to ask is 'when are we done?' (Melody)

The topic of unpaid internships for university students and recent graduates entering the job market is proliferating in US and Canadian news and popular culture (Bellafante, 2012; Carey, 2013; Wayne, 2013; CBC News, 2014), especially related to their ethical and legal status. One humorous example is from HBO's acclaimed series *Girls*, when twenty-something Hannah Horvath, approaches her boss Alistair at the New York magazine where she is an intern, and quietly declares: 'My circumstances have changed, and I can no longer afford to work for free'. Perplexed, Alistair responds that her 'quippy voice' would have been perfect to 'man our Twitter'. Failing to procure a paid position, Hannah laments, 'I just gotta eat' (Dunham, 2012). Lena Dunham's depiction of the Brooklyn hipster Hannah – with her private college degree from Oberlin and aspirations for creative and fulfilling *paid* employment to support her livelihood as a writer – echoes for a generation of young women today.

Unpaid internships in various sectors – government, non-profit, law and policy, and especially the creative sector – have soared in recent decades. The

The Sociological Review, 63:S1, pp. 188–205 (2015), DOI: 10.1111/1467-954X.12249

National Association of Colleges and Employers documented an exponential increase in internships in the United States from 17 per cent of graduating students in 1992 to over 50 per cent in 2008, with 'some experts estimat[ing] that one-fourth to one-half are unpaid' (Greenhouse, 2010). This trend is repeated in Canada, with Toronto lawyer Andrew Langille estimating 200,000 unpaid internships in Canada (De Peuter *et al.*, 2012), of which many are illegal in the Province of Ontario under the Employment Standards Act (Ontario Ministry of Labour, 2014). Kamenetz (2006: n.p.) likens unpaid interns to 'illegal immigrants ... they create an oversupply of people willing to work for low wages, or in the case of interns, literally nothing'.

What youth can afford to undertake an unpaid internship? Elitism reigns such that 'students of privilege cluster in posh unpaid internships that open doors while lower-income students cluster in retail and food preparation jobs' (Thompson, 2012: n.p.). Race, class, and gender are clearly implicated. Perlin, whose 2011 book *Intern Nation* catalysed a vibrant debate about the economics and ethics of unpaid internships, argues that 'internship injustice is closely linked to gender issues, both because of the fields that women gravitate toward and possibly also because female students have been more accepting of unpaid, unjust situations' (Perlin, 2011: 27).

This paper examines how young Canadian women experience unpaid internships in the creative sector. Through a series of interviews with young women, we sought to understand their internship experiences, their ability to secure paid employment in their ideal career, and their knowledge of the legal status of unpaid internships and familiarity with activism against unpaid internships. An objective of the research project was to provide an opportunity for young women to speak for themselves. Despite the plethora of news media covering internships, to date scant research has been undertaken in Canada that explores the experiences of interns to understand the gendered and class-based dynamics of such positions so as to better inform policy and activism. In its focus on gender and labour, this research thus adds to scholarship on labour capitalization in the digital economy (Neff, 2012); the feminization of temp work (Huws, 2003; Hatton, 2011); global studies on precarious work (Hesmondhalgh, 2010; Scholz, 2012; Standing, 2011); and the feminist political economy of communication (McKercher and Mosco, 2008; McKercher, 2014). This research is also a modest contribution to McRobbie's (2011) entreaty to more fully account for gender in nuanced scholarly discussions of precarious, immaterial and affective labour.

The paper will first situate the vexatious reality of securing paid full-time employment for Canadian youth, briefly describe current North American debates about unpaid internships, and then delve into the findings based on our interviews, focusing on our interviewees' experiences and perceptions of unpaid internships. After being in an unpaid internship for over a year, one woman summarized her frustration with the entire internship industry, 'I think it's classist, and it's exploitative, it lets certain people rise in industries that many people want to rise in and other people don't have access to that ...' (Simone).

Youth un(der) employment and the new normal of unpaid internships

For many recent university graduates in North America, where the unemployment rate hovers between 14 and 19 per cent, the entry-level job *is* the unpaid internship. Canada's youth unemployment rate in 2012 was 14.1 per cent, with predictions that high youth unemployment emanating from the 2008 recession will result in 'wage scarring' – a loss of $23.1 billion in wages over the next 18 years (CBC News, 2013). Alongside job precarity amidst higher student debt (CBC Doczone, 2013), Statistics Canada cites an unemployment rate of 16.5 per cent for Ontario youth under the age of 24 (Oved, 2013). Extrapolating from this data, a report from the Canadian Centre for Policy Alternatives detailed that Toronto youth (aged 15–24) had the highest employment rate in the province of Ontario at 43.5 per cent, and the widest gap – 21.8 per cent – between youth and adult employment in the province. More so than in other parts of Ontario, the report stated that Toronto youth have withdrawn from the labour force; one explanation is the rise in unpaid internships and other forms of unpaid labour (Geobey, 2013). Given that Toronto is a major Canadian epicentre for the creative industries (including design, fashion, publishing, film and TV, music, and commercial theatre), employing over 100,000 people (Invest Toronto, 2013), one can speculate that most of these unpaid internships in the creative sector are clustered in Toronto. The US Urban Institute posits that generational differences in precarious employment exacerbate wealth gaps, and that 'for the first time in modern memory, a whole generation might not prove wealthier than the one that preceded it' (Lowrey, 2013).

Precarious youth employment can be, in part, attributed to unpaid internships. In order to secure entry into the paid labour force by gaining work experience, many young people have accepted unpaid internships during their undergraduate and postgraduate years. These white-collar jobs are created by employers to ostensibly provide young people access to professional experience in various labour sectors, allowing the interns to achieve a competitive advantage for scarce paid positions in a contingent job market; yet too often labour standards are lax if not downright illegal (Greenhouse, 2010, 2012; Perlin, 2011; Oved, 2013; Thompson, 2012).

Unpaid internships are a routine component of college and university training in North America, where students receive academic credit (Neff, 2011). In Canada, internships have become so popular at colleges and universities that internship coordinators are hired to advise students on internships, help coordinate internship placements at organizations, develop relationships with partner organizations, and generally oversee students in internships (MacDonald, 2013). Allen *et al.* (2013) describe how in the UK, higher education employability strategies increasingly position young people in work placements, many unpaid, in order to gain experience, especially in the competitive creative sector. Inequality prevails: access to placements is classed, raced and gendered. As well, social class and geographical locale structure access to these opportunities,

The Sociological Review, 63:S1, pp. 188–205 (2015), DOI: 10.1111/1467-954X.12249

affirming 'the enduring significance of class, showing how family capital pertaining to creative careers significantly shapes young people's capacity to inhabit the position of the creative, cosmopolitan worker' (Allen and Hollingworth, 2013: 514). Securing internships is also an entrepreneurial enterprise; internship location site Intern Sushi targets young people, their parents and employers (their motto: 'our philosophy encourages users to be as picky about their internships, or interns for that matter, as they are about their sushi').

The uncritical endorsement of unpaid internships and the cavalier manner in which they are advertised has embarrassed some companies. Facebook COO Sheryl Sandberg's organization, LeanIn.org, backpedalled when their editor posted a call for an unpaid editorial intern: 'Must be HIGHLY organized with editorial and social chops and able to commit to a regular schedule through end of year. Design and web skills a plus!' (Goel, 2013: n.p.). This was a deliciously ironic position for Sandberg's organization to take and unsurprisingly, the mishap was ridiculed on social media. Her bestseller, *Lean In: Women, Work and the Will to Lead*, self-described as a 'sort of a feminist manifesto', entreated women to 'lean in' to reach their full potential and be leaders in their workplaces, and sparked an impassioned conversation about the status of women in the male-dominated workplace (Sandberg, 2013: n.p.).

The legal status of unpaid internships has particularly impacted the creative industries. In the US, Fox Searchlight was sued by two former interns for violation of minimum wage, overtime, and the lack of educational experience under current labour laws (Gardner, 2012); this has since become a class action suit to encompass all unpaid interns that participated in Fox Entertainment Group's internship programme (Gardner, 2013a, 2013b). The viability of class action suits is problematic, as the case of Xuedan Wang illustrates. Wang, a strategic communication graduate and unpaid intern for *Harper's Bazaar* fashion magazine, filed a lawsuit against parent company, Hearst Corporation, alleging violation of federal and state wage and hour laws because the internship was not paid, despite 40–55 hours of work per week (Greenhouse, 2012; Randall, 2012). In seeking class action status for other unpaid interns across the Hearst magazine spectrum (20 US titles and 300 international editions), it was argued that not only were interns denied wages, but also Social Security, unemployment insurance, and workers' compensation benefits. Despite a 2013 ruling from a federal district court judge rejecting the request for class action certification because of a lack of similarity across the class members' tasks and internship venues (Graumlich, 2013), the case, nonetheless, raises critical questions about the legality of unpaid internships in the creative industries. The US situation resonates in Canada, with the Ontario Ministry of Labour shutting down several unpaid internship programmes in the magazine industry (McKnight and Nursall, 2014). As we discuss in our conclusion, recent policy initiatives address the regulation of unpaid internships in Canada.

Young women dominate unpaid internships in the creative industries: arts, fashion and media (Bellafante, 2012; Figiel, 2013; Hatton, 2013; Schwartz, 2013;

The Sociological Review, 63:S1, pp. 188–205 (2015), DOI: 10.1111/1467-954X.12249
© 2015 The Authors. Editorial organisation © 2015 The Editorial Board of the Sociological Review

Seaborn, 2013; Wayne, 2013). Addressing the Ministry of Ontario, the University of Toronto Students' Union (2013) noted this gender difference:

> This disparity sees students in engineering, computer science, technology and business management programs receive paid remuneration more often than students in design, communications, the humanities, the arts or marketing. Students in these programs are finding it increasingly necessary to engage in unpaid labour post-graduation as a precursor or prerequisite to finding paid employment.

In a study conducted for the Canadian Intern Association, Attfield and Couture highlighted the race, class and gender dimension of their findings, derived from a voluntary online survey and telephone interviews: 'underpaid internships are more likely to be taken by those who are from high income, non-visible minority backgrounds.... because survey responses seemed to indicate that more females commit to underpaid work than males, it could slow the closing of the income gap between males and females, or even cause it to grow' (2014: 14).

Bovy argues that young women are perceived to be easily exploitable: 'the problem with unpaid internships isn't that entitled young women are just hanging out in lieu of getting a job. It's that a certain, mostly-female population is signing up for what seems like on-the-job training, with no job in sight' (2013: n.p.). Ross comments that the post-recessionary climate has exacerbated precarity in the cultural sector, with internships a form of 'terminal limbo' characterized by 'a clear class divide' and a gender divide, as 'women are more socialized in the customary ways of doing sacrificial work' (2013: 177). In many instances, our findings confirm this claim.

Research design

For our study, we conducted semi-structured interviews in the summer of 2013 with twelve Canadian women aged 21 to 29 years old. All of them lived and worked in Toronto, with the exception of two women who worked in New York City. A contextual interview guide was prepared with broad and exploratory questions. Interviews took place either offline in a face-to-face context or online using Skype, depending on the informant's location and preference. The interviews were approximately one hour in length. The researcher took notes during the interviews and the audio-recordings were transcribed using a professional transcription service and checked for accuracy. The respondents were encouraged to explain their interning experiences in as much narrative detail as felt comfortable, rather than being restricted to simplistic yes–no answers. The young women were extremely eager to share their stories and were enthusiastic about the opportunity to reflect on their internship experiences.

The twelve respondents had diverse work experiences and were at different stages of their career. Four participants were currently completing their post-secondary education and the other eight participants were either in a job or searching for full-time work. The youngest interviewee was completing her undergraduate degree and the oldest interviewee was in a doctoral programme. All of the participants had some level of post-secondary education, ranging from 3-year college programmes, postgraduate diplomas, 4-year undergraduate degrees, master's, to a PhD.

Participants were recruited using social media, specifically Facebook and LinkedIn. A simple text update was publicly posted on the social networking sites requesting that women who have done an unpaid internship contact us. Interestingly, some people went further to also post current news articles about unpaid internships, which points to their interest in the topic. Others reposted the message on their own social networking page to further spread the call for participants. Many of our participants found the posting directly on the social media platforms. The call for participants was advertised to women who had completed or were currently doing an unpaid internship. As some internships offer a small stipend, such as $100 a month to cover travel expenses, women who received a small honorarium were also permitted to participate, in an attempt to gain diversity of experiences. However, most of the interns received no compensation whatsoever.

Within the context of studying unpaid work, an important research design decision was made to provide modest compensation to show that the researchers appreciated and valued their time. Participants were thus offered an honorarium for participating: a $15 gift voucher to Starbucks or iTunes.

The next sections detail what our participants told us regarding the economic climate and their prospects and experiences for finding paid work, in addition to their perceptions of their internships.

Class matters

In each interview, a topic repeatedly mentioned by participants was the importance of parental support during their unpaid internship. This was articulated most clearly by one participant who stated, 'There's no way that I could have done an internship without my parents' support. I'm speaking from a place of privilege' (Talia). Participants spoke of the liberty to accept an unpaid internship as a 'luxury', a distinction from the self-entitled characteristics often associated with Gen-Yers (a popular North American term to describe those born from the mid-1980s to the mid-1990s, also known as Millennials). As Talia exclaimed, 'I realize that I'm incredibly lucky that I actually had the option . . . '. Others spoke of being 'fortunate' for their family support.

Parental financial support often began well before the start of the internship and extended beyond the end of the internship. Even though participants were not specifically asked about their financial arrangements with their parents, many explained that they received parental support during post-secondary education and were thus not burdened with paying for their tuition and shackled with insurmountable debt immediately after graduation: 'I was lucky that I didn't have any student loans' (Kym). Because student loans accrue interest from the day a student graduates, many recent graduates are forced into the first paid job they can find in order to begin paying off their debt, even if the job is not aligned with their career aspirations. For these students, electing to complete an unpaid internship to help them in their careers is simply not a feasible option.

An unpaid internship does not easily lead to a paid full-time position. Many of the women we interviewed had cycled through various unpaid internships in an ongoing attempt to gain an entry-level position in the industry of their choice. The quest for paid employment typically extends over a year, and can consist of multiple unpaid internships (the typical internship is 4 months) strung together with periods of searching for employment. As a result, the young women are financially dependent on their parents for longer periods of time.

The vast majority of the interns lived at home with their parents during the unpaid internship. One participant stated, 'My parents were like, "this is the experience that you need. As long as you're at home we'll support you until you can support yourself"' (Cara). Another recollected, 'I didn't have expenses, like I didn't have to pay rent or pay for all my groceries at that time' (Naomi). The women questioned how people who do not live at home could possibly intern without family support: 'But if it wasn't for them [my parents] and that support I would not be able to be doing an internship. I don't think anyone would' (Grace). Parents provided different levels of financial support, ranging from allowing their child to live at home for free to full financial support. The women expressed empathy towards classmates and colleagues not as fortunate; 'I know some parents after university just let their kids go. I had that support. Otherwise, I don't know, it would have been a lot harder' (Cara). Parental support thus provides young people with the necessary stability they need during such precarious economic periods.

Throughout post-secondary education, students are encouraged to gain experiential training and for many the unpaid internship provides this pragmatic experience. This is especially true of the creative industries, as discussed by Isabella: 'I have been able to pursue these creative industries and rely on them [my parents] when I've needed to, but I know people who haven't been as lucky and that's not very fair'. Students with the same degree qualifications often find that they are not treated equally or fairly in the job market because many companies require students to have prior job experience, which internships can provide evidence of. Students who cannot accept an unpaid internship can thus be at a disadvantage. One of the interviewees stated:

> I'm a privileged person. My mum was able to support me during that time in my life. I didn't have to not be able to do it because she could help me. But there are a lot of other kids who couldn't do it and then they wouldn't be able to get either the grad school spots they wanted or the career they wanted after college, because maybe they were working full-time when in college because they needed the money to pay for their living. I didn't have to do that. It's a privilege to be able to take an internship like that. It's not something everyone was able to do. (Melody)

Even though all of our interviewees received financial support from their parents, many also worked part-time in minimum wage positions, such as in the restaurant industry or as a swim instructor. One interviewee was attending school, working part-time as a waiter, and also doing an unpaid internship, which meant she worked over 80 hours a week.

The women expressed concern about balancing an unpaid internship and part-time work: 'I know a lot of people that wouldn't be able to do that [an internship] because they'd need that extra time that they'd be spending at the internship to be at their job' (Kaylee).

The interviewees clearly articulated that their unpaid internships aligned with their career aspirations, whereas their paid positions were merely a way to make money for basic necessities. As a result, a binary emerged: skilled unpaid work versus less-skilled paid work. 'Some people will do their internship and also work four nights a week at a restaurant or serving or bartending or whatever it is they have to do, which sucks, but some people just take it for what it is and say, "I just have to do it"' (Naomi).

Family members were also important in providing contacts to industry professionals and in a competitive job market, parents can enable opportunities for their children by linking them with industry professionals and providing them with nuanced knowledge of how the professional and creative sectors operate. Several of the interviewees were given the opportunity to interview with a company because of their parents' business contacts. One interviewee said, 'I talked to different family and friends about what I wanted to do, and they helped me a lot with people they knew' (Cara). Youth with parents in the professional sector thus had a distinct advantage over youth whose parents work in the service sector.

'Paying our dues'

All the women we interviewed recognized the ruthless nature of the current economy and the difficulty in securing paid work. The internship market is equally competitive. The women were determined to succeed in their careers, often sacrificing personal money, such as transit costs to the intern site, and committing a significant amount of time to their internships. One woman, who has already completed a few internships and needs to find another internship to complete her postgraduate certificate, said, 'It's super competitive. You really have to learn how to manage your expectations. But I never really imagined it could be this hard … looking for an internship. Looking for a job is my full-time job right now. I've had a lot of disappointing moments' (Isabella).

The young women conveyed an individual sense of autonomy and responsibility to get ahead. They set realistic expectations and did not express self-entitlement: 'I didn't expect to find a paid position without additional training and also an internship or two' (Talia). Their rationale for seeking an internship and accepting an unpaid internship varied from gaining hands-on experiences, to building contacts in the industry, to merely having the line on their résumé. One interviewee stated that she did an unpaid internship because ' … I feel like the only thing that would put me ahead is really that experience part' (Kym).

Another interviewee, who had a negative internship experience with work that was not intellectually challenging, said that the real value of the internship was merely the ability to add it on her résumé afterwards: 'So it was not even like it actually prepared me. I really don't think it did, but the point is that I had it, and I could say that I had it' (Talia). The internship was thus perceived as a necessary step or rite of passage into the paid workforce, irrespective of the skills acquired or training received.

The young women extensively discussed investing in the future by 'paying their dues': 'If you wanted a chance at being an interesting competitive person in any job market I think the onus was on you to … play that game' (Melody). Paying your dues implies a recognition that everyone has to start 'at the bottom' and work their way up the organizational hierarchy. The internships were equated to an initiation or a pledge to a fraternity/sorority (social organizations for under-graduate students): young pledges need to prove their worth by the sacrifices they are willing to make in order to gain acceptance by and entrance into the group. Many of the women we interviewed even expressed a need to gain hands-on ex-perience *before* they were entitled to paid work.

After years of education and internships, many of our participants expressed frustration because they still could not secure a paid position. As a result, several have been forced to continue to accept multiple unpaid internships in an attempt to build their résumé and become more employable. One woman who completed three unpaid internships said, 'I feel like I have paid my dues and I need a full-time job. I can't live off the salary of not paid' (Cara). Another respondent stated:

> I think pop culturally there is this attitude … we don't want to work and we don't accept these internship positions as happily as we should be. We should just be happy for the work and that we complain. Really what it is, is that all of us have to accept the crappy time in our lives to get to the better positions. I think that's unfair. I've certainly, with all my internships, I have really never worked with what I would call lazy people – which is sort of like the way we get stereotyped. I think most of the problems people had with it were just how expensive it is to live that way. It's not easy and when it doesn't feel rewarding, it sort of extra pisses you off because you're skimping by to try and do this for your future and, sometimes when it feels like there isn't a benefit, it can just be infuriating. (Melody)

Another young woman said about her job search, 'I've done everything in the book and it hasn't worked' (Isabella). While young graduates do not assume their career path will be easy, they are disappointed and feel let down by perpetual rejections and unemployment despite having 'paid their dues'.

Alongside a recognition of the fierce competition in obtaining an internship, the young women also considered the companies to be in positions of power and believe that employers take advantage of the competitive climate for internships: 'I think people are seeing the possibility of making a living in a creative industry nowadays, and these companies know that they can get away without paying people because there's always going to be someone to do it unpaid' (Isabella).

The Sociological Review, 63:S1, pp. 188–205 (2015), DOI: 10.1111/1467-954X.12249

Echoed Scarlett, 'I think especially in the media industry there are always people willing to do the work for less money. It's extremely competitive now'.

Kym suggested that because companies know that parental support is necessary for many youth to take on an unpaid internship,

> ... there's huge potential for our generation to be exploited. We have all been told that the economy is terrible, that there aren't enough jobs for us, that it's really hard for us to find jobs ... there's a billion people applying for that one job. A lot of us have the support of our parents and so ... companies think it's okay for us to take those jobs because we still have the support of our family, plus we're not really going to get paid jobs anyways. That seems to be the thought and I think that puts us at a higher risk.

Despite their frustration, the interns did not blame the individual employers; rather they were frustrated by the capitalist system. One woman stated, 'I don't think it's fair, but I don't even know how one would begin to address this problem, because I think the problem resides at such a high level that it would require re-designing, I don't know, the entire economic infrastructure or something like that' (Talia).

Circuits of credentialism

After years of post-secondary education, many young women are seeking scarce unpaid internships to position themselves for elusive entry-level positions. As a result, the young women believe the value of a post-secondary degree is becoming discounted as the standards for employment continually increase. As Jess stated:

> We are being exploited you know, our generation is extremely educated so there is the under-valued and under-employed ... and you spend thousands and thousands of dollars for an education because you think it's going to get you somewhere, but then you get in to the workforce and you're like ... why don't I have work?

The undergraduate degree, coupled with the internship, is now the minimum expectation for employment. One woman explained:

> So many people have these really down-trodden experiences and in my own job hunt it just made me spin into a life crisis. Oh my god, sending all these applications for things that you know you're right for. You can see and it's evident in your resume that you're qualified and you just don't hear anything. It's just like you throw all of your time and all of your resumes into this vortex of a black hole basically. It's the most disappointing, disheartening experience. And I think it leaves a lot of people really desperate. (Grace)

While the young women acknowledged the importance of post-secondary education, they also recognized that a mere undergraduate degree was insufficient to secure a paid position. To differentiate themselves from other applicants, many of the young women pursued postgraduate degrees. After completing a professional master's degree, Grace remarked that 'you're supposed to be this magical information professional who is so skilled and wonderful and in demand. That's just not [the] reality of the job market, I don't think'. The interviewees were frustrated about how the current labour market and creative industries devalue education: 'It's totally fair [to] think you work really, really, really hard at school and that education shouldn't be discounted because you don't have actual work experience' (Jess).

Because of the competition for internships, employers receive applications from highly qualified applicants with both undergraduate and master's degrees. One respondent stated, 'I think the talent pool they [employers] get is hugely talented and they're just getting so much great resources for free basically' (Grace). Ruefully, the interns were frustrated about the devaluation of their work, but believed that there is nothing they can do about it.

Some interns disavowed extreme menial labour in internships and purposefully sought internships that promised genuine work experience: 'I had an interview at a PR agency before I got this internship and she said to me on the phone, "you're going to be an intern and you're basically going to be like grabbing coffees and making sure the kitchen's clean and such and such" – I didn't like that' (Jess). Others expected coffee-runs and other menial tasks unrelated to the job to be an inevitable part of an internship. However, the young women were also assertive in expressing what they thought was acceptable and unacceptable forms of labour and workplace treatment. One woman emphasized that 'If you're unhappy with the way you're being treated at the workplace you can do something about it, search somewhere else for a different career path. At least that's what I would do' (Madison). Another stated: 'The moment I felt I didn't [get something out of the internship] I quit … That was the moment that I realized that my bank account was almost empty, and that I wouldn't be hired' (Simone). While the vast majority of the young women completed their internship contract, a few left the internship because they recognized that they were not gaining any valuable experience.

Gender matters

There is a palpable recognition that unpaid internships are a gender issue and a continuation of the devaluation of women's work. Unpaid internships are also implicated in a larger and messier precarious contemporary economic structure where free labour is an increasingly routine – and normalized – aspect of the creative sector. As DePeuter *et al.* (2012: n.p.) argue, 'unpaid internships are not an isolated issue. They're one of many forms of free labour flourishing in the most celebrated quarters of the creative industries'. Interestingly, few of the young women we interviewed explicitly mentioned gender in discussing their unpaid internships. However, any time anecdotes about other interns were mentioned, they were generally female.

The gendered nature of unpaid internships was largely ignored by our participants, which may point to the insidious gendered nature of unpaid internships and the repeated history of devaluing women's unpaid work. Yet their perception is that within the creative sector, internships, and specific tasks, are disproportionately gendered. One interviewee who interned in the publishing industry stated, '... the whole industry is mostly women... The intern before me was a woman, the intern after me was a woman...' (Talia). Another interviewee recognized differences between the tasks that male and female interns were given: 'The things that I would be asked to do early on were definitely different than what the male intern was asked to do' (Melody). For example, at the beginning of the internship she was asked to go and buy coffee for a meeting, while the male intern was asked to take the meeting minutes, which the interviewee identified as a gendered difference. This interviewee said that because of her training in gender studies at university she is acutely aware of the gendered dynamic of work.

Similarly, another hidden gender bias emerged in the interviews: when a specific parent was mentioned with regards to providing the intern an industry contact, the interviewees always spoke about their father. For example, 'My dad introduced me to a contact in communications when I was in my undergrad' (Isabella), and '... it turns out that my dad had known someone who worked for [company]' (Madison). This perhaps echoes the traditional gendered binary of men in the public workplace and women in the private home.

Women's employment in the creative industries has been widely reported and anecdotally experienced by the young female interns we interviewed. They interned in various creative sectors including advertising, fashion, publishing, music, radio, television, film, social media, marketing, PR, and communication industries. Henry (2009) argues that women are well-suited to work in the creative industries. Rather than considering women innately well suited for a career in creative industries, some of the young women considered themselves creative types, but more importantly wanted to find meaning and a sense of pride and accomplishment in their work. It was felt that the challenging and fast-paced work environment in the creative industry would allow for this as the industry rewards creativity and ingenuity, and our participants expressed a relentless desire to excel and move up in the industry based on their talents. Gill (2002) found that people are attracted to the creative industries because of the perceived trendy workplace coupled with a flexible lifestyle. Our participants were drawn to the creative industries for various reasons based on their individual interests and skill set. Scarlett reflected on the cool environment of her unpaid internship, 'There was always a bunch of celebrities around; it was a very high calibre environment'. With regards to the creative industry lifestyle, Isabella notes that in the creative industry there is a blurring of one's personal and professional life. While working in the creative industry may be appealing, the creative industry also takes advantage of this reputation, as expressed by Melody: 'The more creative it is the less likely you are to get paid as an intern. The more the industry is focused on finance the more likely you are I think or technical'. Problematically, even though more women are entering the creative industries, it remains the case that women are not seeing increased financial gains and professional stature in comparison to men in the field; however, this disturbing reality was not explicitly expressed by our participants (Henry, 2009).

Unpaid intern rights

Some of the women we interviewed were aware of the legal status of unpaid internships, gleaning information via newspaper accounts, or social media, such as Twitter. Others, mindful of current debates, were unaware of the specific legal implications of unpaid internships. As Cara remarked, 'People are like, "internships are slave labour." It's a vague stigma about it. Are you overworking your interns? You're not paying them and they're doing the same amount of work. There's a lot of controversy around it, but I don't know the legalities of it'.

Unpaid interns are taking over many of the workplace responsibilities previously performed by paid employees. Some companies accept a large number of unpaid interns that are continuously cycled through because basic tasks need to be completed. Despite this, our participants still believed that they gained more from the internship than the company did, which may have to do with their perception that they had to persevere, and be lucky, to obtain the unpaid internship. However, the women also placed trust in the system itself by expecting and hoping that their employers and coordinators would act fairly and legally. Kaylee remarked, 'I never … [felt] uncomfortable or over-worked … I didn't need to worry about the laws'.

At the time we conducted our interviews, our participants expressed little knowledge about emergent activism around unpaid internships. Indeed, heightened media and policy attention to the regulation of unpaid internships occurred just after we concluded our research. In Canada, as in the UK and US, vibrant youth advocacy against unpaid internships is emerging. Intern Labor Rights, a subgroup of Arts & Labor, a working group formed during Occupy Wall Street, targeted unpaid internships in the fashion industry; during Fashion Week 2013 the New York group produced robins-egg blue boxes with swag including buttons, paper slips with Twitter hashtags and information flyers about their campaign. Intern Labor Rights has since petitioned New York City Mayor Bill De Blasio to comply with labour laws that make unpaid internships illegal, and to extend sexual harassment and other anti-discrimination laws to unpaid internships (see http://www.internlaborrights.com/). Alongside creative endeavours, policy interventions, such as contributing to budget consultations to the Province of Ontario have been made by Students Against Unpaid Internships Scams (see http://payyourinterns.ca/)

Moving forward

Overall, the young women we interviewed in our small study articulated a relentless desire to push themselves towards a future goal of secure and meaningful employment in the creative sector. Unpaid internships were seen as an instrumental way to further their career aspirations. Our interviews affirmed that class differences are perpetuated in the system of unpaid internships as upper-class youth with family support were able to take advantage of intern opportunities.

The Sociological Review, 63:S1, pp. 188–205 (2015), DOI: 10.1111/1467-954X.12249

The young women's acquiescent position that unpaid internships are an integral aspect of 'paying our dues' complicates how one can research the nature and degree of 'exploitation'. Siebert and Wilson's (2013) research into unpaid work in the UK creative sector highlights how, given the exclusionary characteristics of unpaid work, only 'surveying those who participate in it is missing the perspectives of the excluded' (2013: 719). Frenette's study of the experiences of unpaid interns in the music industry echoes the need for further research to explore inequality in the cultural industries. Does the 'provisional labor' of unpaid internships: 'a liminal and indeterminate period during which aspirants form a reservoir of excess workers before potentially getting hired as paid employees' (Frenette, 2013: 372), lead to further entrenched inequalities?

Another challenge is determining the parameters of the cultural sector and what constitutes creative economies. Canada, compared to other countries such as the UK, has slowly adopted the concept of the creative economy as a facilitator of economic growth. Sectors that comprise the creative industries include the media, television and film, museum and arts organizations, advertising and public relations, publishing, design and fashion, and videogame and digital arts. Mapping this sector is difficult because of a lack of standardization as labour jurisdiction resides at a provincial level with some federal sharing (Gollmitzer and Murray, 2008).

Labour participation statistics are also out of date; the latest figures on employment in the cultural sector derive from the federal government's Labour Force Survey (LFS), 1996 to 2002. This survey revealed that employment for men in the creative sector (51 per cent) was higher than for women, but when compared to the overall employment in Canada (47 per cent), more women were employed within the cultural sector (49 per cent). Within the cultural sector women were more likely to be situated within support (68 per cent) and production (52 per cent) activities while men were active in manufacturing (62 per cent) and creation (60 per cent) activities (Singh, 2010). As well as lacking currency, these figures do not even account for youth activities in the creative industries and how young people's activities may necessitate a broadening of the traditional notions of creative work (Campbell, 2013).

Challenges to mapping labour participation in the cultural sector are technological and ideological. The sector has transformed to comprise new industries because of globalization and digitization (for instance, the steady growth of the videogame sector in Toronto, Vancouver and Montreal). As well, the federal government, under the austerity measures of the Conservative majority, has curtailed the collection of socioeconomic data, with major funding cuts incurred by the primary agency Statistics Canada.

Murray and Gollmitzer (2012) call for a new policy paradigm to address precarious labour, especially for women and racial minorities, clustered in less secure and lower-income employment relationships, including in the creative sector. In Canada, internships are regulated provincially. In the provinces of British Columbia and Ontario, new guidelines clarify what constitutes legal unpaid internships; interns are exempt from consideration as an employee, do not displace paid workers, and the internship must provide practical training and learning opportunities (Sagan, 2013). Several young activists have challenged the legality of their internships, filing complaints with government entities (Tomlinson, 2013), while NDP Minister Andrew Cash of Toronto recently introduced a private member's bill, the National Urban Worker Strategy, to address the rise in precarious labour. The bill calls for strengthening of labour laws to prevent the misuse of unpaid internships and to extend employment insurance benefits to the self-employed. These are encouraging developments and it is our hope that young women will take a proactive role in advocacy and organization around unpaid internships so that Isabella's sentiment that 'It's not an ideal situation for anyone, but it's just kind of the name of the game' can transform into positive critical activism to challenge 'the name of the game' and to value young women's *paid* labour.

Acknowledgements

This research was funded by the Faculty of Information, University of Toronto. Research ethics protocols were approved by the University of Toronto Office of Research Ethics. All participant names are anonymized for this paper.

References

Allen, K. and Hollingworth, S., (2013), '"Sticky subjects" or "cosmopolitan creatives"? Social class, place and urban young people's aspirations for work in the knowledge economy', *Urban Studies*, 50 (3): 499–517.

Allen, K., Quinn, A., Hollingworth, S. and Rose, A., (2013), 'Becoming employable students and "ideal" creative workers: exclusion and inequality in higher education work placements', *British Journal of Sociology of Education*, 34 (3): 431–452.

Attfield, J. and Couture, I., (2014), 'An investigation into the status and implications of unpaid internships in Ontario', for Canadian Intern Association, available at: https://dspace.library.uvic.ca:8443/handle/1828/5294

Bellafante, G., (2012), 'Seeking chic, brilliant intern to thread needles (no pay)', *The New York Times*, 15 September, available at: http://www.nytimes.com/2012/09/16/nyregion/seeking-chic-edgy-brilliant-intern-to-thread-needles-free.html

Bovy, P. M., (2013), 'Unpaid internships are a rich-girl problem – and also a real problem', *The Atlantic*, 13 February, available at: http://www.theatlantic.com/sexes/archive/2013/02/unpaid-internships-are-a-rich-girl-problem-and-also-a-real-problem/273106/

Campbell, M., (2013), *Out of the Basement: Youth Cultural Production in Practice and Policy*, Montreal: McGill-Queen's University Press.

Carey, K., (2013). 'Giving credit: but is it due?', *New York Times*, 3 February, available at: http://www.nytimes.com/2013/02/03/education/edlife/internships-for-creditmerited-or-not.html?ref=edlife

CBC Doczone, (2013), *Generation Jobless*, Dir. Sharon Bartlett and Maria LeRose, Dreamfield Productions, 31 January, available at: http://www.cbc.ca/doczone/episode/generation-jobless.html

CBC News, (2013), 'Youth unemployment to cost Canadian economy $23 billion', 29 January, available at: http://www.cbc.ca/news/business/story/2013/01/29/business-youth-unemployment-cost.html

CBC News, (2014), 'CBC readers debate unpaid internship crackdown, share own internship tales', 28 March, available at: http://www.cbc.ca/newsblogs/yourcommunity/2014/03/cbc-readers-debate-unpaid-internship-crackdown-share-own-internship-tales.html

The Sociological Review, 63:S1, pp. 188–205 (2015), DOI: 10.1111/1467-954X.12249
© 2015 The Authors. Editorial organisation © 2015 The Editorial Board of the Sociological Review

DePeuter, G., Cohen, N. and Brophy, E., (2012,), 'Interns unite! You have nothing to lose – literally', *Briarpatch Magazine*, 9 November, available at: http://briarpatchmagazine.com/articles/view/interns-unite-you-have-nothing-to-lose-literally

Dunham, L., (2012) Girls, Season 1, Episode 1, 'Pilot', 15 April.

Figiel, J., (2013), 'Work experience without qualities? A documentary and critical account of an internship', *ephemera: Theory & Politics in Organization*, 13 (1), available at: http://www.ephemerajournal.org/contribution/work-experience-without-qualities-documentary-and-critical-account-internship

Frenette, A., (2013), 'Making the intern economy: role and career challenges of the music industry intern', *Work and Occupations*, 40 (4): 364–397.

Gardner, E., (2012), 'Fox's entire internship program now under legal attack', *Hollywood Reporter*, 13 August, available at: http://www.hollywoodreporter.com/thr-esq/fox-black-swan-internship-program-lawsuit-361424

Gardner, E., (2013a), 'Interns win huge victory in labor lawsuit against Fox', *The Hollywood Reporter*, 11 June, available at: http://www.hollywoodreporter.com/thr-esq/interns-win-huge-victory-labor-566360

Gardner, E., (2013b), 'Hollywood interns: Fox lawsuit likely to break ground', *Hollywood Reporter*, 21 February, available at: http://www.hollywoodreporter.com/thr-esq/hollywood-interns-fox-lawsuit-break-422988

Geobey, S., (2013), 'The young and the jobless: youth unemployment in Ontario', Toronto: Canadian Centre for Policy Alternatives / Ontario, available at: http://www.policyalternatives.ca/publications/reports/young-and-jobless

Gill, R., (2002), 'Cool, creative and egalitarian? Exploring gender in project-based new media work in Europe', *Information, Communication and Society*, 5 (1): 70–89.

Goel, V., (2013), 'LeanIn.org offers paid internship after uproar over volunteer position', *The New York Times*, 16 August, available at: http://bits.blogs.nytimes.com/2013/08/16/leanin-org-offers-paid-internship-after-uproar-over-volunteer-position/

Gollmitzer, M. and Murray, C., (2008), 'From economy to ecology: a policy framework for creative labor', research paper for the Canadian Conference of the Arts, available at: http://ccarts.ca/wp-content/uploads/2009/01/CREATIVEECONOMYentiredocument.pdf

Graumlich, B., (2013), 'Unpaid internships lack class, says New York court', *Forbes*, 16 May, available at: http://www.forbes.com/sites/theemploymentbeat/2013/05/16/unpaid-interns-litigation-lacks-class-says-new-york-court/

Greenhouse, S., (2010), 'The unpaid intern, legal or not', *The New York Times*, 2 April, available at: http://www.nytimes.com/2010/04/03/business/03intern.html?pagewanted=all&_r=0

Greenhouse, S., (2012), 'Former intern sues Hearst over unpaid work and hopes to create a class-action suit', *The New York Times*, 1 February, available at: http://mediadecoder.blogs.nytimes.com/2012/02/01/former-intern-sues-hearst-over-unpaid-work-and-hopes-to-create-a-class-action/

Hatton, E., (2011), *The Temp Economy: From Kelly Girls to Permatemps in Postwar America*, Philadelphia: Temple University Press.

Hatton, E., (2013), 'The rise of the permanent temp economy', *New York Times*, 26 January, available at: http://opinionator.blogs.nytimes.com/2013/01/26/the-rise-of-the-permanent-temp-economy/?_r=0

Henry, C., (2009), 'Women and the creative industries: exploring the popular appeal', *Creative Industries Journal*, 2 (2): 143–160.

Hesmondhalgh, D., (2010), 'User-generated content, free labour and the cultural industries', *ephemera: Theory & Politics in Organization*, 10 (3/4): 267–228, available at: http://www.ephemeraweb.org/journal/10-3/10-3hesmondhalgh.pdf

Huws, U., (2003), *The Making of a Cybertariat: Virtual Work in a Real World*, New York: Monthly Review Press.

Invest Toronto, (2013). 'Creative Industries Sector', available at: http://www.investtoronto.ca/Business-Toronto/Key-Business-Sectors/Creative-Industries.aspx#creative-industries-facts

Kamenetz, A., (2006), 'Take this internship and shove it', *The New York Times*, 6 May, available at: http://www.nytimes.com/2006/05/30/opinion/30kamenetz.html

Lowrey, A., (2013), 'Do millennials stand a chance in the real world?', *The New York Times*, 26 March, available at: http://www.nytimes.com/2013/03/31/magazine/do-millennials-stand-a-chance-in-the-real-world.html?pagewanted=1&ref=todayspaper

MacDonald, M., (2013), 'The plight of the unpaid intern', *University Affairs*, 13 September, available at: http://www.universityaffairs.ca/plight-of-the-unpaid-intern.aspx

McKercher C., (2014). 'Precarious times, precarious work: a feminist political economy of freelance journalists in Canada and the United States', in C. Fuchs and M. Sandoval (eds), *Critique, Social Media and the Information Society*, 219–230, London: Routledge.

McKercher, C., and Mosco, V. (eds), (2008), *Knowledge Workers in the Information Society*, Lanham, MD: Rowman & Littlefield.

McKnight, Z. and Nursall, K., (2014), 'Ministry of labour cracks down on unpaid magazine internships', *The Toronto Star*, 27 March, available at: http://www.thestar.com/news/gta/2014/03/27/ministry_of_labour_cracks_down_on_unpaid_internship_programs.html

McRobbie, A., (2011), 'Reflections on feminism, immaterial labour and the post-Fordist regime', *New Formations*, 70: 60–76.

Murray, C. and Gollmitzer, M., (2012), 'Escaping the precarity trap: a call for creative labour policy', *International Journal of Cultural Policy*, 18 (4): 419–438.

National Urban Worker Strategy, (2013), available at: http://petition.ndp.ca/urban-workers

Neff, G., (2011), 'The competitive privilege of working for free: rethinking the roles that interns play in communication industries', Conference presentation at International Communication Association, Boston, May.

Neff, G., (2012), *Venture Labour*, Cambridge, MA: MIT Press.

Ontario Ministry of Labour, (2014), 'Are unpaid internships legal in Ontario?' available at: http://www.labour.gov.on.ca/english/es/pubs/internships.php

Oved, M. C., (2013), 'Unpaid internships: the most precarious work of all', *The Toronto Star*, 5 March, available at: http://www.thestar.com/news/gta/2013/03/05/unpaid_internships_the_most_precarious_work_of_all.html

Perlin, R., (2011), *Intern Nation: How to Earn Nothing and Learn Little in the Brave New Economy*, London: Verso Books.

Randall, E., (2012), 'Former unpaid intern sues Hearst for labor law violations', *The Atlantic Wire*, 1 February, available at: http://www.theatlanticwire.com/business/2012/02/former-unpaid-intern-sues-hearst-labor-law-violations/48172/

Ross, A., (2013), 'Theorizing cultural work: an interview with the editors', in M. Banks, R. Gill and S. Taylor (eds), *Theorizing Cultural Work: Labour, Continuity and Change in the Cultural and Creative Industries*, 175–182, London: Routledge.

Sagan, A., (2013), 'Unpaid internships exploit "vulnerable generation"', *CBC News*, 2 July, available at: http://www.cbc.ca/news/canada/unpaid-internships-exploit-vulnerable-generation-1.1332839

Sandberg, S., (2013), *Lean In: Women, Work, and the Will to Lead*, New York: Knopf.

Scholz, T. (ed.), (2012), *Digital Labor: The Internet as Playground and Factory*, New York: Routledge.

Schwartz, M., (2013), 'Opportunity costs: the true price of internships', *Dissent: A Quarterly of Politics and Culture*, Winter: 41–45.

Seaborn, C., (2013), 'Unpaid internships are a gender issue!', *Babes on Bay Street*, 25 March, available at: http://babesonbaystreet.com/2013/03/25/unpaid-internships-are-a-gender-issue/

Siebert, S. and Wilson, F., (2013), 'All work and no pay: consequences of work in the creative industries', *Work, Employment and Society*, 27 (4): 711–721.

Singh, V., (2010), 'Female participation in the cultural sector workforce', *Focus on Culture*, 15 (2): 5–7, available at: http://www.statcan.gc.ca/pub/87-004-x/87-004-x2003002-eng.pdf

Standing, G., (2011), *The Precariat: The New Dangerous Class*, London: Bloomsbury Academic.

Thompson, D., (2012), 'Work is works: why free internships are immoral', *The Atlantic*, 12 May, available at: http://www.theatlantic.com/business/archive/2012/05/work-is-work-why-free-internships-are-immoral/257130/

The Sociological Review, 63:S1, pp. 188–205 (2015), DOI: 10.1111/1467-954X.12249

Tomlinson, K., (2013), 'Bell accused of breaking labour law with unpaid interns', *CBC News*, 24 June, available at: http://www.cbc.ca/news/canada/british-columbia/bell-accused-of-breaking-labour-law-with-unpaid-interns-1.1356277

University of Toronto Student Union (UTSU), (2013), 'Letter to Yasir Nagvi, ON Minister of Labour', 8 April, available at: http://www.utsu.ca/content/3433

Wayne, T., (2013), 'The no limits job', *New York Times*, 1 March, available at: http://www.nytimes.com/2013/03/03/fashion/for-20-somethings-ambition-at-a-cost.html?pagewanted=1&_r=0

Notes on contributors

Ana Alacovska holds a doctoral degree from the Copenhagen Business School in Denmark (2013), a master's degree in Communication Studies from Roskilde University (2007) and a degree in Comparative Literature from Ss. Cyril and Methodius University in Skopje, Macedonia (2003). Her research interests revolve around the sociology of culture and literature, cultural and creative work, and media production. She is currently embarking on her post-doctoral project on the production of Scandinavian crime fiction in the publishing industry, generously funded by the Danish Research Council for the Humanities. e-mail: aa.ikl@cbs.dk

Sarah Baker is Associate Professor of Cultural Sociology in the School of Humanities, Griffith University, Australia. She previously held Research Fellow positions at the University of Leeds and the Open University, UK, and the University of South Australia. Sarah is the co-author of *Creative Labour: Media Work in Three Cultural Industries* (with David Hesmondhalgh; Routledge, 2011) and *Teaching Youth Studies through Popular Culture* (with Brady Robards; ACYS, 2014) and co-editor of *Redefining Mainstream Popular Music* (with Andy Bennett and Jodie Taylor; Routledge, 2013) and *Youth Cultures and Subcultures: Australian Perspectives* (with Brady Robards and Bob Buttigieg; Ashgate, 2015). She is the inaugural Reviews Editor of *Journal of World Popular Music* and former co-editor of *Journal of Sociology*. e-mail: s.baker@griffith.edu.au

Miranda J. Banks is Assistant Professor of Visual and Media Arts at Emerson College. Her research focuses on Hollywood's creative labour and American media industry history. She is the author of *The Writers: A History of American Screenwriters and their Guild* (Rutgers, 2015). She is co-editor of *Production Studies: Cultural Studies of Media Industries* (Routledge, 2009) as well as the forthcoming *Production Studies 2*. Her work has appeared in *Television & New Media, Popular Communication, The Journal of Popular Film and Television,* and *Montage/AV,* as well as the anthologies *Teen Television: Genre, Consumption, and Identity* (BFI, 2008) and *How to Watch Television* (NYU, 2013). She serves on the board of Console-ing Passions. e-mail: miranda_banks@emerson.edu

The Sociological Review, 63:S1, pp. 206–210 (2015), DOI: 10.1111/1467-954X.12250
Editorial organisation © 2015 The Editorial Board of the Sociological Review. Published by John Wiley & Sons Ltd, 9600 Garsington Road, Oxford OX4 2DQ, UK and 350 Main Street, Malden, MA 02148, USA

Bridget Conor is a lecturer in the Department of Culture, Media and Creative Industries at King's College London and has previously taught at Goldsmiths College and AUT University in Auckland. She recently completed her first monograph, *Screenwriting: Creative Labour and Professional Practice* (Routledge, 2014) and has also published in journals such as *Television and New Media* and the *Journal of Screenwriting*. Her previous work focused on the globalization of the New Zealand film industry and the production of *The Lord of the Rings* trilogy. e-mail: bridget.conor@kcl.ac.uk

David Hesmondhalgh is a professor in the School of Media and Communication at the University of Leeds. He is the author of *Why Music Matters* (Blackwell, 2013), *Creative Labour: Media Work in Three Cultural Industries* (Routledge, 2011, co-written with Sarah Baker), and *The Cultural Industries*, now in its third edition (Sage, 2012). He is also editor or co-editor of five other books, including *The Media and Social Theory* (with Jason Toynbee, Routledge, 2008). He recently co-edited (with Anamik Saha) a special issue of the journal *Popular Communication* on 'Race, Ethnicity and Cultural Production'. e-mail: D.J.Hesmondhalgh@leeds.ac.uk

Ursula Huws is Professor of Labour and Globalisation at the University of Hertfordshire and the editor of *Work Organisation, Labour and Globalisation*. She has written extensively on the impact of technological change on labour, including the gender division of labour and her publications have been translated widely, including into Chinese, French, German, Greek, Hindi, Korean, Norwegian, Portuguese, Serbo-Croat, Spanish, Swedish and Turkish. e-mail: u.huws@herts.ac.uk

Rosalind Gill is Professor of Social and Cultural Analysis at City University. She is interested in contemporary cultural and academic labour, in sexuality and intimate life, and in questions about the dynamics of inequality in post-feminist and neoliberal times. She is author of several books including *Gender and the Media* (Polity Press, 2007) and *Mediated Intimacy: Sex Advice in Media Culture* (Polity Press, 2015) (with Meg John Barker and Laura Harvey). e-mail: rosalind.gill.2@city.ac.uk

Jenna Jacobson is a PhD candidate at the University of Toronto in the Faculty of Information. Her research interests lie at the intersection of new media, identity and community. In her dissertation, Jenna analyses community management with a focus on the dynamics on personal branding, labour, and social media privacy. Find her on Twitter: e-mail: jenna.jacobson@mail.utoronto.ca

Deborah Jones is an associate professor in the School of Management in Victoria Business School, Victoria University of Wellington, New Zealand. She is interested in critical and interdisciplinary work which links organizational studies to cultural studies. Her research is centred on working lives and the political contexts in which they unfold, especially in terms of gender, ethnicity and nation. A major recent focus has been on film work in the New Zealand film industry, at the level of individual life histories and in the context of cultural and labour policies and practices. Other recent projects include 'biculturalism' in New Zealand organizations; deciphering menstruation in the workplace; and the ethics of sea slavery in New Zealand chartered fishing vessels. She teaches on organizations and ethics, and organizational behaviour more widely. She is an associate of the Centre for Labour, Employment and Work at Victoria University. e-mail: Deborah.jones@vuw.ac.nz

George Morgan is a researcher at the Institute for Culture and Society, University of Western Sydney, whose current research deals with the struggles of working-class and minority youth who aspire to creative careers. He has published recent papers on this theme in *Ethnic and Racial Studies, Journal of Youth Studies, Journal of Urban Affairs, Economic and Labour Relations Review* and *Journal of Cultural Economy.* e-mail: george.morgan@uws.edu.au

Pariece Nelligan recently completed her doctorate at the Institute for Culture and Society at the University of Western Sydney. Her research interests include precarious employment in the creative industries, labour relations, networking and communities of practice in the new economy as well as identity formation and biographical narrative analysis. She has also trained as a ballet dancer and teacher and looks forward to conducting research in this area. e-mail: pariecenelligan@yahoo.com.au

Judith K. Pringle is Professor of Organisation Studies, initiator and co-ordinator of the Gender and Diversity Research Group at AUT University, and also adjunct professor at Griffith University. Her research focuses on women's experiences in organizations, workplace diversity, intersections of social identities (gender/ethnicity/sexuality/age), bi-cultural research teams and reframing career theory. She is co-investigator of a 3-year funded project 'Glamour and Grind: New Creative Workers' exploring how film industry workers construct their career identities. Judith is on the editorial board of *British Journal of Management.* She was co-editor of the Sage *Handbook for Workplace Diversity* (2006) and co-author of *The New Careers* (1999). She has published numerous book chapters, and in scholarly journals such as *British Journal of Management, Equality, Diversity and Inclusion, Journal of World Business, International Journal of HRM, Women in Management Review, Career Development International,* and *Asia Pacific Journal of HR.* e-mail: judith.pringle@aut.ac.nz

Keith Randle is Professor of Work and Organisation and Associate Dean (Research) at the Hertfordshire Business School. He has research interests in the work, employment and organization of graduate-level employees and his PhD was on the management of research scientists in pharmaceutical R&D. For the past 15 years he has researched and written on the creative industries, especially

208

film and television, with a particular interest in issues around diversity and exclusion. In 2013 he co-established the interdisciplinary Creative Economy Research Centre (CERC) at the University of Hertfordshire with the aim of bringing together research interests in Business, Humanities and the Creative Arts. e-mail: k.r.randle@herts.ac.uk

Leslie Regan Shade is an associate professor at the University of Toronto in the Faculty of Information. Her research focus since the mid-1990s has been on the social and policy aspects of information and communication technologies (ICTs), with particular concerns towards issues of gender, youth and political economy. Her work has been published in numerous journals including the *Canadian Journal of Communication, Signs, First Monday*, the *International Journal of Media and Cultural Politics*, and *Feminist Media Studies*, alongside numerous chapters on topics surrounding gender and ICTs. e-mail: leslie.shade@utoronto.ca

Christina Scharff is a lecturer in the Department of Culture, Media and Creative Industries, King's College London. Her research interests include gender, media and culture and she is author of *Repudiating Feminism: Young Women in a Neoliberal World* (Ashgate, 2012) and, with Rosalind Gill, co-editor of *New Femininities: Postfeminism, Neoliberalism and Subjectivity* (Palgrave Macmillan, 2011). Her publications have appeared in various international journals, including *Sociology, Feminism & Psychology, Feminist Media Studies*, and *The European Journal of Women's Studies*. She recently won an ESRC Future Research Leaders grant and is currently conducting research on gender, cultural work and entrepreneurial subjectivities. e-mail: christina.scharff@kcl.ac.uk

Lauren Steimer is Assistant Professor of Media Arts in the School of Visual Art and Design at the University of South Carolina. Her recent work on stunt workers in transnational media industries has been published in *Discourse* and the *Transnational Star Reader*. Her work examines the distinctive corporeal spectacles of stars as working bodies in transnational articulations of the action genre. She previously taught in the Department of Film and Media Studies at the University of California, Irvine, where she was named 'Professor of the Year for the School of Humanities' in 2007 and in 2012. e-mail: lsteimer@mailbox.sc.edu

Stephanie Taylor is Senior Lecturer in Psychology, Social Sciences at the Open University. Her research employs a narrative-discursive approach to investigate the constitutive processes and constraints around identity and subjectification which operate in specific social sites (creative work, places of residence, the nation), exploring in particular the issues confronted by women in the contexts of late modernity and neoliberalism. Her books include *Contemporary Identities of Creativity and Creative Work,* with Karen Littleton (Ashgate, 2012) and *Theorizing Cultural Work: Labour, Continuity and Change in the Creative Industries,* co-edited with Mark Banks and Rosalind Gill (Routledge, 2013). She has also written extensively on qualitative research methods, most recently in *What is Discourse Analysis?* (Bloomsbury, 2013). e-mail: Stephanie.Taylor@open.ac.uk

Leung Wing-Fai is a lecturer in Contemporary Chinese Studies at the University College Cork, Ireland, with an interest in Chinese language film and media, as well as work and employment in the creative and online economy. Her monograph on multimedia stardom in Hong Kong will be published by Routledge (2014). She has co-edited *East Asian Cinemas: Exploring Transnational Connections on Film* (2008) and *East Asian Film Stars* (2014). Her articles have appeared in *Canadian Journal of Film Studies, Journal of Asian Cinema,* and *Asian Ethnicity.* She is a member of the EU COST Action on Dynamics of Virtual Work, and is currently researching new media start-ups, entrepreneurship and gender in Taiwan. e-mail: wf.leung@ucc.ie

Natalie Wreyford is a third year PhD candidate in the Department of Culture, Media and Creative Industries at King's College London. Her research is borne over 14 years working in the UK film industry, including as a senior development executive at the UK Film Council. Natalie is exploring the scale of the gender imbalance in feature film screenwriting in the UK and attempting to unpack why the situation is not changing. Her empirical research examines the employment practices and working conditions to which screenwriters in the UK film industry are subject, and analyses how established industry discourses around gender and creativity might uphold, justify and reinforce patterns of inequality. Natalie has read, advised on and script edited hundreds of film scripts, and worked with a hugely diverse range of screenwriters, producers and directors, from Academy Award-winners to those trying to get their first break. e-mail: natalie.wreyford@kcl.ac.uk

The Sociological Review, 63:S1, pp. 206–210 (2015), DOI: 10.1111/1467-954X.12250
Editorial organisation © 2015 The Editorial Board of the Sociological Review

Gender and creative labour index

academic work, and precariousness, 129
Acker, Joan, 1, 38, 39, 43–44, 46
Adkins, Lisa, 6, 68
advertising, 3, 6, 13, 24, 28, 33, 34, 54, 117, 122, 132, 199, 201
aesthetic skills, 73, 76, 80
ageism, 149–50
Ahl, Helene, 181, 182
Alacovska, Ana, 14, 17, 128–43, 206
Aldoory, L., 27
Alsop, Marin, 97
Amabile, Teresa, 5
Anderson, A.B., 89
Anker, R., 29, 30
anxiety, 9, 17, 54, 62, 85, 114, 166; and travel writing, 129, 137–38, 140; genre anxiety, 140
apprenticeship, 16, 70–71, 72–73, 77, 80; artisanal, 74–75; cultural, 71; rituals, 72
architecture, 2, 6, 7
Aronowitz, Stanley, 167
audiences, 17, 91, 114, 121, 122, 129, 135, 154
Australia, 2006 census, 7; 'Creative Nation' policy, 2; creative work, 66–83

Babbage, Charles, 163
Bain, Alison, 181, 183
Baker, Sarah, 5, 9, 12, 15, 23–36, 67, 129, 206
Banks, Mark, 158, 180
Banks, Miranda, 2, 14, 17, 28, 128–57, 206
Baron, J.N., 85
Bean, Henry, 114
Bean, J., 147
Bechdel Test, 120–21
Beck, Ulrich, 51
Beeching, A., 99
below-the-line workers, 37, 42–46
Bem, Sandra, 181
benefits, 9, 98, 191
Beveridge, William, 165
Bielby, D.D., 85, 89, 93, 122
biographies, 132–33, 134, 135–36

Bird, Antonia, 60
Black List 3.0, 121
Blair, Helen, 39, 56, 86, 92
book publishing, 85
boundaries, 3, 13, 14, 34, 50, 168, 177, 181
Bourdieu, Pierre, 130
Bovy, P.M., 192
Brah, A., 8, 51
BRIC nations, 2
Broadcast Training & Skills Regulator, 55
Brouillette, Sarah, 4–5, 13
Browne, Jude, 24, 30, 35
Burt, R.S., 92
Butler, Judith, 116

Cage, Nicholas, 117
Caldwell, J.T., 123
Canada, creative industries, 201; Labour Force Survey, 201; National Urban Worker Strategy, 202; women interns, 188–205
Cantor, M., 131
Carter, Lynda, 152, 156
Cash, Andrew, 202
Chadha, Gurinder, 60
chess, 5
childcare, 12, 44, 59–61, 62, 63, 85
children, 7, 44, 52, 53, 59–61, 63, 85, 177, 179, 182
China, 2
Christopherson, Susan, 85, 86, 124
classical musicians, 2–3, 7, 14, 16–17, 97–112
Clawson, M.A., 131
Cohen, P., 70
collaboration, 5, 76
commodities, intangible, 168; new, 168, 171
Communication Act 2003, 55
communications sector, 32, 176, 192, 199
community of practice, 66–83; and education, 72; lost, 75–76
computer games, 6
Comte, Auguste, 161
Connell, R.W., 72

The Sociological Review, 63:S1, pp. 211–216 (2015), DOI: 10.1111/1467-954X.12309

Conor, Bridget, 1–22, 41, 52, 113–27, 207
'Cool Britannia', 2
Cooper, Chris, 114
cottage industries, 178
Creative and Cultural Skills, 24
creative labour, 3, 98; and boundaries, 14–15; and gender, 10–15; and informality, 8–10; and working class masculinity, 66–83; in Canada, 201; scope, 4; working for oneself, 174–87
craft collaboration, 76
craft labour, 80
creativity, 1, 2, 10, 38, 42, 66, 70, 79, 90, 132, 160, 161, 164, 167, 180, 199; and commerce, 34–35; and psychology, 4–5; and screenwriting, 122–24; entrepreneurs, 3; in context, 5; masculinist, 15, 33; of labour, 164; scope, 4
Crenshaw, K., 51
Culkin, N., 85
cultural and creative industries (CCI), 1–3, 5, 6–8, 9, 10, 11, 12, 13; and inequality, 1–3; and working for oneself, 174–87
cultural labour, *see* cultural work
cultural studies, 38, 85
cultural work, 3, 10, 14, 16, 18, 23–36, 38–39, 98–99; and division of labour, 158–73; and entrepreneurialism, 98–99, 100, 116, 123; and utopian visions, 158–73; as product, 100–102, 109; masculine, 161
cybernetics, 170

D'Arcy, C., 185
DeFillippi, R.J., 50, 61, 62, 63
dentists, 25
Department for Culture, Media and Sport, 2, 3, 180
Derrida, Jacques, 130
design, 16, 72–74
developing economies, 2
Dex, Shirley, 176
DiFazio, William, 167
digitization, 201
disability, 57, 63
discrimination, 52, 58, 85
discursive strategy, 97–112

division of labour, 159–60; and economic classes, 160–61
documentary researchers, 30
Du Gay, Paul, 123
Dunham, Lena, 118
Dyer-Witheford, Nick, 169–70

Ebert, Roger, 114
economization, of subjectivity, 99, 101, 110, of the self, 110
education, 5, 34, 40, 55, 67, 71, 73, 129, 131, 162–63, 164, 190, 191, 192–93, 194, 196, 197, 198; music, 98; *see also* training
Eikhof, Doris, 59
Ekinsmyth, Carol, 177
employment policy, 34, 55
Engels, Fredrich, 161, 163, 164
engineering contractors, 129
entrepreneurialism, 98, 105, 109, 123, 174–87; mumpreneurs, 177, 179; new entrepreneurs, 178–80
Epper, Jeannie, 149
equal opportunities legislation, 58–59
Equalities and Human Rights Commission, 52, 58
Evans, Debbie, 149
Evans, Marian, 39

fashion, 1, 8, 67, 138, 139, 190, 199; designers, 2, 14, 178, 180, 181; internships, 200, 201
Faulkner, R.R., 89
Fawcett Society, *Sex and* Power, 7
feminization, 24, 27, 28, 35, 174–87; temporary work, 189
femininity, 17, 25, 33, 98, 102–106, 109, 130, 133, 137, 181, 182, 183; 'normative', 129
film industry, 1, 6, 7, 15, 16, 17; BBC, 87; British Film Industry, 7, 40; British Film Institute, 52, 87, 120, 122; Film Four, 87; freelancing in, 51–65; gender inequalities, 52–53; location scouts, 78; New Zealand industry, 12, 15, 37–49; producers, 86; project-based work, 39, 51, 54, 59, 76, 85–87; recruitment practices, 84–96; risk reduction, 89–91; sexism in, 37–49; stunt work, 128–57; UK

The Sociological Review, 63:S1, pp. 211–216 (2015), DOI: 10.1111/1467-954X.12309

Film Council, 40, 120; women in, 7, 11, 119–20, 131
flexibility, 11, 66–83, 179
Florida, Richard L., 1, 4, 10
Fordism, 6, 16
Fourier, Charles, 163–64
Fox Searchlight, 191
Fraser, Nancy, 30
freelancing, 3, 9, 11, 15, 51–65, 101, 107–108; in London, 55; in Scotland, 55; *see also* working for oneself; working from home
Frenette, A., 201
Friedan, Betty, 174, 175, 183–84
Frölich, R., 32–33
Fuller, G., 4

game industries, 24
Gardiner, L., 185
Geena Davis Institute for Gender and Media, 121
gender, and creative labour, 10–15, 66–83; and genre, 130–41; and racial segregation, 135; and the creative artist, 115–17; inequality, 1, 6–8, 11–12, 15, 52–53, 128–43; performativity, 116; 'retraditionalization' of roles, 66; regime, 38; work segregation, 23–36
genre, 17; gendered, 129, 133–35; ideology, 131–32; travel writing, 128–43; women's genres, 129–30
Gill, Rosalind, 1–22, 38, 43, 51–65, 85, 86, 87, 122–23, 199, 207
Gilligan, Carol, 35
globalization, 201
Goldberg, Steven, 35
Goldman, William, 91
Gorz, André, 167, 168
Green, L., 98
Gregg, Melissa, 10, 57, 77, 177
Griswold, W., 131
groups, 5; of men, 72; semi-permanent, 56, 57

Hakim, Catherine, 35
Hansard Commission, 86
harassment, 138, 139
Haukka, S., 68–69
Hearst Corporation, 191

Henry, C., 199
Henry, Lenny, 8
heritage, 3
Hesmondhalgh, David, 3, 4, 5, 9, 12, 15, 23–36, 67, 84, 89, 129, 189, 207
hiring practices, 10, 11; informality in, 11
Hirsch, P., 3
Holgate, Jane, 6, 8, 58
Hollands, R., 71
home, 182, 183
homeworking, *see* working from home
homophily, 11, 50, 51, 57, 88, 91–93
House of Lords Select Committee on Communications, 54
Huws, Ursula, 15, 18, 158–73, 207
Huxley, Aldous, 166, 168

Ibarra, H., 92
identity-making, 1, 3, 13–14
Illich, Ivan, 167, 168
individualism, 37, 80, 123, 185
inequality, and language, 38–39, 51, 123; and pay, 25, 52–53; and recruitment, 84–96; as psychosocial phenomenon, 3; in creative and cultural industries, 6–8; in film industry, 37–49; in television, 52–53; new forms, 38; regimes, 1; unmanageable inequalities, 11, 51, 56–59; *see also* gender
informality, 3, 8–10, 15, 51–65; in recruitment, 11, 84–96
information exchange, 169
information technology, 169; 3D printers, 168; app development, 6
internet, 168, 170
internships, 8, 188–205; academic qualifications, 197–98; and elitism, 189; and gender, 1989–199; and inequality, 190–91; and social class, 193–95, 200; Canadian Intern Association, 192; legal status, 200; parental support, 193–95, 200; statistics, 188–89, 190; young women, 191–93
intersections, 51, 53

Jacobson, Jenna, 15, 18, 188–205, 207
Janes, Lauren, 147
job insecurity, 8, 54
John-Steiner, Vera, 5

Johnson-Hill, E., 98
Jones, Deborah, 11, 12, 15, 37–49, 59, 61, 62, 207–208
Jones, John Chris, 170
journalism, 13, 27, 32; working conditions, 35

Kanter, R.M., 91
Kaufman, Charlie,113, 114–15, 116–17, 118, 119, 121, 123, 124; *Adaptation*, 17, 113, 114–19, 121, 122, 123, 124
Kaufman, Donald, 114, 116–17, 118, 119, 121, 124
Kelan, Elizabeth, 40

labour, 'labile', 68; Taylorist, 68
labour market, and youth transitions, 67, 71; churning, 69, 71
language, and inequalities, 38–39; of statistics, 39–40
Lauzen, M., 7, 40, 42, 44, 52, 120, 121, 131
Lawless, Lucy, 144, 153
Le Guin, Ursula, 167
'life history', interviews, 67, 135; studies, 35, 69
Littleton, Karen, 70
Lury, Celia, 68

Macdonald, I.W., 119
McKay, Sonia, 6, 8, 58
magazine publishing, 5, 24, 25, 33, 191; men's magazines, 33
Mahar, Karen, 122
Mäkinen, K., 99
manual labour, 16, 71, 163, 164
marketing, 23, 26, 27, 29, 30, 35, 99, 102, 106, 129, 145, 192, 199; self-marketing, 99, 101, 105; strategies, 107, 122
management, 28, 29, 35, 59, 129, 192; style, 33; Taylorist, 71
Marlow, Susan, 181, 182
Marx, Karl, 164
masculinity, 15, 16, 33, 79; and creative work, 66–83; and screenwriting, 113–27; entrepreneurs, 181; Fordist, 67; itinerant, 133; 'protest', 72; residual, 72–79; working class, 66–83
Maslow, Abraham, 5

Mato, Daniel, 4
Mayer, R.C., 91
McGuire, G.M., 86, 87
McKee, Robert, 114, 117, 118, 124
McRobbie, Angela, 38, 42, 70, 79, 100, 116, 123, 173, 181, 189
media, and genre, 128–143; and segregation, 12; digital, 33; industries, 2, 7, 9, 17, 24, 27, 53, 128–43; new media, 11, 85, 118; news media, 189; social media, 178, 191, 193, 199, 200; technologies, 4; women in, 224, 28, 52, 53
mentorship, 68, 72
meritocracy, 16, 38, 39, 70, 88, 93
Miller, Toby, 4
minority ethnic groups, 8, 11, 58, 86, 87, 98, 120
modesty, 102–105
More, Thomas, 158, 161, 168; *Utopia*, 159–60
Morgan, George, 5, 11, 14, 16, 66–83, 184, 208
Morris, William, 164, 165, 167, 169
Moss, Carrie Anne, 149
multimedia, 6
museums, 2
music industries, 1, 34, 77
music publishing, 35
Musicians' Union, 98

narrative codes, 70
Neff, Gina, 54
Negus, Keith, 27, 30
Nelligan, Pariece, 5, 11, 14, 16, 66–83, 184, 208
neoliberalism, 3, 15, 37, 46, 122–23, 185; neoliberal economy, 174–87
'network sociality', 3, 10
networking, 10, 11, 51, 56–57
New Enterprise Allowance, 181, 185
New Lanark, 162
New Zealand, below-the-line film workers, 37–49; film industry, 40–43; New Zealand Film Commission, 41
newspaper editors, 7
NGOs, 6
Nixon, Sean, 28, 33, 34
Nolan, E., 42
novel-publishing, 131

The Sociological Review, 63:S1, pp. 211–216 (2015), DOI: 10.1111/1467-954X.12309

O'Connor, Kate, 53
Oakley, Kate, 181
Orwell, George, 166, 168
Osborne, T., 2
Owen, Robert, 162–163

parenting, 51–65
pay, 6, 9, 25, 29, 38, 41, 46, 52, 58, 150, 184; inequality, 53; low pay, 2, 9, 16, 78, 98, 129
Perkins Gilman, Charlotte, 166–67
Perrons, Diane, 11
Peters, Tom, 5, 13
Petrenko, Vasily, 97
Phoenix, Ann, 8, 51
Pickering, M., 30
Piercy, Marge, 167
Pollock, Griselda, 33
post-feminism, 6, 39, 40, 122, 125, 153
post-Fordism, 6
Pratt, A.C., 9, 60, 85
precariousness, 3, 8–10, 44, 51, 54, 69, 77, 129, 185; and anxiety, 128; internships, 188, 189, 190, 202
Preston, Gaylene, 41
Pringle, Judith, 11, 12, 15, 37–49, 59, 61, 62, 208
Proctor-Thomson, Sarah, 33, 40
production staff, 2, 11, 16, 27–28, 45, 54, 86
prostitution, 107–109
PR staff, 27, 30
PRS for Music, 24
psychology, and creativity, 4–5
public sector broadcasters, 55

quality of life, 26
Quesnay, F., 160, 161

radio, 6, 85
Randle, Keith, 11, 15, 51–65, 85, 208–209
recruitment, 30, 50, 56–57, 58, 84–96; and risk reduction, 89–91
refusal of work movement, 14
Ricoeur, Paul, 130
Rifkind, Jeremy, 167, 168
Robeyns, I., 30
rock music, 131
Rose, Nikolas, 68

Ross, Andrew, 2, 51, 192
Rowlands, L., 44
Rousseau, Jean-Jacques, 161
Rudman, L.A., 99, 102–103
Ruskin, John, 164, 165, 169

Saint-Simon, comte de, 161, 162
Sandberg, Sheryl, 191
Saner, Emine, 178, 179, 180, 182, 184–85
Scharff, Christina, 7, 14, 16, 58, 97–112, 123, 209
screenwriting, 2, 11, 14, 16, 17, 84–96, 113–27; manuals, 113, 117, 119; portrayed in film, 115–19; sex-typing, 116; socio-economy, 119–122
segregation, 15; by age, 163; forms, 27–29; explaining, 29–34; gender, 5, 7, 34, 35, 39, 41, 130; occupational, 23–36, 46; racial, 135
self-representation, 3, 13–14, 16, 58
self-promotion, 97–112; and commerce, 106–107, 109; and racial background, 104–105, 109; and art, 105–106, 109
Sennett, R., 6, 69
sex work, 24
sexism, 3, 11–12, 23–36, 61, 62, 87, 97, 98; Everyday Sexism Project, 11; definition, 38; in film industry, 37–49
sex-typing, 113
sexual difference, 25
sexualization, 97, 108, 109
Shade, Leslie Regan, 15, 18, 188–205, 209
Single Equalities Act, 51
skills sector councils (SSCs), 6, 23, 24
Skillset, 23, 24, 40, 45, 52, 53, 54, 62, 85, 98, 120
Smith, Adam, 160, 161
social media, 178, 191, 193, 199, 200
social psychology, 5
socialism, utopian, 161–64, 168
socialized workers, 84
Steimer, Lauren, 14, 17, 128–57, 209
stereotypes, 15, 23–36
studios, 182–83
stunt work, 2, 14, 17, 128–57; ageism, 149–50; certification, 155; discrimination, 148; history, 147–49; injuries, 150–51; nature of work, 149–52; pay, 150; screen credits, 154–55; stunt

coordinators, 147–49; Stuntman's Association of Motion Pictures (SAMP), 147; 'utility' stunts, 155
stuntwomen, and action heroine, 144–45, 149, 152–54; discrimination, 149–50; erasure, 144–45, 146, 152–54; physique, 151–52; risks, 154; skills, 150; Stuntwomen's Association of Motion Pictures, 146, 148, 156
subjectivities, labouring, 3

Taylor, Frederick Winslow, 163
Taylor, Stephanie, 1–22, 70, 103, 174–87, 209–210
technology, 28–29, 169
television, 1, 3, 6, 7, 15; deregulation, 55; freelancing in, 51–65; gender inequalities, 52–53; student interns, 77; stunt work, 128–57; women in, 7–8, 24, 27–28, 31, 32, 40, 85
theatre, 2, 8, 9, 190
Tomsic, M., 41
'trade pain', 123
trade unions, 13, 167
training, 13, 40, 42, 52, 55–56, 68, 73, 74, 75, 79, 80, 150; on-the-job, 192, 194, 196, 202
travel writers, 3, 14, 17, 128–43; and masculine ideology, 133–35; and race, 134–35
Trollunteer, 42
trust, 11, 16, 57, 88, 89, 90; and homophily, 91–93
Tuchman, G., 131, 140
Tunstall, J., 130, 131

unions, 13, 41; Equity, 13; National Union of Journalists, 13
United Nations, 6
University of Hertfordshire, 51
University of Toronto Students' Union, 192

unpaid labour, 170–71; *see also* internships
US Urban Institute, 190
utopians, 158–73; history, 159–71

Walby, Sylvia, 35
Warhurst, C., 59
web design, 6
Weeks, Kathi, 14–15
Wells, H.G., 165–66, 168, 169
Wharton, A.S., 24, 30
Wing-Fai, Leung, 11, 12, 15, 51–65, 210
Wittel, A., 3, 10, 54
Wolff, Janet, 133
Wollestonecraft, Mary, 161
women, 6, 7, 11–13; and parenting, 12; as caring, 29–30, 33; at BBC, 131; communication skills, 31; in creative media, 23–24, 66–67; in senior roles, 53; organizational skills, 31–32; self-employed, 176; television writers, 120; training, 52; women's genres, 129–30
Women in Film and Television NZ, 41–42
Wood, J., 70
work experience, 55
working class men, and creative labour, 66–83
working for oneself, 174–87; older people, 176, 185; statistics, 174–76, 185; women, 176
working from home, 18, 19, 174, 175, 186
working patterns, 3, 9–10, 60, 62
Working Title, 93
workshops, 182, 183
Wreyford, Natalie, 11, 14, 16, 52, 59, 84–96, 122, 210
Writers' Guild of America West, 120

Yoshihara, M., 108
youth employment, 188–205

The Sociological Review, 63:S1, pp. 211–216 (2015), DOI: 10.1111/1467-954X.12309